A Manager's Guide to Blockchains for Business:

From Knowing What to Knowing How

A Manager's Guide to Blockchains for Business:
From Knowing What to Knowing How

Mary C. Lacity

SB Publishing
United Kingdom

A 'SB Publishing' book
www.sbpublishing.org

Cover design:
Nick Sample
www.nicksample.com

Cover image:

Victory Boogie Woogie by Pieter Cornelis 'Piet' Mondriaan, (1872 - 1944)
1944, oil and paper on canvas (unfinished)
State property of the Netherlands, through the Stichting Nationaal Fonds Kunstbezit
(National Art Foundation); in public domain; copyright expired 1st February 2014

Author:
Mary C. Lacity

Published in 2018 by:
SB Publishing
60 Loxley Road
Stratford-upon-Avon
Warwickshire CV37 7DR
United Kingdom
Tel: +44(0)1789 267124

A CIP catalogue record for this book is available from the British Library
ISBN 978-0-995682-04-7

Printed and bound in Poland by Latitude Press Ltd

Contents

Figures & Tables   7

Foreword   11

Author's Acknowledgements   13

Introduction: The Inspiration, Research Base and Focus of this Guide   15

1. The Blockchain Landscape   **19**

1.1. Introduction   19

1.2. Why should managers care about blockchains?   21

1.3. How big is the blockchain landscape today?   23

1.4. Blockchain's technology hype cycle   34

1.5. Conclusion: The landscape shifts rapidly   36

2. The Blockchain Application Framework   **41**

2.1. Introduction   41

2.2. Centralized systems vs. distributed blockchain applications   42

2.3. Bitcoin: The first blockchain application   45

2.4. The blockchain application framework   47

2.5. Blockchain's distributed ledger vs. traditional distributed databases   65

2.6. Mapping Bitcoin to the blockchain application framework   67

2.7. Conclusion   70

3. Business Application Examples   **75**

3.1. Introduction   75

3.2. Blockchain applications in financial services   77

3.3. Blockchain applications in the energy sector   97

3.4. Blockchain applications in supply chains   107

3.5. Conclusion   121

Contents

4. Technical Challenges and Emerging Solutions   **133**
4.1. Introduction   133
4.2. Security challenges   134
4.3. Performance and scalability challenges   143
4.4. Anonymity challenges   147
4.5. Confidentiality challenges   150
4.6. Interoperability challenges   153
4.7. Resource consumption challenges   157
4.8. Conclusion   156

5. Mindshifts, Strategies and Action Principles: Making   **163**
Enterprise Blockchains Real
5.1. Introduction   163
5.2. Mindshifts: The blockchain mindset   166
5.3. Phase I: 'Cart before the horse' exploration   172
5.4. Phase II: 'Horse before the cart' strategic intent   184
5.5. Phase III: Critical mass   199
5.6. Conclusion   201

Glossary   **211**

Book details – *Robotic Process and Cognitive Automation: The Next Phase*   **239**

Book detais – *Robotic Process Automation and Risk Mitigation:*   **240**
       The Definitive Guide

Book details – Service Automation: Robots and The Future of Work   **241**

Website details – *www.RoboticandCognitiveAutomation.com*   **242**

Figures

1.1   The blockchain landscape as of beginning of 2018
1.2   Equity funding vs. Initial Coin Offerings (ICOs)
1.3   Blockchain-related patent filings
1.4   US GAO map of US regulatory environment
1.5   Gartner's mapping of blockchains through its technology hype cycle
2.1   Multiple-centralized systems vs. a shared blockchain application
2.2   Components of a blockchain application
2.3   A permissioned blockchain with a gatekeeper to enforce the rights of access
2.4   Conceptual picture showing different access rights within a blockchain network
2.5   Parties' access rights varied by smart contract rules
2.6   Examples of three distributed ledger structures
2.7   Proof of digital asset ownership using private-public key pairs
2.8   Blockchain use cases
2.9   Example of a private-public key pair
2.10   The 'trust boundary' as a distinguishing difference
2.11   Bitcoin is a blockchain application fopr payments
2.12   Example of a digital wallet interface to Bitcoin
2.13   A screenshot of a website to view Bitcoin's blockchain
3.1   A simplified example of cross-border payments before blockchains
3.2   A high-level depiction of two banks using Ripple
3.3   Ripple mapped to the blockchain application framework
3.4   Stellar mapped to the blockchain application framework
3.5   A blockchain application for cross-border payments
3.6   Attributes of ASX's proposed blockchain application
3.7   Overview of an LO3 Microgrid comprising hardware and software
3.8   Example of LO3 Hardware
3.9   Example of mobile app interface for Brooklyn Microgrid project
3.10   Site of proof-of-concept test on President Street in Brooklyn, New York

3.11   Gowanus and Park Slope neighborhoods of Brooklyn, New York

3.12   Flow of tokens and dollars in Exergy Blockchain application

3.13   Innogy charging station with embedded Etherum node

3.14   Global supply chains before a blockchain application

3:15   Everledger's digital identifier for a fair trade diamond

3.16   Provenance's blockchain application for tracking and tracing tuna from sea to table

3.17   Moog Aircraft's blockchain application for verifying 3-D printed parts

3.18   Business and technical domains of a blockchain application

4.1   Bitcoin's largest winning mining pools on December 28th 2017

4.2   Concentration of power in a permissioned blockchain

4.3   A Bitcoin transaction that occurred in Block 400000 on February 25th 2016

4.4   Meta patterns that can arise from a blockchain's transparency

4.5   Monero transaction displayed with amount masked and input address displayed as a key image

4.6   Quorum's architecture for separating public and private transactions

4.7   Channels in Hyperledger Fabric

4.8   Wanchain's proposed solution for blockchain interoperability

4.9   Cosmos' proposed solution for blockchain interoperability

4.10   Bitcoin mining site in Bowden, Sweden

5.1   The roadmap for making enterprise blockchains real

5.2   The blockchain mindset

5.3   A screen shot of Barclay Bank's prototype for a legal contract that automatically codes a smart contract for deployment on a blockchain

5.4   Criteria for identifying multiple use cases for POCs

5.4   Three influences that pressure institutions to conform

G.1   Example of a block header for bitcoin

G.2   Distributed ledger structured as a chain of blocks

G.3   Distributed ledger structured as a tangle of transactions

G.4   Bitcoin's elliptic curve cryptography

G.5   Hard fork vs. soft fork

G.7   Three network structures

G.8   The 'proof-of-work' mining competition algorithm

G.9   Three examples of the SHA-256 hash function

G.10   Silk Road website screenshot

Tables

2.1   Permissionless blockchains
2.2   Permissionless vs. permissioned blockchains
2.3   Three common consensus protocols
2.4   Size of code bases for various blockchains
3.1   Blockchain application examples
5.1   Strategic intents of blockchain applications

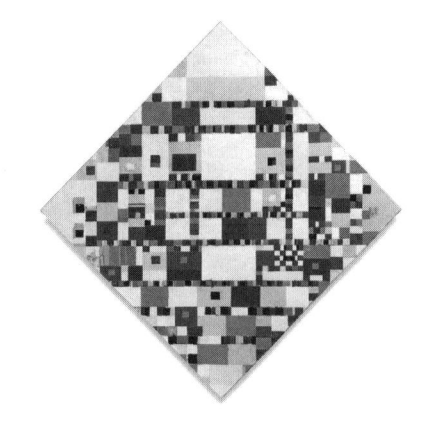

Foreword

The amount of column inches in newspapers and magazines, bytes in the Twittersphere, and the subsequent hand-wringing that has been devoted to a thing called 'blockchain' has been unprecedented, surpassing the interest – and confusion – in any other technology topic of the last decade. Blockchain has been called everything from the 'new internet,' and 'industry disruptor,' to 'much ado about nothing' and a 'dangerous trend'. The truth, as with most things in technology and in life, lies somewhere in between.

In this book, Professor Mary Lacity seeks to demystify the world of blockchain, both releasing some of the incumbent pressure attached to the topic, while also revealing and exploring many of the possibilities the technology holds. Through fascinating and highly pertinent case studies and a clear-eyed voice beyond the noise, Professor Lacity provides real life illustrations in blockchain's art of the possible. Using a thorough exploration of various challenges, approaches and outcomes, she presents blockchain in a truly three-dimensional way.

By focusing on the practical outcomes and true innovations of blockchain – such as smart contracts, which can be applied even where only a notional contract exists – this book creates a roadmap to using this technology for real world outcomes and aspirational ideas in equal measure. Readers will come away with a stronger sense of what a 'blockchain future' looks like, without all of the *sturm und drang* that the dialogue has featured thus far.

One key dimension of particular interest to readers that will be explored in these pages is that of blockchain outside of the technology itself, and more squarely about the environment in which it lives and functions. With 'trust-less systems' supported by blockchain, most industries have independent or regulated parties that enable trust-based interactions. Professor Lacity helps to unlock and explain what these ecosystems can, and should, look like.

Given the myriad of opinions around this topic, it is easy to lose sight of the basic proposition and look only at blockchain from the top down – as a concept. But as Professor Lacity clearly states, things like distributed ledger technology (DLT), smart contracts and trust-less systems are where the rubber truly meets the road. These are not concepts searching for an application. They are actionable, tangible approaches which take the underlying concepts of blockchain and extrapolates them into new ways of doing business, which are smarter, faster and more efficient and frictionless. By creating a new type of payment metaphor, blockchain is exactly as aspirational as it has been reported. But through discussions such as this, the aspiration is something that any business person or consumer can understand and begin to conceive of ways to implement in their daily work and personal lives.

By juxtaposing examples and experiences from multiple industries, readers will begin to understand how the basics of blockchain can unlock new models and efficiencies previously untold. Professor Lacity's articulate and crystal-clear narrative applies academic rigor and practical experience to the industry. While there are many books and articles – and nearly limitless different points of view – on this topic, this book is different. It provides and in-depth, practical view of the concepts and the commensurate applications. And in doing so, breathes fresh life and a more refined lens into the conversation on blockchain.

Nilesh Vaidya

Executive Vice President
Financial Services
Capgemini

Author's Acknowledgements

Many people informed and shaped this research program. Lee Coulter, CEO of Ascension Shared Services, was the first to explain blockchains to me, on the back of a napkin, at a dinner in San Francisco. Joining MIT's Center for Information Systems Research (CISR) in 2017, as a Visiting Scholar to study enterprise blockchains, fulfilled a long-time aspiration to work with people I had admired for so long – most notably Dr. Jeanne Ross and Dr. Peter Weill. On our blockchain team, Kate Moloney was the person who kept the project running smoothly and the one who asked the tough questions. I am indebted to the directors and staff at CISR for their support, including Executive Director Leslie Owens for thinking outside the box; Dr. Barb Wixom for her sparkle and unwavering support; Dr. Kristine Dery for sharing her social capital; Chris Foglia and Amber Franey for making all my trips to MIT magical; and Cheryl Miller for her editing. Thanks also to Dr. Nils Fonstad; Dr. Stephanie Woerner; Dr. Ina Sebastian; Dr. Lynne Markus; and Dr. Cynthia Beath, for their collegiality. Thank you to Ian Barkin and other friends from Symphony Ventures for pleasant dinners and long walks around the historical streets of Boston.

I profoundly thank Christine Ferrusi Ross, whom I first met when she was a Research Vice President at HfS Research studying blockchains. She and I took this blockchain journey together in so many ways – from a research trip to an innovation center, to editing drafts of early papers. Christine was the one who convinced me of the value of a glossary.

Thank you to Saurabh Gupta, Chief Strategy Officer, and Phil Fersht, CEO and Chief Analyst at HfS, for sharing their research results and the stage at HfS events. Thank you Nilesh Vaidya, Executive Vice President at Capgemini and Debi Hamill, CEO of the IAOP, for disseminating the work.

For over a quarter century, I have had the full support of the University of Missouri-St. Louis. Dr. Dinesh Mirchandani, Chair of the Information Systems Department, and Charles Hoffman, Dean of the College of Business, supported every request to enable this research. Other

Author's Acknowledgements

colleagues engaged in thoughtful conversations about the research, most notably: Dr. Nasser Arshadi, Professor of Finance; Dr. Tom Eyssell, Associate Dean and Director of Graduate Studies; Dr. Joseph Rottman, Chair of Global Leadership and Management; Dr. Shaji Khan, Assistant Professor of Information Systems; and Dr. Steve Moehrle, Chair of the Accounting Department.

This research has brought collaborations with other like-minded folks from The Sam M. Walton College of Business at the University of Arkansas, including Dr. Rajiv Sabherwal, Dr. Paul Cronan, Dr. Zach Steelman, and Dr. Varun Grover.

Many thanks to my publisher, SB Publishing. Your services bring our best work to market faster than any traditional publishing route.

I am especially thankful to all of the executives interviewed for this research. I hope this guide fittingly trumpets your visions and achievements.

I proclaim my heartfelt gratitude to my circle of family and friends. This work consumed much of my time, resulting in neglect on my part to people who enrich my life in every way. Thank you to my long-time colleague, coauthor and friend, Professor Leslie Willcocks at the London School of Economics. Leslie took up the slack on our robotic process and cognitive automation projects while I focused on blockchains. Christine Emma Cotney Benson, thank you for entertaining me during my many research trips to New York City. My thanks to my parents, Dr. Paul and Joan Lacity, my sisters Karen, Diane and Julie, and my dear friends, Michael McDeviitt, Beth Nazemi, and Val Graeser for your unwavering support. To Michael Christopher, whom I hold in my heart every hour of every day. Finally, to the man who makes all this worthwhile, I thank Jerry Pancio. In the words of Ricardo Montalban, *"True love doesn't happen right away; it's an ever-growing process. It develops after you've gone through many ups and downs, when you've suffered together, cried together, laughed together."* Jerry will likely view that as too serious, so I'll leave my final message to him as this: *"Who's my future?"*

Introduction:
The inspiration, research base and focus of this guide

Think back to the early 1990s. Are you old enough to remember the first time you saw the Internet through the friendly interface of a web browser? I do. It was 1994. I was sitting in my office at Templeton College at Oxford University when my colleague showed me Mosaic, one of the first web browsers. I viewed it with curiosity for a few moments, but then went back to my 'day job'. I venture to say I was not alone in initially ignoring – and certainly underestimating – the Internet's long-term economic, social and political effects. The Internet changed everything, everywhere.

Jump ahead to 2009 when Bitcoin, the first blockchain application was released. It remained a curiosity for many years. I finally took serious notice in June of 2016 while attending Cognizant Community in Austin Texas. On stage, large global enterprises were talking about how to adapt Bitcoin's underbelly of protocols, collectively known as a 'blockchain', to improve business. Beyond the hype and splashy headlines Bitcoin garnered, something interesting for organizations was indeed afoot: Bitcoin was proving that a crowd could securely maintain a completely distributed transaction processing application. This time around, I did not ignore blockchain's potential to change everything, everywhere. After the Cognizant conference, 'blockchains for business' became my primary research focus.

Research base

I've been studying blockchains since the summer of 2016. I spent the first six months learning about the protocols that specify the rules for blockchains, like Bitcoin, Ethereum, Ripple, Stellar, Corda, Fabric and Quorum. The learning curve was brutal – it's easy to fall down the technical rabbit hole. Terms like: elliptic curve cryptography; proof-of-work; mining; digital wallets;

native digital assets; smart contracts; hashing; Merkle roots; Byzantine fault tolerance; and zero-knowledge proofs, make it difficult to climb out and really understand what the technology enables for businesses. ***One of the aims of this guide is to shortcut the technical learning curve for managers.***

In 2017, I joined MIT's Center for Information Systems Research (CISR), housed in the Sloan School of Management, as a Visiting Scholar to study how enterprises were exploring blockchains. The research team included Dr. Jeanne Ross, Principal Research Scientist, and Kate Moloney, Research Specialist. During interviews, we asked managers about their blockchain adoption journeys, their participation in blockchain ecosystems, and the practices and lessons they have learned so far. We asked the following types of questions:

- What strategies are being considered? How is the organization building blockchain capability? Which applications are deemed to be the most promising, are already under development, or have been deployed?
- Does the organization participate in industry consortia? Open-source projects? Invest in startups or FinTechs? What needs to happen to create the minimum viable ecosystem for applications relevant to the organization?
- What challenges do organizations need to overcome to deploy blockchain applications? What are the key project and change management practices? How well have expectations been met? What are the preliminary outcomes and lessons learned?

As of this writing, we have interviewed executives from 30 global enterprises currently exploring blockchains, from the professional services firms that sell services to them, and from the startups that want to disrupt them. The enterprises we studied primarily represent global financial services, but also include manufacturing and healthcare firms. The professional services firms include representatives from large organizations like Deloitte, KPMG, Capgemini, Cognizant, IBM, and Wipro, as well as boutique consulting firms. The startups include companies seeking to advance general blockchain technical capabilities and specific business-focused blockchain applications.

I also participate in (or more accurately observe) the Center for Supply Chain's three studies[i] to define blockchain standards for tracking and tracing pharmaceuticals. Bob Celeste leads

---

(i) See Center for Supply Chain's website at https://www.c4scs.org/

the group of about 50 participants who represent pharmaceutical manufacturers, wholesalers, distributors, and retail and hospital pharmacies. This experience has helped me to understand the perceived benefits and concerns that supply chain partners have about shared blockchain applications.

Focus of this guide

While there are many books on blockchains, this guide focuses on ***blockchain applications for business***. The target audience is managers, business students, and other people who want to learn about the overall blockchain landscape – the investments, the size of markets, major players and the global reach – as well as the potential business value of blockchain applications and the challenges that must be overcome to achieve that value. We present use cases and derive action principles for building enterprise blockchain capabilities. Readers will learn enough about the underlying technologies to speak intelligently to technology experts in the space, as the guide also covers the blockchain protocols, code bases and provides a glossary of terms. Throughout the guide, we also point to helpful sites to monitor this rapidly evolving space. Although many students seek investment advice, this guide does not focus on cryptocurrencies or blockchains as an investment opportunity. Those interested in that space might consult Chris Burniske and Jack Tatar's book, *Cryptoassets: The Innovative Investor's Guide to Bitcoin and Beyond* (McGraw-Hill Education, 2017).

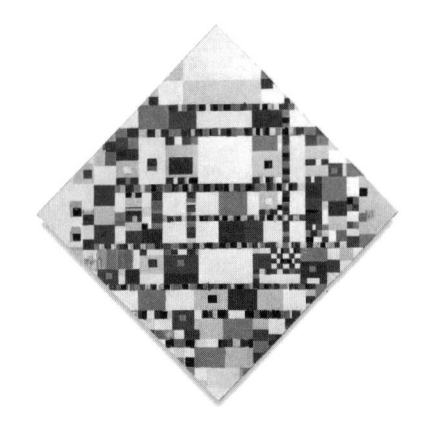

Chapter 1

The Blockchain Landscape

"I'm a big believer in the ability of blockchain technology to effect fundamental change in the infrastructure of the financial service industry."

Bob Greifeld, CEO of NASDAQ in 2015[1]

"I believe that Blockchain will do for trusted transactions what the Internet has done for information."

Ginni Rometty, CEO of IBM in 2017[2]

"There are only a few dozen exciting [blockchain] projects [in Silicon Valley]. I see really silly ideas being issued as coins that would not merit a Master's degree at MIT or Cornell, but they are garnering millions of dollars of investment."

Emin Gün Sirer, Associate Professor, Cornell University in 2017[3]

1.1. Introduction

By now, most people are aware of Bitcoin, the first blockchain application for payments that went live in 2009. Invented by the mysterious Satoshi Nakamoto, blockchain is the technology that makes the cryptocurrency Bitcoin work. Bitcoin, and other blockchain applications similar to it, allows people to transact directly with each other without needing third-party intermediaries like banks and credit card companies. Instead of relying on institutions to facilitate transactions, a blockchain application relies on computer algorithms. Bitcoin proved (so far) that a crowd could securely maintain a completely distributed application – no one person or institution owns or controls it. Even if the Bitcoin bubble bursts, other viable business cases already exist and many new ones are emerging.

"The current blockchain landscape is clearly shaping up to be the tsunami of hype cycles in the technology field. Many of the claims and use cases assigned to Blockchain by its proponents are, on their face, overly hyped and destined to fail. I hear these claims repeated by large numbers of people, many of them with little or no technical experience."

Arthur J. Riel, Director, Middleware Engineering and Rapid App Development, The World Bank in 2017[5]

There's no question that blockchain is an exciting new development. The idea of taking third-parties out of the equation opens up a whole new world of automation and efficiency that should (rightly) have most C-suite executives doing their homework. Executives are mainly concerned with the threats and opportunities blockchains pose to their business models. During the course of this research, managers expressed heated opinions as to whether blockchain technologies could be adapted to add value for traditional enterprises. As the first two quotes of this chapter attest, blockchains promise to radically change the economic, social, and political landscape of our world, in much the same way that the Internet has already done so. However, the last two quotes temper expectations with some shrewd insights from technical experts. Blockchain's dissenters have responded with such statements as, *"There are no legitimate use cases"*, and *"Blockchains are over-hyped"*. Which set of quotes is more telling? We've been studying the space for over 18 months to find out more (see 'Research Base' in the Author Introduction). Wading through the arguments and evidence, we grant that as we enter 2018, blockchains for business are indeed following a traditional technology hype cycle. However, the point is that most technologies eventually do mature; managers eventually learn to adapt them for purposeful use; and ultimately, innovations like blockchains become institutionalized as part of our technical architecture. Moving to business purpose will require overcoming both technical and non-technical challenges.

Executives interviewed for this research are confident the cadre of bright people in working groups and startups will successfully address the technical challenges. They are more concerned with the required mindshifts, new shared governance models, standards, and regulatory challenges that need to be addressed before more blockchain applications are widely deployed and scaled across industries and geographies. Managers from traditional enterprises will need to take an active role in addressing industry challenges for the particular blockchain applications that affect their business models – as discussed in final chapter of this guide.

While the learning curve is quite steep, this guide will help managers, business students, and other inquisitive people learn about blockchains for business. Depending on one's needs, the guide may be read in parts or in its entirety. The guide answers these questions:

Chapter 1 answers: Why should managers care about blockchains?
How big is the blockchain landscape today?

Chapter 2 answers: What exactly are blockchain applications? Where did they come from?

Chapter 3 answers: What are examples of actual blockchain applications for business?

Chapter 4 answers: What are the technical challenges and emerging solutions?

Chapter 5 answers: What mindshifts, strategies and action principles should an enterprise consider?

While it is too soon to foresee all that will unfold, we've learned that despite the billions of dollars in blockchain investments worldwide[5], the thousands of proofs-of-concepts across all industries, and the high-profile groups working to define standards and to develop code, there were very few enterprise blockchains applications in production in 2017. A 4th quarter 2017 study of 200 blockchain projects by HfS, a research and consulting firm, corroborates our findings. HfS found that 90 to 95 percent of enterprises were still conceptualizing blockchains, conducting proof-of-concepts or piloting applications. Only 5 to 10 percent of pilots were progressing to production.[6] Many people strongly believe that blockchain applications will go live across many industries over the next few years. So while we agree it is early days, it's time to learn about blockchain applications now.

1.2. Why should managers care about blockchains?

Thoughtful managers, business students, and other people with business interests have many reasons to learn about blockchain applications:

1. **Boards of Directors** are asking questions about the efficacy and strategic implications of enterprise blockchains. They want insights to separate hype from reality, and a deeper understanding as to the opportunities and threats blockchains pose.
2. **Heads of Innovation** are already exploring business use cases. Such evangelists need considerable support to move blockchains from ideas to live applications that deliver real business value.
3. **Employees** in many organizations are excited by blockchain's possibilities, so it's a way to invigorate and develop talent. According to Upwork, the world's largest freelancing website, blockchain skills were the second-fastest growing, sought-after skills following robotics in 2017.[7] Enterprises that foster skills today may indeed gain an advantage.
4. **Customers** are demanding them. Unlike other enterprise applications that were developed within companies and then foisted upon consumers, consumers used blockchain applications first. As of September 2017, over 15 million consumers had blockchain wallets[8] and now they want to buy products and services with their cryptocurrencies. Corporate customers also want blockchain services – some hedge fund clients demand that fund managers add cryptoassets to their portfolios.
5. Incumbent enterprises need to watch the space closely for competitive threats from traditional **competitors** and **newcomers.** In particular, a vibrant, global start-up community has secured billions of dollars of investment, some of which will succeed at disrupting current business models.
6. Leaders have an opportunity **to help architect the future** rather than be overcome by it. At the very least, managers need to know enough about blockchains to decide whether they want to lead, be fast followers, or explore enterprise blockchains at a slower pace.
7. Beyond the profit motive, many people in the space have worthwhile **social missions** like bringing financial services to the two billion people who lack access, protecting both the property rights of people with low economic status, and the integrity of political elections. As citizens of the world, managers can contribute to such worthy causes.

Beyond these lists of reasons, managers simply want to know, to paraphrase the great Gertrude Stein, "*Is there any 'there' there?*" Our position is yes, absolutely. There are simply too many great brains focused upon blockchains, and too many investment dollars being spent to conclude otherwise. Next we explore the scale of the market as of the start of 2018.

1.3. How big is the blockchain landscape today?

To answer this question, we'll examine the players involved and the money invested in the space. Across venture capital, corporate and token sales, over $5 billion has been invested in blockchain technologies as of the beginning of 2018. Overall, the United States (US) dominates the market, but blockchain players and investments are indeed global, with investments in 24 countries as of 2016, according to the World Economic Forum.[9]

Looking across the global landscape, there are several groups investing their time and resources in developing blockchain technologies (see Figure 1.1). On the investment side, venture capitalists have invested over $2 billion, and corporations have invested over $1.2 billion, by year-end 2017.[10] Most interestingly, a new financing model called an Initial Coin Offering (ICO) is being used to fund startups. According to CB Insights, 250 ICOs raised over $2 billion between January 2016 and October 2017.[11] On the services side, service providers and consulting firms have been building blockchain capabilities and selling services to corporate clients to the amount of $1 billion a year.

In addition to startups, investors, service providers and consulting firms, there are other important players shaping the blockchain landscape. We focus on working groups and regulators in this chapter, but academics, philanthropists, meet-up groups, technology journalists, politicians, lawyers, and other stakeholders are making significant contributions as well.

1.3.1. The blockchain investment market

Blockchain startups. As of January 2018, the website www.angel.co identified 1,548 blockchain startups, with an average valuation of $4.5 million.[12] Which ones show the most promise? According to Ameer Rosic, an investor in the space, the most promising blockchain startups are Blockstream (to speed blockchain transactions); Ethereum (now the largest blockchain platform); Auger (distributed prediction market that runs on Ethereum); Lisk (rival to Etherum, written in JavaScript); Everledger (tracks high-valued assets like diamonds and art); Ripple Labs (commercial applications for the Ripple protocol); and Coinbase (the largest cryptocurrency exchange).[13]

Figure 1.1: The blockchain landscape as of beginning of 2018

[1] https://angel.co/blockchains

[2] *Blockchain in Review: Investment Trends and Opportunities,* CB Insights, October 2017

[3] Price volatility is very high. See https://coinmarketcap.com/all/views/all/ for today's values

[4] *Enterprise Blockchain Services,* Gupta, S. and Mondal, T., HfS Blueprint Report, 2017

CEX ranked the top 50 blockchain startups to follow in 2017. Its top ten were: BitPesa (payments to African-based businesses); Provenance (tracking goods in a supply chain); Storj (encrypted cloud storage); Cambridge Blockchain (identity compliance); Hijro (marketplace); OpenBazaar (Ecommerce platform); Blockstack (distributed applications platform); Chronicled (encrypted identities for physical things; business processes automation using smart contracts);[14] Hashed Health (focused on healthcare); and Slock.it (universal sharing network for rides, rentals).[15]

Rise.global lists 100 of the most influential blockchain companies. As of December 2017, its top picks were Coindesk (blockchain news); Kik Interactive (social media); Blockchain (finance); CoinTelegraph (blockchain news); Coinbase (an exchange); Ripple (finance application); and Bittrex (exchange).[16] We'll encounter several of these startups throughout this guide.

Venture Capital Investment. From 2012 to 3rd quarter 2017, CB Insights reported that 650 equity deals were made, totaling over $2 billion.[17] Early investments focused on public blockchain technologies like digital wallets and currency exchanges – few of which will prevail. Only 28 percent of startups were able to achieve additional funding after the initial angel investments, according to CB Insights. Later investments focused on private blockchains for business.

According to CB Insights, the top venture capital investors over a five-year period were Digital Currency Group; Blockchain Capital; Pantera Capital; Draper Associates; 500 Startups; RRE Ventures; Fenbushi Capital; Andreessen Horowitz; Plug and Play Ventures; Liberty City Ventures; Union Square Ventures; and FuturePerfect Ventures.[18] While the US investment market is by far the largest, equity investors are funding startups all over the world. For example, The Digital Currency Group has made investments in companies in Africa, Asia, Australia, Europe, North America and South America.[19] The biggest blockchain investments by country were, in descending order, the US, United Kingdom (UK), China, Singapore, Canada, South Korea, Japan, Switzerland, the Netherlands and Germany.

Corporate Investment. CB Insights reported that corporations have invested over $1.2 billion in blockchain companies between 2012 and 2017. Financial services firms were the early investors, including such companies as USAA, NYSE, CME Group, Wells Fargo, JP Morgan, Visa, MasterCard, Citi, DTCC and Nasdaq to name just a few. Since 2014, more than 50 of the world's largest financial services companies have made direct investments in blockchain startups. By the third quarter of 2017, corporate investment was nearly equal to venture capital investment. In 2017, SBI holdings, Google, Overstock.com, Citi, and Goldman Sachs were the most active corporate investors.[20]

Initial Coin Offerings. An interesting new investment model gained traction in 2017: Initial Coin Offerings (ICO) (see Figure 1.2). With an ICO, startups announce that they want to raise cash using an ICO by launching a new coin or token, i.e. a new cryptocurrency. Investors buy the coins instead of shares in a company, which bypasses many onerous regulations – for now. According to CB Insights, 250 ICOs raised over $2 billion between January 2016 and October 2017.[21]

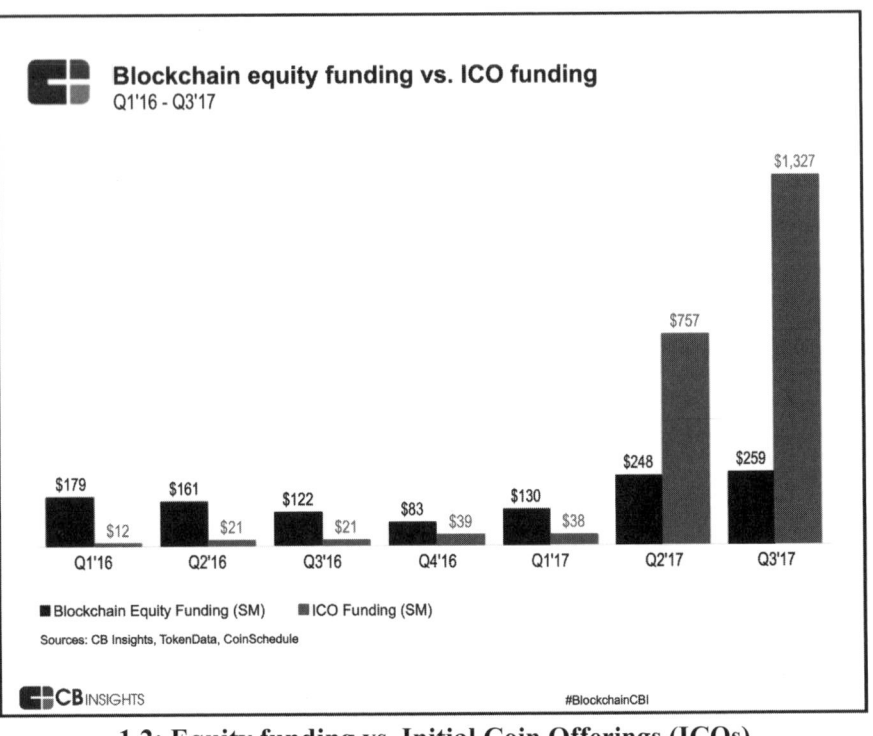

1.2: Equity funding vs. Initial Coin Offerings (ICOs)

Source: CB Insights[22]

The bellwether ICOs occurred in 2014 when Mastercoin raised $5.5 million and Ethereum raised $18 million.[23] The largest ICO as of December 2017 raised $257 million for the Filecoin project, which aims to store files on a distributed network analogous to the way Bitcoin stores transactions. The second largest ICO was $232 million for the Tezos Blockchain project, which aims to put more governance around blockchains to prevent forks such as occurred at Ethereum (a story told later in this guide).[24] According to Merkle, the other top ICOs in 2017 were EOS (raised $185 million); Bancor (raised $153 million); Status (raised $90 million); TenX (raised $64 million); SONM (raised $42 million); Aeternity (raised $37 million); and Monetha (raised nearly $37 million).[25]

As a new funding tool, the risks around ICOs are significant. Swindlers have entered the space aiming to scam investors. For example, the unknown founder(s) of Confido disappeared with nearly $400,000 raised through an ICO.[26] For another example, some investors in Tezos are suing its organizers for fraud. Tezos was supposed to have released a new coin to investors called a Tez, but it had not done so as of 2017.[27] Apparently, investors were told they were making a donation and that they may never receive any – a claim the founders dispute.[28]

In response to such scams, Jay Clayton, Chairman of the US Securities and Exchange Commission (SEC), warned investors in December of 2017:

> *"Investors should understand that to date no initial coin offerings have been registered with the SEC. The SEC also has not to date approved for listing and trading any exchange-traded products (such as ETFs) holding cryptocurrencies or other assets related to cryptocurrencies. If any person today tells you otherwise, be especially wary."*[29]

The SEC has also halted ICOs, including Plexcoin, which raised $15 million by promising a 1300 percent return on investment with a month.[30] Some countries, most notably China and South Korea, have banned ICOs.

For the casual investor, Techcrunch contributor Deep Patel identified these red flags to spot ICO scams: the early release of coins goes primarily to the founders, not investors or miners; the founders are anonymous or have little credible experience; the project's white paper is missing details; the project has no clear timelines; the project claims the programming code will be open sourced but it does not exist on GitHub – the de facto repository for open-sourced blockchain source code.[31] The SEC has a more comprehensive list of questions investors should ask about ICOs before investing.[32] In short, *caveat emptor*.

1.3.2. The cryptocurrency market

While most people are familiar with the popular cryptocurrencies like Bitcoin, Ether (Ethereum's coin), and Litecoin, many people are surprised to learn that there were over 1300 cryptocurrencies trading as of December 2017. Where did all these digital coins come from? Many of them were created as offshoots from Bitcoin, including Namecoin and Litecoin. So called 'Altcoins' because they are alternatives to Bitcoin, aimed to either improve on Bitcoin (such as decreasing settlement times) or to serve different purposes,[33] like funding blockchain platforms.

The market capitalization of existing cryptocurrencies, calculated by multiplying the price in US dollars times the number of coins in circulation, is another way to consider the size of the blockchain space. Market prices fluctuate considerably, sometimes rising or falling by hundreds of billions of dollars within a few weeks. For example, 1,320 cryptocurrencies[34] had a combined market capitalization of $324 billion on December 2nd 2017 and just 30 days later, the market cap exceeded $600 billion (see https://coinmarketcap.com/all/views/all/ for today's values). By January 21st, 2018, Bitcoin captured the lion's share at nearly $207 billion, followed by Ethereum, Ripple, and Bitcoin Cash with market capitalizations of $109 billion, $58 billion, and $31 billion respectively.[35] To place this activity in context, the world's fiat money supply – the value of all banknotes, coins, money market accounts, savings accounts, checking accounts and Certificates of Deposit (CDs) – was $81 trillion in 2017.[36] *The value of all the cryptocurrencies combined equaled about 0.4 percent of the global fiat money supply in December 2017.*

During 2017, the high price volatility of cryptocurrencies overshadowed the business uses of blockchain technologies. Certainly, Bitcoin's price breaking marks dominated news cycle when it reached $1,000 per bitcoin in November 2013[37], $2,000 per bitcoin in May 2017[38], $10,000 in November 2017[39] and then over $19,000 in December 2017.[40] Bitcoin was not the only cryptocurrency to see wide spreads in price. In 2017, Ethereum's price fluctuated between $7.13 and over $800.[41] Litecoin started out at $4.51 in January 2017 and hit over $370 by December.[42] The noisy, irrational exuberance over investing in cryptocurrencies leaves many people with the false impression that the entire blockchain space is only attracting risk-tolerant speculators.

The high price volatility of cryptocurrencies impedes widespread acceptance of cryptocurrencies as forms of payment. Overstock.com, Microsoft, the DISH network, Intuit, and PayPal are the few examples of companies that accept bitcoins as payments. What is more worrying is that some merchants that initially accepted bitcoins ceased to do so because of high price volatility. For example, Steam, the online gaming platform, dropped bitcoin as a payment method in December of 2017.[43] If Amazon accepted bitcoins as payment, it would undoubtedly boost adoption, but as of 2017, the company had no plans to do so.

1.3.3. The enterprise blockchain services market

Service providers and consulting firms are key players in the market because they have built considerable blockchain capabilities; some have hundreds of employees ready to advise enterprises on blockchain strategies. Several research firms have estimated the revenues generated from the global sales of blockchain services by firms like Accenture; Capgemini; Cognizant; Deloitte; Ernst & Young; IBM; KPMG; NTT; PwC; and Wipro. Most recently, HfS estimated the blockchain market for enterprise services to be $1 billion in 2018.[44]

Grand View Research, a US-based market research and consulting company, valued the global blockchain market at $509 million in 2015 and $605 million in 2016.[45] Financial services applications dominated the market, followed by transportation, tech/media/telecom, consumer products, healthcare, and public sector applications. Statista, a German-based research firm, had lower estimates of $210 million in 2016 and $340 million in 2017, but it is unclear as to what they measure.

All research firms predict growth between 50 and 100 percent per annum. To put these numbers in perspective: ***Blockchain global sales represented about .0001 percent of the world's $75 trillion GDP in 2017***.

1.3.4. Working groups

Working groups, including consortia and non-profits, are defining blockchain standards and developing code bases for business applications. As of year-end 2016, William Mougayar, the author of *The Business Blockchain*, analyzed 25 of the top global consortia. Over half were focused on financial services, 10 were based in the US, and the average number of members was 25. His top 20, in alphabetical order, were Accounting Consortium; B3i; BlockRx Project; Blockchain Study Group; CULedger; ChinaLedger Alliance; Digital Asset Holdings; Dutch Logistics Group; FCA Sandbox Project; Financial Blockchain Shenzhen Consortium; Fundchain; Global Blockchain Council; Hashed Health; Hyperledger; Hyperledger Healthcare Working Group; ISITC Blockchain Working Group; ISO/TC 307; Kinakuta; Post-Trade Distributed Ledger Group; and Project Jasper.[46]

As of August 2017, Deloitte identified 40 major consortia, of which 26 were focused on financial services, 10 were cross-sector, and three were in healthcare. In their survey of 308 executives, eight percent of those who were aware of blockchains were already participated in a consortium, 45 percent were likely to join one soon, and 14 percent were considering forming one.[47]

To get a sense of these consortia, we briefly cover R3, the Hyperledger Project, JBI, B3i, and the Enterprise Ethereum Alliance.

R3. Founded in 2014 by David Rutter, R3 is one of the first consortia of significance. R3 was launched with nine large banks: Barclays; BBVA Francés; State Street; JP Morgan; Commonwealth Bank of Australia; Goldman Sachs; Royal Bank of Scotland; Credit Suisse; and UBS. Eventually growing to 60 members, R3 developed an enterprise-grade blockchain platform called Corda, for global financial institutions. Corda is designed to increase privacy, reduce data redundancy (not everyone needs to see a transaction), and scalability (see Glossary for more on Corda).[48]

Hyperledger Project. The Linux Foundation launched this non-profit organization in December of 2015. Brian Behlendorf, the developer of the Apache Web server, serves as Executive Director. As of December 2017, 177 corporate members are listed on its website. It aims to advance the application of enterprise-grade blockchains across industries.[49]

Thus far, Hyperledger Project has five major blockchain frameworks: Fabric (see Glossary for overview), Sawtooth, Iroha, Burrow, and Indy. Fabric, much of whose code was donated by IBM, is commonly used by enterprises, including IBM, Wal-Mart, and Maersk.[50] The Hyperledger Project is also developing four tools: Cello, Composer, Explorer, and Quilt.[51]

JBI. The Jiangsu Huaxin Blockchain Research Institute (JBI) was founded in September of 2016 in Nanjing. JBI is owned and operated by the Chinese government. Within six months of launch, it claimed to have 100 employees working on creating blockchain applications for the Chinese market. Their ambitions include the training and accreditation of blockchain professionals.[52]

B3i was founded in October 2016 in Zurich Switzerland to focus on blockchain standards for the insurance sector. As of 2017, its 15 members were Achmea; Aegon; Ageas; Allianz; Generali;

Hannover Re; Liberty Mutual; Munich Re; RGA; SCOR; Sompo Japan Nipponkoa Insurance; Swiss Re; Tokio Marine Holdings; XL Catlin; and Zurich Insurance Group. In March 2017, B3i began working on a proof-of-concept for catastrophic property insurance. The product, called Property Cat XOL contract, is being built with IBM on Hyperledger Fabric.[53]

Enterprise Ethereum Alliance. Many companies want an enterprise-grade blockchain based on the Ethereum protocol. To this end, Microsoft, Accenture, JP Morgan, BNY Mellon, CME Group, MasterCard, Santander, Wipro and 26 other enterprises founded The Enterprise Ethereum Alliance in February 2017.[54] Within the first year, 200 organizations joined the alliance. The Alliance is seeking solutions to Ethereum's scalability, performance and privacy challenges.[55] To help make progress given the size of the alliance, working groups focus on particular areas of interest. As of mid-2017, the active working groups focused on: the advertising industry, banking, healthcare, insurance, legal industry, supply chain, and token working groups.[56]

While our coverage is far from exhaustive, it underscores the point that people are taking blockchains for business seriously across sectors and across the globe.

1.3.5. Patents filed

Juxtaposed to the open-sourced, libertarian, cypherpunk roots of Bitcoin, adapting public blockchains for enterprise blockchains requires a significant amount of private investment. Therefore, it is no surprise to learn that over 1600 patents have been filed since 2010 because companies want to protect the intellectual property generated from their investments (see Figure 1.3). According to Derwent Innovation, 75 percent of patent applications were granted. Security First Corp, Microsoft, and IBM held the most patents with 64, 40, and 25 respectively.[57]

1.3.6. Regulators

> *"Regulators are still trying to manage this machine with rules devised for the industrial age."*
>
> **Don and Alex Tapscott, authors of *Blockchain Revolution*[58]**

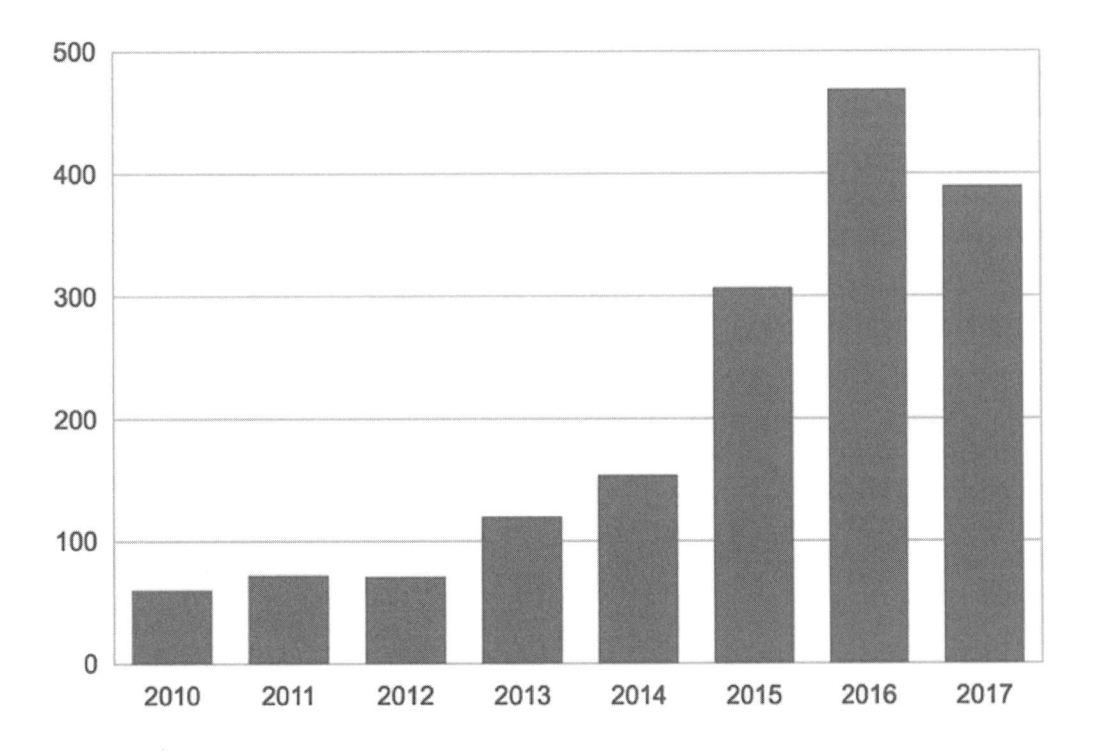

Figure 1.3: Blockchain-related patent filings

Source: https://www.coindesk.com/rate-blockchain-patent-applications-nearly-doubled-2017/

Regulators all over the world are examining the blockchain space. Some regulators are supportive, some are not, and still others have yet to deliberate.

Regulations on cryptocurrencies. In the US, a complex web of federal and state regulators oversees financial services (see Figure 1.4). The US Treasury Department was one of the first regulators to enact a policy. In 2013, it classified Bitcoin as a convertible, decentralized, virtual currency, and therefore subject to property taxes.

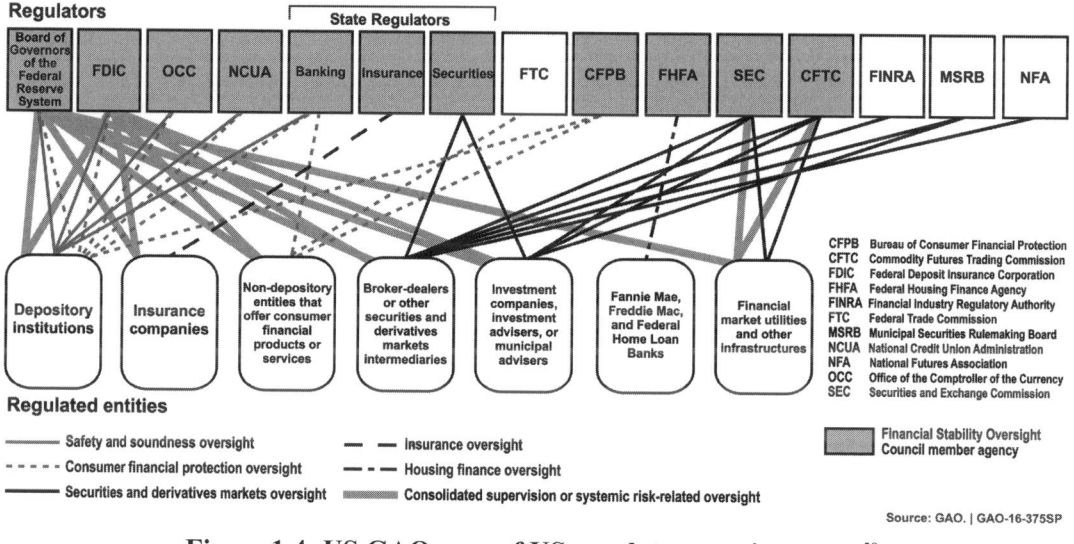

Figure 1.4: US GAO map of US regulatory environment[59]

Besides US federal regulations, US States agencies[60] can also impose cryptocurrency regulations, some of which are controversial. One notable example was a regulation published in June of 2015 by the Department of Financial Services (DFS) for New York State that required companies to get a BitLicense for virtual currencies. Many small firms found compliance to be too expensive (or too invasive) and stopped operating in the state. A further controversy happened when the chief architect of the regulation, Benjamin Lawsky, left the DFS to start his own consulting process to help clients maneuver through the onerous process to obtain a BitLicense.[61] The arguments for regulations are reasonable – the BitLicense, for example, required companies to: store transaction receipts; disclosure risks; publish a customer complaint policy; maintain a cybersecurity program; hire a compliance officer; and abide by anti-money-laundering rules.[62] While regulations can seem to stall innovation, they are designed to protect consumers.

Beyond the US, China banned financial institutions from accepting, using, or selling virtual currencies. Bangladesh, Bolivia, Ecuador, Kyrgyzstan, and Nepal explicitly banned bitcoins.[63] Russia banned cryptocurrencies in 2016 and Nigeria did so in 2017, but both may change course. Saudi Arabia has warned investors that cryptocurrencies are a high-risk asset. Japan recognizes Bitcoin as a method of payment. Estonia is one of the most forward-looking countries in terms of promoting cryptocurrencies and blockchain technologies.[64] For specific regulations by country, Wikipedia maintains a list of legal rules for Bitcoin.[65]

Regulations on ICOs. Many regulators don't quite know what to make of ICOs yet. Some regulators are reacting negatively to ICOs; China and South Korea banned them in 2017[66]. Other regulators in Switzerland, Singapore and Japan seem more favorable.[67] Estonia has even gone so far as to support an ICO for the creation its own crypto tokens called estcoins.[68] Regulators in the US, Singapore, Hong Kong and UK, have warned investors that an ICO may violate securities laws and that investors may lose their money.[69] To help reduce the risks of the new funding model, The Safe Agreement for Future Tokens (SAFT) project was launched in the US to establish a compliant token sale framework. The goal is *'to develop an industry standard that protects the interests of network creators, investors, and users.'*[7]

1.4. Blockchain's technology hype cycle

As we enter 2018, enterprise deployments of live blockchains applications have been slow, leading many to conclude that the buzz around enterprise blockchains is nothing but hype. Our response is that emerging technologies all pass through a well-established cycle of hype, and is thus to be expected. So while indeed blockchain technologies may be hyped as we enter 2018, eventually some forms of them will be widely deployed and certainly will generate value. To get a sense of where blockchains are in the hype cycle, we'll look at Gartner's assessment.

Gartner, a US information technology firm, branded a particularly well-known version of the hype-cycle. Gartner's model comprises five phases that map the level of expectations about the innovation over time (see Figure 1.5). During the **technology trigger phase**, early proof-of-concepts capture media attention and interest, but there are no real applications. During the **peak of inflated expectations phase**, a few early successes garner even more attention; senior executives start to take notice, new entrants jump into the market, and the technology may be viewed as a silver bullet, i.e. something that promises to instantly solve a long-standing problem. Many organizations start testing the technology, but enter the **trough of disillusionment phase** when instant success is not achieved. Organizations regroup. They learn to apply sound project management, change management, and what we call 'action principles' to deliver successful applications. In other words, it's hard work to get value from a new innovation. As time passes, upgraded versions of the technology are released, the market producers consolidate, and organizational consumers learn how to gain value from the innovations. Gartner calls this the **slope of enlightenment phase**. The last phase, called the **plateau of productivity phase**, sees market maturity, wide-spread adoption, and integration into the enterprises' standard technology portfolios.

Every year, Gartner updates its map of current emerging technologies through the five phases. In 2015, blockchains were not yet on Gartner's map. However, by July of 2016, Gartner placed blockchains as past the 'technology trigger phase' and was indeed approaching the apex of the 'peak of inflated expectations phase'. A year later in July 2017, Gartner placed blockchains as nearly finished with that phase; blockchains were headed for the 'trough of disillusionment'. While we cannot forecast with certainty when blockchain technologies will become mainstream, Gartner predicted that blockchains would not reach of the 'plateau of productivity' until after 2022. Again, our point is that blockchain technologies, while immature as of the start of 2018, will become mainstream.

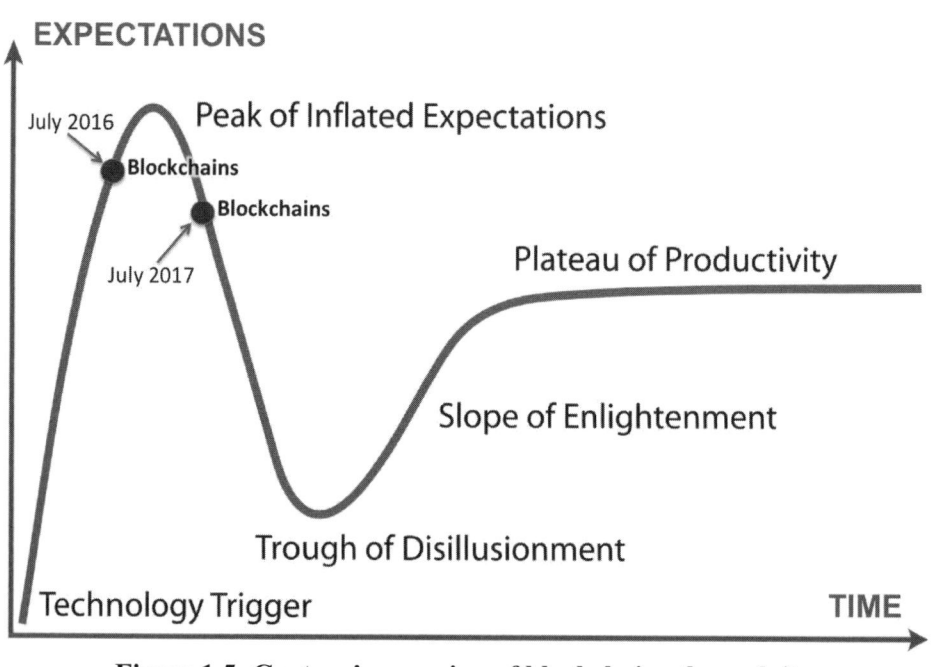

Figure 1.5: Gartner's mapping of blockchains through its technology hype cycle[71]

1.5. Conclusion: The landscape shifts rapidly

The particular context we are studying – blockchain applications for business – is built upon a rapidly shifting landscape. This guide has been tempered with phrases such as 'as of the beginning of 2018' and 'so far' to reflect that fact. Our review of the blockchain landscape found nearly $5 billion in investment and many active stakeholders. Although this level of activity has not yet produced many live business application deployments yet, we have argued that managers, business students, and other people with business interests need to learn about blockchains now.

This chapter did not define a blockchain application by design. We did not want to discourage readers with technical jargon before showing them that the blockchain landscape was signification enough to warrant their attention. The next step in climbing the learning curve is learning the answers to these two questions:

- What exactly are blockchain applications?
- Where did they come from?

Once the basics are understood, managers will be in a good position to understand blockchain's promised business value. By the end of this guide, managers will be able to assess how aggressively their enterprises should be exploring and building blockchain applications.

Citations

1. Quote from Prisco, G. (2015), Nasdaq to Push Forward with Blockchain Applications, *Bitcoin Magazine*, available at https://bitcoinmagazine.com/articles/nasdaq-push-forward-blockchain-applications-1432680278/
2. Quote from CEO's speech at IBM's Interconnect Conference, March 21st 2017
3. Quote from Emin Gün Sirer's presentation, *What Could Go Wrong? When Blockchains Fail*, at the Business of Blockchain conference, April 18th 2017, https://www.technologyreview.com/s/604219/blockchains-weak-spots-pose-a-hidden-danger-to-users/
4. Riel, A. (2017), *Blockchain: Reality Versus Hype*, white paper
5. See Blockchain in Review: *Investment Trends and Opportunities*, October 2017 by CB Insights
6. See Gupta, S. and Mondal, T. (2017), *HfS Blueprint Report: Enterprise Blockchain Services*
7. McKendrick, J. (December 2nd 2017), *Decision time is here for blockchain, but are enterprises ready?* http://www.zdnet.com/article/for-blockchain-decision-time-approaches/

8. Source: *Number of Blockchain wallet users worldwide from 1st quarter 2014 to 3rd quarter 2017*, https://www.statista.com/statistics/647374/worldwide-blockchain-wallet-users/

9. World Economic Forum (August 2016), *The Future of Financial Infrastructure: An Ambitious Look at How Blockchain Can Reshape Financial Services*, http://www3.weforum.org/docs/WEF_The_future_of_financial_infrastructure.pdf

10. Blockchain in Review: *Investment Trends and Opportunities* CB Insights webinar October 27th 2017, http://support.citrixonline.com/en_US/Webinar

11. Blockchain in Review: *Investment Trends and Opportunities,* CB Insights webinar October 27th 2017, http://support.citrixonline.com/en_US/Webinar

12. Blockchain Startups, https://angel.co/blockchains

13. Rosic, A. (July 4th 2016), *The 7 Most Valuable Blockchain Startups In The World*, available at : http://www.ameerrosic.com/the-7-most-valuable-blockchain-and-bitcoin-startups-in-the-world/#ixzz50DhoSFuZ

14. https://blog.cex.io/cryptonews/top-50-blockchain-startups-2017-16158

15. https://blog.cex.io/cryptonews/top-50-blockchain-startups-2017-16158

16. https://www.rise.global/blockchain-100

17. *Blockchain in Review: Investment Trends and Opportunities*, CB Insights webinar October 27th 2017, http://support.citrixonline.com/en_US/Webinar. See also: Levi, A. (May 21st 2017), 'Corporate Trends in Blockchain', CB Insights webinar presentation.

18. See *Blockchain in Review: Investment Trends and Opportunities*, October 2017 by CB Insights

19. See: http://dcg.co/portfolio/

20. See *Blockchain in Review: Investment Trends and Opportunities*, October 2017 by CB Insights

21. *Blockchain in Review: Investment Trends and Opportunities*, CB Insights webinar October 27th 2017. http://support.citrixonline.com/en_US/Webinar

22. See *Blockchain in Review: Investment Trends and Opportunities*, October 2017 by CB Insights

23. Griffith, E. (May 5th 2017), Why Startups are Trading IPOs for ICOS, *Fortune Magazine,* http://fortune.com/2017/05/05/ico-initial-coin-offering/

24. Higgins, S. (2017), *$232 Million: Tezos Blockchain Project Finishes Record-Setting Token Sale.* Posted on July 13th 2017, https://www.coindesk.com/232-million-tezos-blockchain-record-setting-token-sale/

25. See *Top 10 Cryptocurrency ICOs of 2017 (So Far)*, https://themerkle.com/top-10-cryptocurrency-icos-throughout-2017-to-date/

26. Kharpal, A. (November 21st 2017), *Cryptocurrency start-up Confido disappears with $375,000 from an ICO, and nobody can find the founders,* CNBC News, https://www.cnbc.com/2017/11/21/confido-ico-exit-scam-founders-run-away-with-375k.html

27. Goodman, L. (2014), *Tezos – a self-amending crypto-ledger*, White Paper, https://www.tezos.com/static/papers/white_paper.pdf

28. Irrera, A. and Stecklow, S. (November 3rd 2017), *Tezos organizers sued in California over crypto currency project*, Reuters, https://www.reuters.com/article/us-bitcoin-tezos-battles/tezos-organizers-sued-in-california-over-crypto-currency-project-idUSKBN1D325A

29. Clayton, J. (December 11th 2017), *Statement on Cryptocurrencies and Initial Coin Offerings,* https://www.sec.gov/news/public-statement/statement-clayton-2017-12-11

30. Shin, L. (December 4th 2017), $15 Million ICO Halted By SEC For Being Alleged Scam, *Forbes Magazine*, https://www.forbes.com/sites/laurashin/2017/12/04/15-million-ico-halted-by-sec-for-being-alleged-scam/ - 1728c7141569

31. Patel, D. (December 7th 2017), *Six red flags of an ICO scam*, Techncrunch, https://techcrunch.com/2017/12/07/6-red-flags-of-an-ico-scam/

32. Clayton, J. (December 11th 2017), *Statement on Cryptocurrencies and Initial Coin Offerings*, https://www.sec.gov/news/public-statement/statement-clayton-2017-12-11

33. Burniske, C. and Tatar, J. (2017) *Cryptoassets: The Innovative Investor's Guide to Bitcoin and Beyond*, McGraw Hill, United States

34. Most cryptocurrencies are created as hard forks from existing open source code, most commonly Bitcoin. Litecoin, Zcash, and Dash, are Bitcoin hard forks. Monero and NEM, both among the top ten cryptocurrencies by market capitalization as of July 2017, have different code bases. Monero uses proof-of-work based on CryptoNote protocol, which masks origin, destination, and transaction amount (see https://moneroblocks.info/); NEM is based on new code, https://www.nem.io/

35. This website tracks the trading price of cryptocurrencies in $US dollars and the total number of coins in circulation to calculate a market cap: https://coinmarketcap.com/all/views/all/

36. *Here's all the money in the world, in one chart*, posted January 29th 2016, http://www.marketwatch.com/story/this-is-how-much-money-exists-in-the-entire-world-in-one-chart-2015-12-18

37. Jeffries, A. (November 27th 2013), *Bitcoin hits $1,000 for the first time*, https://www.theverge.com/2013/11/27/5151396/bitcoin-hits-1000

38. Russell, J. (May 20th 2017), *Bitcoin just surged past $2,000 for the first time*, https://techcrunch.com/2017/05/20/btc2k/

39. Cheng, E. (November 28th 2017), *Bitcoin surpasses $10,000 for the first time*, https://www.cnbc.com/2017/11/28/bitcoin-surpasses-10000-for-the-first-time.html

40. Cheng, E. (December 6th 2017), *Bitcoin tops record $19,000, then plunges in wild 2-day ride*, https://www.cnbc.com/2017/12/06/bitcoin-tops-13000-surging-1000-in-less-than-24-hours.html

41. https://coinmarketcap.com/

42. To put these numbers in context, price volatility indices that calculate the standard deviation of a price from its mean during a certain time period may be used to compare historical price fluctuations. Using the price volatility index of a 30-day window, Bitcoin's 2017year end index was 7.14 percent and Ethereum's was 5.26 percent. For comparison, the volatility of gold averages around 1.2 percent and the volatility major fiat currencies averages between 0.5 and 1.0 percent. '*The Bitcoin Volatility Index*', tracked at https://www.buybitcoinworldwide.com/volatility-index/

43. Higgins, S. (December 7th 2017), *Steam Drops Bitcoin Payments Citing High Fees and Price Volatility*, Coindesk, https://www.coindesk.com/steam-drops-bitcoin-payments-citing-high-fees-price-volatility/

44. Gupta, A. and Mondal, T. (2017), *HfS Blueprint Report: Enterprise Blockchain Service*, https://www.hfsresearch.com/blueprint-reports/hfs-blueprint-enterprise-blockchain-services

45. *Blockchain Technology Market Analysis,* http://www.grandviewresearch.com/industry-analysis/blockchain-technology-market/, posted December 2016

46. Mougayer, W. (December 11th 2016), *The State of Global Blockchain Consortia*, Coindesk, https://www.coindesk.com/state-global-blockchain-consortia/

47. Gratzke, P., Schatsky, D., and Piscini, E. (August 2017), *Banding together for blockchain. Does it make sense for your company to join a consortium?*, https://dupress.deloitte.com/dup-us-en/focus/signals-for-strategists/emergence-of-blockchain-consortia.html - endnote-sup-7

48. See https://www.r3.com/

49. The Linux Foundation (January 22nd 2016), *The Hyperledger Project Charter*, https://www.hyperledger.org/about/charter

50. Connell, J. (2017), *On Byzantine Fault Tolerance in Blockchain Systems*, posted June 2017, https://cryptoinsider.com/byzantine-fault-tolerance-blockchain-systems/

51. https://www.hyperledger.org/projects

52. Rizzo, P. (April 25th 2017), *Inside the JBI: China's Massive New Blockchain Research Effort*, Coindesk, https://www.coindesk.com/chinas-government-backing-massive-blockchain-research-effort/

53. See https://b3i.tech/home.html

54. *Enterprise Ethereum Alliance Becomes World's Largest Open-source Blockchain Initiative*, posted July 17th 2017, https://entethalliance.org/enterprise-ethereum-alliance-becomes-worlds-largest-open-source-blockchain-initiative/

55. https://entethalliance.org/

56. *Welcome EEA Members*, https://entethalliance.atlassian.net/wiki/display/EEA/Welcome+EEA+Members

57. Chiu, H. (November 8th 2017), *An Overview of the Blockchain Patent Landscape*, https://clarivate.com/blog/overview-blockchain-patent-landscape/

58. Tapscott, D., and Tapscott, A. (2016), *Blockchain Revolution*, Penguin Random House, NYC, 56.

59. Source: http://www.gao.gov/modules/ereport/handler.php?1=1&path=/ereport/GAO-16-375SP/data_center/General_government/5._Financial_Regulatory_Structure

60. As an example of a US Federal regulation, The Financial Crimes Enforcement Network (FinCEN) bureau of the United States Department of the Treasury stated that virtual currency operators must abide by the regulations established for money transmitters

61. *Banking on Bitcoin*. Movie directed by Christopher Cannucciari, released November 22nd 2016

62. https://en.wikipedia.org/wiki/Legality_of_bitcoin_by_country

63. https://en.wikipedia.org/wiki/Legality_of_bitcoin_by_country_or_territory

64. *Global Regulations On Cryptocurrencies* (August-September 2017), https://www.cyberius.com/global-regulations-on-cryptocurrencies-aug-sep-2017/

65. This website tracks major bitcoin regulations by jurisdiction: https://en.wikipedia.org/wiki/Legality_of_bitcoin_by_country_or_territory

66. Russell, J. (September 28th 2017), *First China, now South Korea has banned ICOs*, Techcrunch, https://techcrunch.com/2017/09/28/south-korea-has-banned-icos/

67. Keane, J. (July 13th 2017), *The State of ICO Regulation? New Report Outlines Legal Status in 6 Nations*, Coindesk, https://www.coindesk.com/state-ico-regulation-new-report-outlines-legal-status-6-nations/

68. *Global Regulations On Cryptocurrencies* (August-September 2017), https://www.cyberius.com/global-regulations-on-cryptocurrencies-aug-sep-2017/

69. Russell, J. (September 28th 2017), *First China, now South Korea has banned ICOs*, Techcrunch, https://techcrunch.com/2017/09/28/south-korea-has-banned-icos/

70. The SAFT Project: https://saftproject.com/

71. Figure was created from Gartner's generic hype cycle and 2015, 2016, and 2017 versions:

    https://upload.wikimedia.org/wikipedia/commons/thumb/9/94/Gartner_Hype_Cycle.svg/1200px-Gartner_Hype_Cycle.svg.png

    http://na2.www.gartner.com/imagesrv/newsroom/images/emerging-tech-hc-2016.png;

    https://blogs.gartner.com/smarterwithgartner/files/2017/08/Emerging-Technology-Hype-Cycle-for-2017_Infographic_R6A.jpg

Chapter 2

The Blockchain Application Framework

A ***blockchain application*** is a distributed, peer-to-peer system for validating, time-stamping, and permanently storing transactions on a ***distributed ledger*** that uses ***cryptography*** to authenticate ***digital asset ownership*** and ***asset authenticity***, and ***consensus*** algorithms to add validated transactions to the ledger and to ensure the ongoing integrity of the ledger's complete history. Enterprise blockchains also use ***smart contracts*** that apply rules to automatically execute transactions based upon pre-agreed conditions.

2.1. Introduction

In this chapter, we'll gradually climb the learning curve to understand the meaning of our imposing definition above. The context we are studying – ***blockchains for business*** – is particularly challenging to understand because blockchains are not just one technology. Rather a blockchain application comprises a set of components that allow people to do some remarkable things, like transact directly with each other without needing third-party intermediaries, instantly tracking items across partners in a supply chain, and automatically executing the terms of a contract.

This chapter begins by explaining the relative advantage of blockchain applications compared to the centralized trading systems that dominate the coordination of today's businesses. Next, we'll provide a quick overview of Bitcoin, the very first blockchain application that went live in 2009. Every manager should know Bitcoin's story because all subsequent blockchains are an extension of or departure from the original Bitcoin blockchain. Since that hallmark event, other types of blockchains have been proposed and deployed, some with significant departures from Bitcoin's protocol. Consequently, many people now call the space 'distributed ledger technologies', as some blockchains are not even structured as a chain of linked blocks. Still

41

others contend that if the space is called 'distributed ledger technologies', it fails to capture the notion of smart contracts that automatically execute agreements in blockchains like Ethereum.[1] The debates over nomenclature become more comprehensible after first understanding the components of a blockchain application, including protocols, code bases, use cases, and application interfaces. Finally, we'll illustrate the framework by mapping Bitcoin to it. By the end of this chapter, managers will be able to map any blockchain application to the framework and understand the trade-offs of different choices among its component parts.

2.2. Centralized systems vs. distributed blockchain applications

"Distributed ledger technology will significantly increase transparency between market participants."

World Economic Forum Report[2]

When individuals or organizations want to trade in today's world, they engage trusted third parties to facilitate transactions. Trusted third parties – like banks, certificate authorities, and credit card companies – exist to mitigate counterparty risks, i.e. the risk each party bears that the other party will not fulfill its contractual obligations. Trusted third parties perform many vital functions, but here we focus upon two: ***trusted third parties authenticate asset ownership and make sure accounts are funded to prevent double spending***. While these functions are imperative, they come with some serious limitations.

Centralized trading systems have many versions of the truth. Each party to the transaction – the trading partners and the trusted third parties upon which they rely – maintain their own electronic records, i.e. digital ledgers, to record business transactions. These centralized records do not talk to each other (see Figure 2.1). Reconciling ledgers across trading partners can be onerous, particularly for applications like trade finance. With so many players involved in trade finance – customers, suppliers, banks, customs, transporters, and warehousers – the pain points in the process are significant.

Centralized trading systems provide little transparency as a consequence of each institution maintaining its own ledgers. Consider cross-border payments, the transfer of funds from an entity in one legal jurisdiction to an entity in another jurisdiction. When a manufacturer in one country sends payment to a supplier in another country, the manufacturer and the supplier's financial institutions, national payment systems, and corresponding banks process the transaction. Parties to an exchange have no access to the status of the transaction, the fees being charged, or even which institution controls a transaction as it works its way through the system. Furthermore, owners of centralized systems may modify records after-the-fact, so partners cannot be confident they are dealing with the same historical record of transactions through time.

Before blockchains:
Every organization has their own Ledger and relies on a trusted third party ...

After a blockchain:
Every participating organization has an identical copy of a shared ledger and transacts directly ...

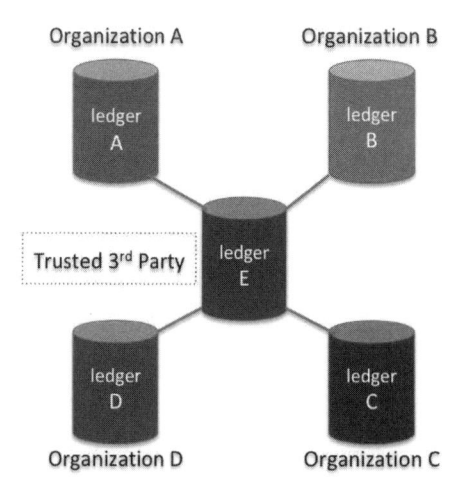
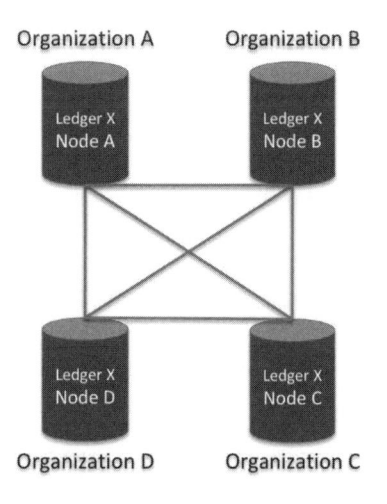

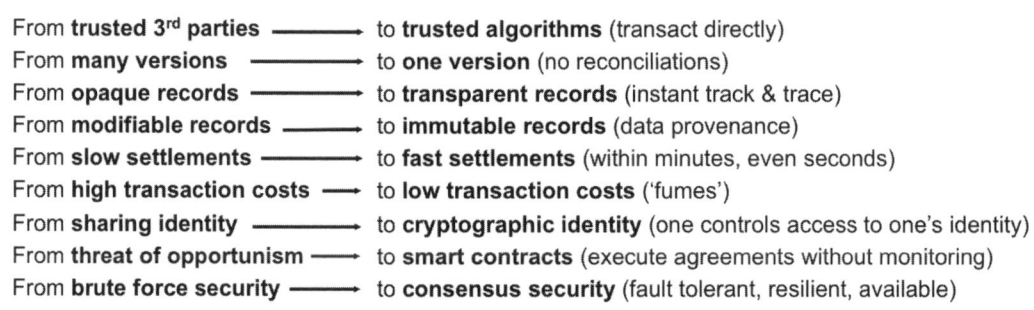

From **trusted 3rd parties** ⟶ to **trusted algorithms** (transact directly)
From **many versions** ⟶ to **one version** (no reconciliations)
From **opaque records** ⟶ to **transparent records** (instant track & trace)
From **modifiable records** ⟶ to **immutable records** (data provenance)
From **slow settlements** ⟶ to **fast settlements** (within minutes, even seconds)
From **high transaction costs** ⟶ to **low transaction costs** ('fumes')
From **sharing identity** ⟶ to **cryptographic identity** (one controls access to one's identity)
From **threat of opportunism** ⟶ to **smart contracts** (execute agreements without monitoring)
From **brute force security** ⟶ to **consensus security** (fault tolerant, resilient, available)

**Figure 2.1: Multiple-centralized systems vs.
a shared blockchain application**

Centralized trading systems have slow settlement times. Trading partners spend a lot of time and money reconciling and settling transactions to make sure records agree. Some transactions, like cross-border payments and trade finance, can take days or weeks to settle. For example, the European Central Bank reported that the average time to settle cross-border credit transfers was 4.8 working days in 1999.[3] McKinsey found little progress by 2015, as the average settlement times were still between three to five business days.[4]

Centralized trading systems have high transaction costs. In the current global financial system, fees accumulate with each step in the process. Trading partners do not always know the fees in advance, which can become quite substantial. The World Bank estimated that sending remittances cost an average of 7.99 percent of the amount sent.[5] Some banks charged 13 percent of the transaction value for round-trip exchanges between the UK and Europe in 2013.[6] Transaction costs are also high because parties need to monitor each others' activities to prevent opportunism and to ensure agreements are executed as promised. There are also additional costs associated with compliance reporting.

Centralized trading systems provide little privacy because of the way trading partners and trusted third parties establish identity. Consumers, for example, routinely turn over much of their personal data, including national identification numbers, home addresses, credit card numbers, birth dates, employment records, utility bills, and more, simply to verify identity to the financial institutions that sit in the middle of their transactions. Furthermore, each party's financial institution has access to every transaction associated with an account to prevent double spending. The risk of information leakage is high, as any partner might use the data for something other than the original transaction.[7]

Centralized trading systems are vulnerable to attack and can cost an organization billions of dollars to protect or remedy. High profile attacks include Heartland Payment Systems in 2009 that cost the company $2.8 billion to remedy, Citibank in 2011 that cost $19.4 million, and JP Morgan Chase in 2014 that cost $1 billion.[8] Think also about the security breeches at Equifax, Target, Sony, and Netflix… the list goes on.

In summary, centralized trading systems provide vital functions, but come with many limitations. Blockchain applications are distributed trading systems that aim to overcome them.

A distributed blockchain application promises to perform the vital functions of trusted third-parties without relying on institutions, allowing **trading partners to transact directly.** Instead, a blockchain application uses computer algorithms to confirm **asset authenticity**, authenticate **asset ownership** and to **validate transactions**, such as making sure accounts are funded before transferring value. With a distributed blockchain application, **every** participating organization has an exact copy of the same digital ledger. Each copy is called a 'node'. Computer algorithms sequence transactions, time-stamp them and permanently store them on the shared distributed ledger. Transactions on the shared ledger are **immutable**, thus every party can be confident they are dealing with the same data. With **one version** of the truth **transparent** to all parties, there are no reconciliations, enabling **faster settlement times** and **lower transaction costs.** Consumers and institutions control their own identity with cryptographic digital signatures, reducing the risks of information leakage and identity theft. Enterprise blockchain applications use smart contracts that apply rules to **automatically execute agreements** based on pre-agreed conditions, thus no more monitoring and worrying that trading partners are not fulfilling their obligations. Furthermore, blockchain applications promise **heightened security**. All of the nodes constantly chatter with each other to maintain agreement. Blockchain applications still function properly even if a high percentage of nodes are faulty – or even malicious – **enabling resiliency** and 100 percent **availability**. In theory, the only way to break a blockchain application is to commandeer more than 50 percent of the nodes before any of the other nodes notice.

Now that we've explained a blockchain application at a high level, let's understand where it first came from.

2.3. Bitcoin: The first blockchain application

"Bitcoin is a remarkable cryptographic achievement and the ability to create something that is not duplicable in the digital world has enormous value."

Eric Schmidt, CEO of Google[9]

"I think the fact that within the bitcoin universe an algorithm replaces the functions of [the government] ... is actually pretty cool. I am a big fan of Bitcoin."

Al Gore, 45th Vice President of the United States[10]

"As bitcoin becomes more mainstream, the social consensus around what bitcoin should be may change. If this occurs, we may not see the libertarians turn on bitcoin so much as bitcoin turn on the libertarians. It is for this reason that I believe it is incredibly important that we teach bitcoin users the history behind cryptocurrency in order to instill Cypherpunk values in them."

Jameson Loop, Coindesk[11]

Among the dozens of blockchains that exist today and the hundreds more on their way, all blockchains are a reaction to the original Bitcoin blockchain as articulated by Satoshi Nakamoto in a 2008 white paper.[12] Satoshi Nakamoto, a pseudonym used by an unknown person or persons who remains anonymous to this day, posted a paper entitled, '*Bitcoin: A Peer-to-Peer Electronic Cash System*' to a cryptographic mailing list in 2008. This remarkable nine-page paper is the foundation for all we have today in the blockchain world. Quite simply, Nakamoto proposed *"an electronic payment system based on cryptographic proof instead of trust, allowing any two willing parties to transact directly with each other without the need for a trusted third party."*[13] Nakamoto was solving this problem: How can a payment system be created that performs the vital functions of trusted third parties without using them? Rather than rely on institutions, Nakamoto proposed to rely on computer algorithms.

The cryptocurrency 'Bitcoin'. If transactions were to exchange value electronically, the first thing needed was something of electronic value. Nakamoto thus created an 'electronic coin' called a 'Bitcoin'. Contrary to popular belief, Bitcoins are not the first cryptocurrency. David Chaum launched DigiCash in 1990, the first live cryptocurrency.[14] While an important breakthrough, DigiCash was centrally controlled in that the company's system performed the validations. Nakamoto resurrected Chaum's idea of blind digital signatures as a way to verify asset ownership, but this time with distributed validation and control.[15]

Like DigiCash, bitcoin's blockchain relies on cryptography to authenticate asset ownership. Specifically, bitcoin relies on a digital signature, which is a mathematical process that uses two related numbers called a 'private-public' key pair. A form of the public key is stored on the permanent distributed ledger. The private key is stored off the blockchain. Both keys are needed to 'digitally sign' a transaction to prove ownership (more on this below). Anonymity is achieved because, while anyone can see the transactions, the identity of the transacting parties is not revealed; one only views values being transferred between addresses.

Independent validators. Validating transactions to prevent double spending was a bit trickier to solve without trusted third parties. We can't trust senders to verify that they have enough currency to fund their transactions. We need an independent verifier. Here was Nakamoto's brilliant solution: reward other nodes in the network with newly issued bitcoins when they validate all the recently submitted transactions by searching the ledger to make sure all the senders' addresses have enough coins to fund their transactions. So that validator nodes take the task seriously, Nakamoto proposed a competition in which competing nodes race to find a computationally intensive number that meets some specific criteria. These validators, called 'miners', are going to put some skin in the game as far as using their own computing power to perform the validations. The validation process is called a 'proof-of-work'. The winning node sequences and organizes all the recently validated transactions into a new block that has a pointer to the previous block, thus creating a chain of blocks through time, called a 'blockchain' (more on this below).

Early users. After this white paper was posted to a listserve in 2008, the bitcoin application was coded – presumably by Nakamoto – and went live in January of 2009. At first, Bitcoin was used by just a few folks, most notably by the programmer Hal Finney, the creator of b-money, Wei Dai, the creator of smart contracts, Nick Szabo, and the eventual head of the open-sourced Bitcoin Foundation, Gavin Andresen. (For managers interested in the details, read Nathaniel Popper's book, *Digital Gold: Bitcoin and the Inside History of the Misfits and Millionaires Trying to Reinvent Money,* (2015), Allen Lane, UK.)

Bitcoin's blockchain delivered a payment system that had: a single version of the truth; full transparency; full anonymity; rapid settlement times; predictable and lower transaction fees; democratic and predictable rules controlled by an open source community; and heightened security, when compared to the current global financial system.

Now that we've explained where the idea for blockchain applications came from, let's peek under the hood to examine its component parts.

2.4. The blockchain application framework

A blockchain application comprises protocols, code bases, use cases, and application interfaces (see Figure 2.2). As one becomes more familiar with blockchain technologies, one appreciates that protocols are the real innovations in the space. **Protocols** specify rights of access and the rules for how transactions in a blockchain application authenticate asset ownership, and how transactions are structured, addressed, transmitted, routed, validated, sequenced, secured, and added to the permanent record. Once rules are established, protocols are programmed into **code bases**, like Ethereum, Hyperledger Fabric, Corda, Chain, or Multichain. From there, organizations can adapt the code base for a particular **use case**, like tracking and tracing items in a supply chain or for cross-border payments. Finally, all blockchain applications have **interfaces** where users access the system.

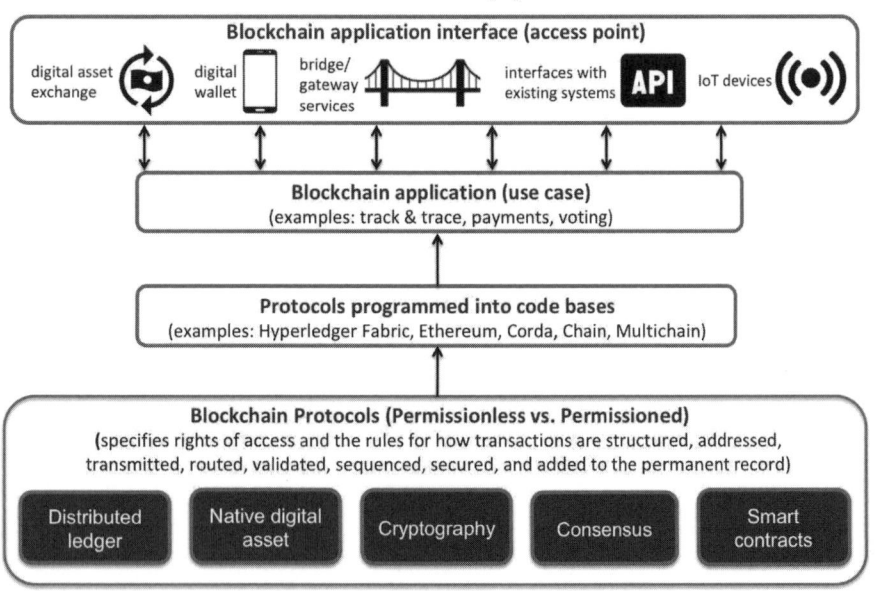

Figure 2.2: Components of a blockchain application

2.4.1. Protocols

A blockchain protocol is often called the 'Trust Protocol'. However, the word 'trust' is narrowly defined to mean: 'trust that the records on the distributed ledger agree across copies.' Trust here has nothing to do with the faith or confidence that trading partners are benevolent or will play by the rules. In fact, it is more accurate to say that we can assume many actors will indeed be malevolent. **'Trust that the records on the distributed ledger agree across copies'** equates to **'trust that the computer algorithms will reject faulty transactions, ignore faulty nodes on the network, and never modify the valid transactions once they have been added to the ledger.'** For a given blockchain application, protocols serve as the blueprints to ensure the correctness and ongoing integrity of records. In general, blockchain protocols can be divided into 'permissionless' and 'permissioned' protocols.

A **permissionless** protocol does not restrict access, and for this reason, they are also referred to as 'public' blockchains.[16] Anyone with access to the Internet can observe a permissionless blockchain to see all the transactions that have taken place over time (see Table 2.1 for websites to observe Bitcoin, Ethereum, and Stellar blockchains). Anyone can submit transactions to the blockchain provided they obtain some of the native digital assets (e.g. cryptocurrency). For the Bitcoin, Ethereum, and Stellar blockchain applications, people can buy their native digital assets – bitcoins, ether, or lumens, respectively – from an exchange like Coinbase (US-based), Kraken (US-based), Bittrex (US-based), BitFinex (Hong Kong-based), Bitstamp (Luxenbourg-based), CEX.IO (UK-based), Coinmama (Virgin Islands-based), and Binance (China-based). Additionally, anyone can buy the necessary hardware, download the entire Bitcoin or Ethereum codebase, become a miner, and compete for block rewards paid in bitcoins or ether (see Table 2.1 for instructions). Additionally, people can apply for a grant from the Stellar Foundation, as it will give away 95 percent of the lumens over the next years. People can also run Stellar validation nodes to help secure the network.

Blockchain	Native Digital Asset (Cryptocurrency Symbol)	Website to observe all transactions	Instructions to download code to operate a node
Bitcoin	bitcoins (BTC)	https://blockexplorer.com/	https://www.bitcoinmining.com/
Ethereum	ether (ETH)	https://etherscan.io/	https://github.com/ethereum/wiki/wiki/Mining
Stellar	lumens (XLM)	https://stellarchain.io/	https://www.stellar.org/developers/stellar-core/software/admin.html

Table 2.1 Permissionless blockchains

A **permissioned** protocol restricts access. Nearly all enterprise blockchains are permissioned, as businesses must comply with regulations and need more control than permissionless blockchains provide. Regulators, for example, require that financial institutions know their customers, so the anonymity of permissionless blockchains will not likely comply with current regulations. As far as control, enterprises do not want competitors to see every transaction they've made with customers; they want some control over who views records.

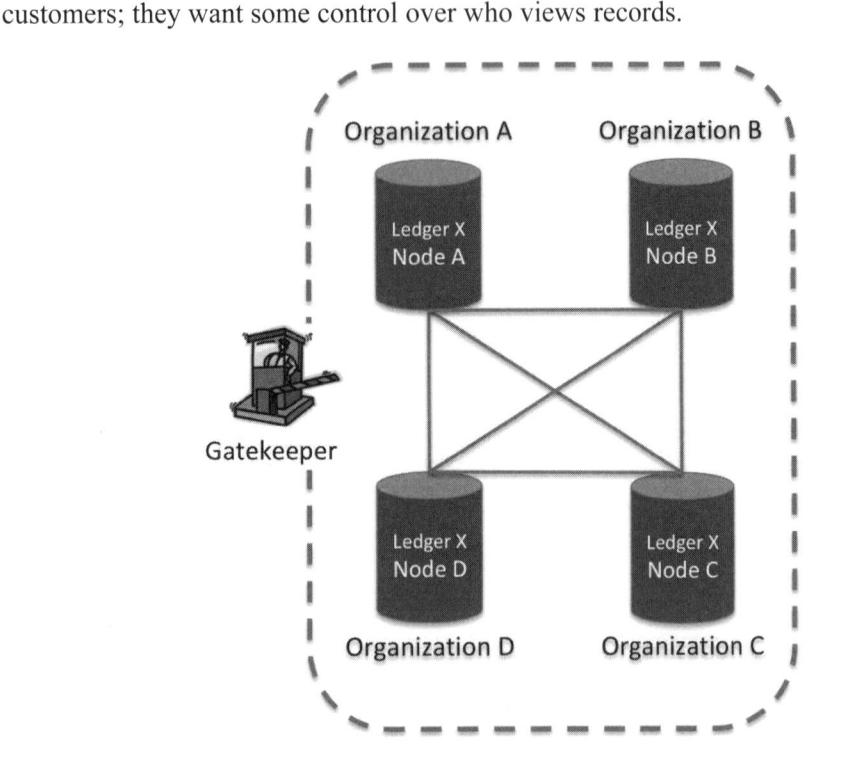

**Figure 2.3: A permissioned blockchain with a gatekeeper
to enforce the rights of access**

Permissioned blockchains rely upon a front-end gatekeeper to enforce the rights of access (see Figure 2.3). Unlike a trusted-third party that sits in the middle of transactions, the gatekeeper is like a security guard that checks a badge before allowing entry. It has no ability to alter the ledger or to stop smart contracts from executing.[i] The gatekeeping function may be governed

---

(i) This is true provided that the organization that serves as the gatekeeper operates fewer than 50 percent of the nodes; If a gatekeeper does operate 50 percent or more of the nodes, there is little point in using a blockchain except under specific circumstances, such as an intra-organizational blockchain across divisions.

collaboratively by the trading partners or by a single enterprise, such as a regulatory authority that issues licenses for participation: '*existing participants could decide future entrants; a regulatory authority could issue licenses for participation; or a consortium could make the decisions instead.*'[17] Once participants are past the gatekeeping function, they enter the distributed blockchain application.

Permissioned blockchains can also use smart contracts (explained below) to nuance roles within a blockchain application. Particular parties may play different roles within different smart contracts, such as observe, transact, validate, and add transactions to the ledger (see Figures 2.4 and 2.5). For example, Hyperledger Fabric uses smart contracts to create separate channels, which can be thought of as multiple mini-ledgers within a blockchain network; A given node within a HyprerLedger Fabric blockchain network only has access to the channels which it created or to which it was invited to participate.

One shared blockchain network with different access rights

PUBLIC STATES:
Every member of the permissioned blockchain network may view the public state transactions

PRIVATE STATES:
Only parties to the particular smart contract can view the private state transactions

Figure 2.4: Conceptual picture showing different access rights within a blockchain network

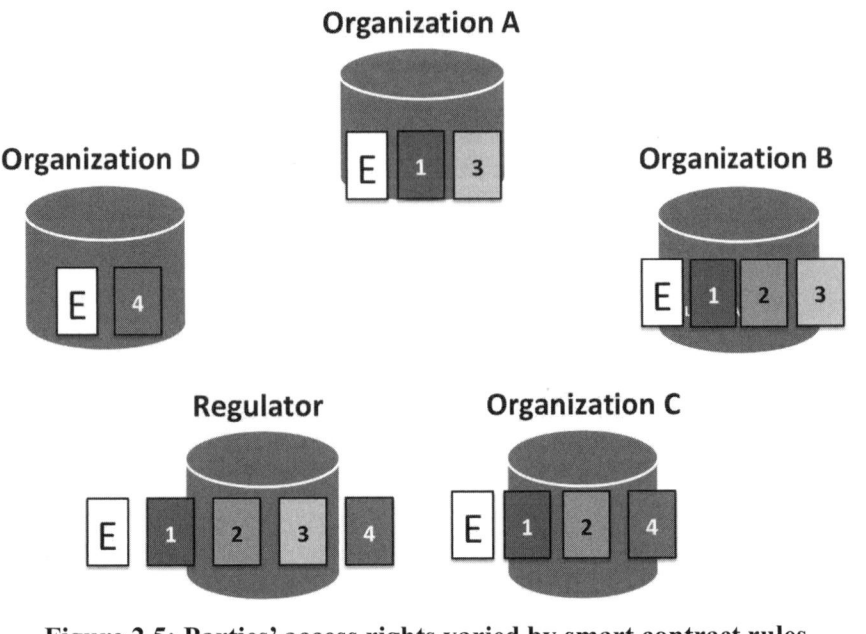

Figure 2.5: Parties' access rights varied by smart contract rules

Organization A is party to smart contracts 1 and 3, but cannot observe smart contracts 2 and 4;
Organization B is party to smart contracts 1, 2, and 3 but cannot observe smart contract 4;
Organization C is party to smart contracts 1, 2, and 4 but cannot observe smart contract 3;
Organization D is part to smart contract 4 but cannot observe smart contracts 1,2, and 3;
The regulator in this example is granted observation-only access to all transactions.

Let's examine the trade-offs between permissionless and permissioned blockchains more closely…

Permissionless vs. permissioned blockchains. The choice between permissionless and permissioned blockchains comes down to this question: For a given application, do we need or have a *priori* faith in trading partners?

Permissionless blockchains require zero external faith or confidence in trading partners because trust – again 'trust' is defined as 'trust that the records on the distributed ledger agree across copies' – is established completely by the computing power of the network. In contrast, permissioned blockchains use the gatekeeper to establish a level of faith or confidence in trading partners upfront (see Table 2.2). By establishing some level of faith up front, permissioned protocols need less computationally-intensive computer algorithms to ensure that the records on the distributed ledger agree. Transactions running on a permissioned blockchain application settle faster, scale bigger, and consume fewer resources compared to transactions running on a permissionless blockchain.

Many people ask which type of protocol is more secure. No technology is one hundred percent secure, and therefore security has to be assessed against the risks associated with a specific context. The context of voting in a US Presidential election will have a significantly different risk profile than the context of voting for our favorite potato chip flavor. Security risks are mitigated with a combination of technology, processes, and people. Permissionless blockchains rely more on technology than permissioned blockchains. Of course, people play a role in securing permissionless blockchains – open source communities define the protocols and build the codes bases, and miners verify and add transactions to the blockchain. The protocols incentivize the miners to play by the rules.[18]

	Permissionless Blockchains	Permissioned Blockchains
Do we need or have *a priori* faith in trading partners?	No	Yes
Source of 'trust' that the records on the distributed ledger agree across copies	'Trust' is completely established by computationally intensive computer algorithms	Gatekeeping function and centralized list of validator nodes require less computationally-intensive computer algorithms in the blockchain application to establish 'trust'
Resource consumption (e.g. electricity to run computers)	Higher	Lower
Scalability	Lower	Higher
Transaction Settlement Speed	Slower	Faster
Security	Relies more on technology than people and processes	Relies on a mix of technology, people, and processes
Examples	Bitcoin, Ethereum, Stellar	Hyperledger Fabric, Chain, Multichain Quorum, Corda

Table 2.2: Permissionless vs. permissioned blockchains

Be forewarned: many people think that permissionless blockchains are incongruous with the original purpose and spirit of blockchains. While this guide focuses on enterprise uses of blockchain, it is important to realize that the Bitcoin community was founded on cypherpunk and libertarian values. After the 2008 Global Financial Crisis – possibly the greatest economic disruption since the Great Depression of 1929 – people became increasingly distrustful of financial institutions. Movements like Occupy Wall Street ranted against wealth inequality and the influence of large financial intuitions on government policy. People rallied against the government's power to control money; governments can print fiat money at will, causing inflation, and can change regulations on a whim. Even more distressing, governments can freeze, seize, or restrict access to one's assets. For example, the Greek banks would not allow account holders to withdraw more than 60 euros a day in 2015.[19] Understanding this cypherpunk and libertarian history will shed light on the debates against enterprises adapting blockchain applications with 'permissioned' blockchains. Consider these various views:

> *"The banks and the corporations say, "Oh, Bitcoin's awesome. We want that – only without the open, decentralized, peer-to-peer, borderless, permissionless part. Could we instead have a closed, controlled, tame, identity-laden permission version of that please?"*
>
> **Andreas Antonopoulos, Bitcoin Guru[20]**

> *"A permissioned blockchain is about as special as a car being drawn by a horse: impractical and unlikely to show the innovation of the product."*
>
> **Bas Wisselink, Co-founder of Blockchain Workspace[21]**

> *"The permissioned blockchain isn't looking to overthrow the political system, or remove the need for established financial institutions."*
>
> **Devon Allaby, Fjord Australia[22]**

Now that we explained the two general types of protocols – permissionless and permissioned – we can examine the specific protocols. A given blockchain application specifies rules for the structure of the ***distributed ledger***; the rights of use for its ***native digital asset (***e.g. cryptocurrency); the rules to secure data using ***cryptography***; the rules to maintain ***consensus*** among nodes; the rights of different nodes to observe, transact, verify and add transactions to distributed ledger; and the rules for how trading partners can code agreements that will be automatically executed by ***smart contracts*** (see Figure 2.2).[(ii)] We examine each of these protocols a bit more below.

(ii) There are other ways to categorize the protocols, such as 'network', 'transaction', and 'consensus'.

Distributed ledger. Protocols define the structure of the distributed ledger. The most common structure is a ***chain of blocks*** – thus the name 'blockchain' (see Figure 2.6). With a blockchain structure, recently approved transactions are sequenced and collected into a block. The block is secured with a unique identifier that points to its immediate predecessor to form a linked chain. Bitcoin, Ethereum, Quorda and Hyperledger Fabric use blockchains to structure their ledgers.

Distributed ledger structured as a chain of blocks:

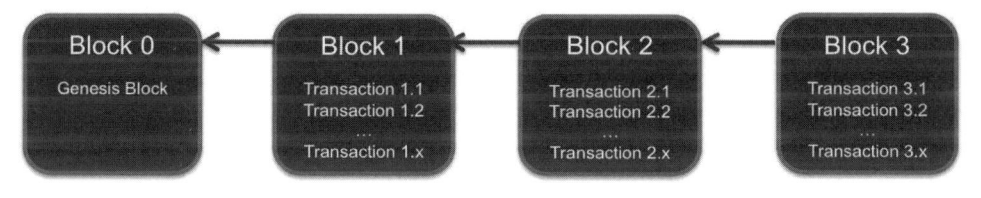

Distributed ledger structured as
a growing list of transactions:

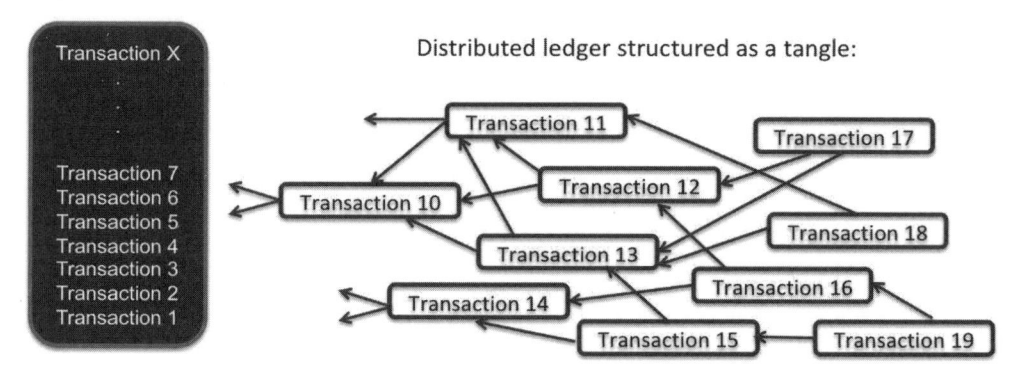

Figure 2.6: Examples of three distributed ledger structures

Another common structure is a ***continuous stream of transactions***, one after the other, through a process of continual ledger close. Ripple and Stellar use continual ledger close processes.

The startup IOTA recently proposed to structure its distributed ledger as a ***tangle*** of transactions.[23] Different structures have tradeoffs between security and speed of transaction settlement. In general, the chain of blocks is the most secure; the tangle promises to be the quickest.

Why is a blockchain structure the most secure? Within a block, not only is each transaction secured with a cryptographic hash (see Glossary), but each pair of transactions is cryptographically hashed, and then each pair of transaction pairs is cryptographically hashed, and so on until the last hash, called the Merkle root (see Glossary), is stored in the block header. All this hashing securely locks the time sequence and value of transactions in a way that if one piece of information were altered, it would be immediately detected. (Visually, the opening sequence of the US TV comedy show, Get Smart, comes to mind, where the spy has to pass through locked door after locked door to get to his destination).

Why does a tangle promise to be the fastest ledger? Because each new transaction only has to validate two other transactions, compared to, say, Bitcoin, that relies on a separate mining function to validate all the recently submitted transactions, which could be hundreds or even thousands of transactions. Serguei Popov, author of the IOTA white paper explains:

> *"The main idea of the tangle is the following: To issue a transaction, users must work to approve other transactions. Therefore, users who issue a transaction are contributing to the network's security. It is assumed that the nodes check if the approved transactions are not conflicting. If a node finds that a transaction is in conflict with the tangle history, the node will not approve the conflicting transaction."[24]*

Native digital asset. A protocol defines the uses of a blockchain application's native digital asset – an asset that exists only in digital form and comes with rights of use. Native digital assets can serve multiple functions in blockchains. Five common uses are:

1. As a **cryptocurrency**, a native digital asset serves the same functions as fiat money, namely as a medium of exchange for payment of debts, as a common measure of value, and as a store of value that should retain its worth over time.

2. Native digital assets can also be used as a **token** to represent anything of value. For example, anyone can download Bitcoin's source code and create an AltCoin (Bitcoin Alternative) that might be used to represent loyalty rewards points, airline miles, or shares in a company. The same goes for Ethereum – Auger, Golem, and Aragon are three examples of tokens created in Ethereum.[26]

3. Blockchains rely on participants to operate nodes to validate transactions and constantly re-check the integrity of the ledger's records. Native digital assets are a way to **compensate participants for securing the network**.

4. Native digital assets can be used to **discourage people from over-using a shared resource** by requiring a small fee to submit transactions to the network. Ethereum, for example, uses its native digital asset – 'ether' – to pay for specific actions on the blockchain network.

5. Additionally, native digital assets serve as a **counter-measure to Denial of Service (DoS) attacks**, as a malicious actor trying to spam millions of transactions would run out of funding.[27]

Cryptography. Blockchains rely heavily on cryptography, the science of securing data in the presence of third party adversaries. There's quite a bit of imposing mathematics that secure blockchains, but a digital signature is the most important cryptographic feature to understand because consumers are ultimately responsible for their own digital signatures. If consumers don't protect them, they risk losing their digital asset.

Here's how a digital signature works. When a consumer buys a native digital asset, let's say a bitcoin, the system generates a unique pair of numbers that are mathematically related, called a private-public key pair. The public key is the address we see stored on the blockchain (well actually, it's a hashed version of the public key; see the Glossary for a description of hashes). The private key is stored off the blockchain, most typically in a digital wallet. To move value out of the address stored on the blockchain, one needs to verify he or she owns the address by using his or her private key stored off the blockchain. Computer algorithms verify that the private key is indeed the mathematical mate to the public key. Both keys are needed to digitally sign the transaction (see Figure 2.7). Thus, a blockchain uses digital signatures to verify asset ownership and thus does not need to rely on a trusted third party to provide this function.

Validating transactions to prevent double spending is a bit trickier to solve without trusted third parties. We can't trust senders to verify that they have enough currency to fund their transactions – we need an independent verifier. This brings us to consensus protocols.

Consensus. As the name implies, consensus protocols are the rules that make sure all the nodes in a blockchain network agree, that is, that nodes are using the same, exact copy of the digital ledger. A consensus protocol assures '*a common, unambiguous ordering of transactions and blocks and guarantees the integrity and consistency of the blockchain across geographically* *distributed nodes.'*[28] Many consensus protocols have been proposed, including: proof-of-work; proof-of-stake; proof-of-activity (which combines proof-of-stake with proof-of-work); proof-of-authority; proof-of-burn; proof-of-capacity; proof-of-listening; proof-of-elapsed time[29]; proof-of-luck; … the list goes on.[30]

Digital Signature

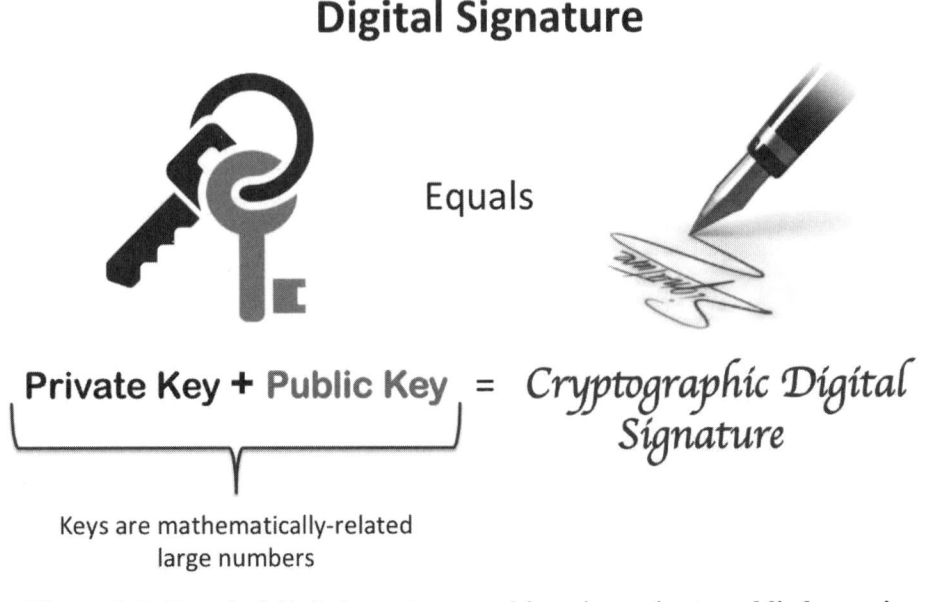

Equals

Private Key + Public Key = *Cryptographic Digital Signature*

Keys are mathematically-related
large numbers

Figure 2.7: Proof of digital asset ownership using private-public key pairs

Although consensus protocols vary in their validation procedures, in general, all consensus protocols seek to verify legitimate transactions, reject unverifiable transactions, ignore faulty nodes on the network, and prevent modifications to the ledger. The process of validation begins when a new transaction is broadcast to the network. Computer algorithms on the other nodes verify legitimate ownership of the asset (based on the owner's digital signature with his or her private key) and check that the asset has not been given away before by scanning the digital ledger, thus preventing double spending. Which particular node gets to collect verified transactions, sequence them and add them to the official ledger depends on the network's specific consensus protocol.

Commonly used consensus protocols are 'proof-of-work' (used by Bitcoin and Ethereum); 'proof-of-stake' (used by NXT and possibly Ethereum in the future); and 'Byzantine Fault

Tolerance (BFT)' (used by Ripple, Stellar, Hyperledger Fabric, and Tendermint) – see Table 2.3. Few managers will probably be interested in the details, but for those who are, see the Glossary.

Consensus Protocol	Description	Pros	Cons	Blockchains
Proof-of-work	Open competition among nodes; the first computer node that finds a valid block identification number wins a reward in the form of digital coins.	• Allows trustless concensus • Prohibitively expensive to hack	• High electricity consumption • Time to confirm and add a transaction to the blockchain - takes longer than other protocols	• Bitcoin • Ethereum • Monero
Proof-of-stake	Semi-random selection of a verifier node that favors those with the greatest investments or 'stake'.	• Less electricity consuption than proof-of-work • Faster settlement than proof-of-work • Once scaled, very safe from attacks	• Validators with little at stake might double-sign transactions[31]	• Peercoin[32] • NXT[33] • Ethereum may move to PoS
Byzantine Fault Tolerance[34] (BFT)	Only authorized nodes are allowed to validate and add transactions to the official ledger.	• Less electricity consuption than proof-of-work • Faster settlement than proof-of-work • Network performs well as lomg as not more than 33% of nodes are faulty[35]	• More centralized that other protocols because governance is needed to maintain lists of authorised nodes	• Ripple • Stellar • Hyperledger • Tendermint

Table 2.3: Three common consensus protocols

Smart Contracts. A smart contract – a concept developed by Nick Szabo in 1994 – is *"a piece of software that stores rules for negotiating the terms of a contract, automatically verifies the contract and then executes the terms."*[36] Anything that can be coded, can be coded into a smart contract that is secured and permanently stored on a blockchain. Ethereum was the first major blockchain to include 'smart contracts', thus escalating blockchains from peer-to-peer payment systems to platforms that can execute machine-to-machine agreements. As of February 2018, over 14,000 contracts were running on Ethereum.[37]

Smart contracts' magic (and danger) is that, once deployed, they execute automatically and cannot be stopped. Therefore, parties must agree to all the terms of the contract before deploying it. Smart contracts are commonly used to automatically move value around accounts based on agreed upon conditions. As we shall see, use cases abound: lotteries; voting; crowdsourcing, asset sharing (lookout Uber, Airbnb, and Spotify), asset tracking, identity management, bidding; rating; gaming; and gambling. In general, smart contacts can be classified as either 'deterministic' or 'non-deterministic'.

A deterministic smart contract means that the contract, once deployed on the blockchain, can execute autonomously without the need for any outside information. A lottery is a good example. A smart contract for a lottery could define the time period when people could send value to the smart contract account to 'buy' lottery tickets. The smart contract could specify how the winning lottery number would be selected, perhaps by taking the hash of a randomly selected block and awarding the account that is closest to that number as the winner. The smart contract could automatically transfer the money to the winning account. If the lottery was regulated, the smart contract could be coded to deduct taxes.

A non-deterministic smart contract means that outside information is needed to execute the contract. Horse race betting is an example. Like a lottery, a smart contract for horse race betting could be coded to define when people could send value to the smart contract account to place their bets. The rules for adjusting odds could also be mechanized in the contract. However, smart contracts for horse racing cannot run autonomously; they need outsiders (called '*oracles*') to inform the smart contract of the winning animal. Unlike trusted third parties, an oracle in this scenario does not control the funds, the smart contract does.

Autonomous execution of organizations. One special kind of smart contact is called a Decentralized Autonomous Organization (DAO):

> *"The idea of a DAO is to create a completely independent entity that is exclusively governed by the rules that you program into it and 'lives' on the chain. This is more than using the blockchain to manage a company; instead, the code is the entire company. And it cannot be stopped."*

Henning Diedrich, author of Ethereum: Blockchains, Digital Assets, Smart Contracts, DAOs[38]

The concept of a DAO is intriguing. As the name implies, the idea is to create a new organization that runs automatically based on codified rules encrypted in a smart contract. It runs without anyone controlling it, and it cannot be modified or rescinded once it is launched. ***Think of a decentralized autonomous organization as a completely digital 'company' with no managers or employees***. The 'owners' are the ones who transferred cryptocurrencies to the DAO's accounts during an initial funding period. Their investments are subject to the rules of the contract, such as limiting when accounts can be liquidated. How well did this idea work in practice? Well the coders of one particular DAO created such havoc, it resulted in a huge battle within the Ethereum open source community, resulting in a 'hard fork' (see Glossary). The story, covered in Chapter 4, is an important reminder of the challenges of shared governance over distributed systems.

2.4.2. Code bases

Open source communities, consortia, or even private companies and individuals can program protocols into ***code bases***. A code base is the set of programming instructions based on the agreed upon rules, i.e. the protocols. Many code bases are and managed by an open community who decides what changes can be made to the code base. Open source code bases also allow people to download the code and play with the code in a test environment called a 'sandbox'.

Of course Bitcoin was the first blockchain code base, but most businesses will use open-source code bases for permissioned versions like Hyperledger Fabric, enterprise Ethereum, Corda, Multichain or Quorum. The most commonly used code bases for business, as of first quarter 2018, were Hyperledger Fabric, Ethereum, and Corda. A study of 52 blockchain projects by HfS Research, in the 4th quarter of 2017, found that half were based on Etherum, followed by R3 Corda, Hyperledger Fabric, Quorum, Chain, and several others. HfS expected that Hyperledger Fabric adoption would soon accelerate.[39] Multichain has also gained momentum by partnering with companies like Accenture, Cognizant, and Mphasis to help build blockchain applications.

GitHub, a version-controlled repository hosting service, manages many open source blockchain code bases. Code bases are released in stages, such as alpha, beta, release candidate, and general availability. Upgrades are released and tracked using version control. From a manager's perspective, the immaturity of the code bases may be a concern, as software vulnerabilities may takes months or years to be fully identified (see Table 2.4).

Codebase	Released	Approximate # Lines of Code
Bitcoin Core	Initial release: 2009 More recent versions	100,000[40] 495,000
Ethereum	General Availability: 2015	768,000
Chain	Initial release: 2016	1,186,784
Quorum	Beta: 2017	785,000
Corda	Beta: 2017	220,000
Hyperledger Fabric	Beta: 2017	842,000
Multichain	Pre-Beta 2017	174,782
Notes: Stats are from Github unless otherwise stated; *Lines of code vary by client, release date, etc.*		

Table 2.4: Size of code bases for various blockchains

The number of lines of code serves as a proxy as to the complexity of the code base. For example, Google has 2 billion lines of source code, Facebook has 62 million lines of code[41], and Microsoft Windows has about 50 million lines of code.[42] In contrast, blockchain code bases contain fewer lines of code. Table 2.4 also provides some estimates of numbers of lines of code, but the actual figures vary by client. For example, Ethereum protocols have been coded in various computer languages like Go, Rust, C++, Python, Java, Ruby, etc.

2.4.3. The blockchain application 'use case'

Code bases can be used to develop *blockchain use cases*, i.e. applications. Figure 2.8 provides examples of use cases across industries, collected from press announcements and Google alerts. Firms from the financial services industry were the first to take serious notice of blockchain's opportunities and threats, and therefore have explored more use cases than other industries. Insurance, healthcare, supply chain and governments are quickly catching up.

As noted in Chapter 1, thousands of blockchain applications have been built, but, as of the end of 2017, many of these were still in sandboxes, or in test environments. These 'test' applications – also called Proof-of-Concepts (POC) – have occurred across industries and geographies.

Moving blockchain applications from the isolation of innovation labs into full-scale live productions will take time, due to the inescapable issue of 'technology embeddedness'.[43] Technology is never neutral, but rather technologies are developed and deployed in a dynamic legal, political, organizational, regulatory, social, economic, and physical world. It is technology embeddedness that makes predictions about the future of enterprise blockchains so speculative. These technology embeddedness challenges are discussed in Chapter 5.

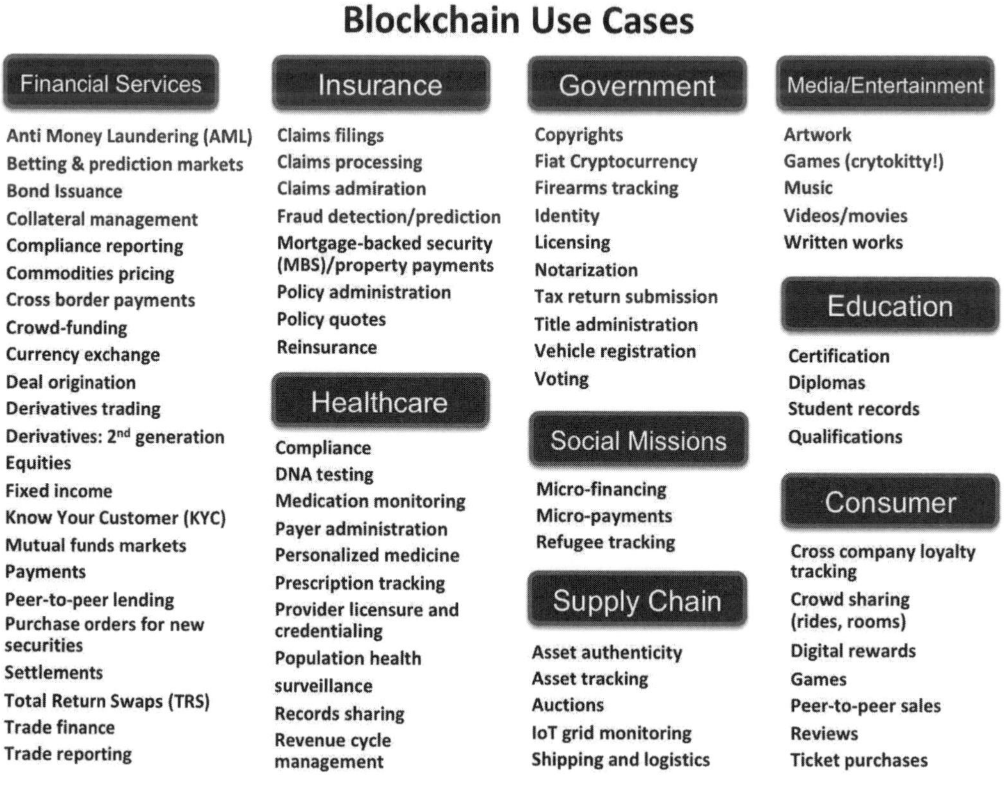

Blockchain Use Cases

Financial Services

Anti Money Laundering (AML)
Betting & prediction markets
Bond Issuance
Collateral management
Compliance reporting
Commodities pricing
Cross border payments
Crowd-funding
Currency exchange
Deal origination
Derivatives trading
Derivatives: 2nd generation
Equities
Fixed income
Know Your Customer (KYC)
Mutual funds markets
Payments
Peer-to-peer lending
Purchase orders for new securities
Settlements
Total Return Swaps (TRS)
Trade finance
Trade reporting

Insurance

Claims filings
Claims processing
Claims admiration
Fraud detection/prediction
Mortgage-backed security (MBS)/property payments
Policy administration
Policy quotes
Reinsurance

Healthcare

Compliance
DNA testing
Medication monitoring
Payer administration
Personalized medicine
Prescription tracking
Provider licensure and credentialing
Population health surveillance
Records sharing
Revenue cycle management

Government

Copyrights
Fiat Cryptocurrency
Firearms tracking
Identity
Licensing
Notarization
Tax return submission
Title administration
Vehicle registration
Voting

Social Missions

Micro-financing
Micro-payments
Refugee tracking

Supply Chain

Asset authenticity
Asset tracking
Auctions
IoT grid monitoring
Shipping and logistics

Media/Entertainment

Artwork
Games (crytokitty!)
Music
Videos/movies
Written works

Education

Certification
Diplomas
Student records
Qualifications

Consumer

Cross company loyalty tracking
Crowd sharing (rides, rooms)
Digital rewards
Games
Peer-to-peer sales
Reviews
Ticket purchases

Figure 2.8: Blockchain use cases

Sources: various press announcements, Google alerts

2.4.4. The blockchain application interface ('access point')

To access permissionless blockchain applications, users need a digital wallet they download themselves or go through an exchange like Coinbase or Kraken. To access permissioned blockchains, enterprise users typically interface through gateway services or build their own interfaces to existing systems using Application Programming Interfaces (APIs), pieces of software that connect two software applications so that one application can send a message to and receive a response from another application. Increasingly, enterprises are interested in connecting sensors and other IoT (Internet of Things) devices directly to a blockchain application. In food tracking, for example, and IoT sensor could inform a blockchain application if the temperature of the food ever deviated from agreed upon ranges.

Interfaces are blockchains' main points of vulnerability. Nearly all of the hacks one hears about occur at the access points. We've already introduced the notion of a digital signature that comprises private-public key pairs. Hackers don't waste their time trying to calculate the private key because it's theoretically impossible to figure out the private key if one only has the public key. Hackers find it much more lucrative to *steal* the private keys. Because consumers are responsible for their own keys, it is worth taking a moment to examine a legitimate private-public key pair (see Figure 2.9). The numbers look strange because they are written in hexadecimal format (base 16) rather than decimal format. Notice how long the public key is… the public key gets shortened through a hashing process, so it would look like this on a blockchain: **'31uEbMgunupShBVTewXjtqbBv5MndwfXhb'**.

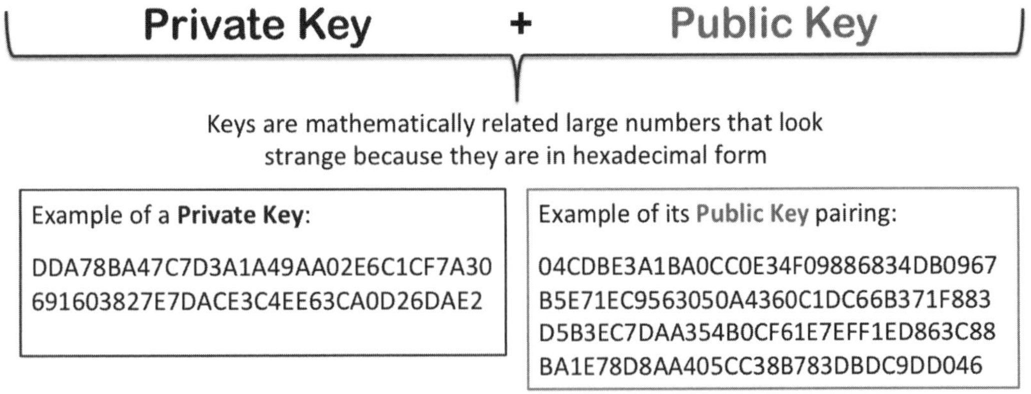

Private Key   +   Public Key

Keys are mathematically related large numbers that look
strange because they are in hexadecimal form

Example of a **Private Key**:	Example of its **Public Key** pairing:
DDA78BA47C7D3A1A49AA02E6C1CF7A30 691603827E7DACE3C4EE63CA0D26DAE2	04CDBE3A1BA0CC0E34F09886834DB0967 B5E71EC9563050A4360C1DC66B371F883 D5B3EC7DAA354B0CF61E7EFF1ED863C88 BA1E78D8AA405CC38B783DBDC9DD046

Figure 2.9: Example of a private-public key pair

(Don't bother searching for this address on a blockchain, a program created the private-public key pair for illustrative purposes.)[44]

Source: http://minetopics.blogspot.com/2013/01/hiding-bitcoins-in-your-brain.html

Many consumers do not realize just how vulnerable they are to theft or loss of their private keys. Many people keep their private keys in digital wallets stored on their mobile devices, again, not realizing that if the phone breaks or is lost or is hacked, they lose their private keys. As a general rule, private keys cannot be recovered – there is no help desk to call to retrieve them, like when one forgets a password, and no credit card company to report and recover damages from fraud. That said, new services are emerging that may help with recovery of private keys, but it is still early days and therefore difficult to find a provider with a strong historical track record. The safest places to store private keys are on a USB drive that is not connected to the Internet and, quite ironically, on a piece of paper that is locked in a fireproof safe.

Other people trust their centralized exchanges to store and protect their keys. However, hackers most commonly target exchanges because they can steal large numbers of private keys. One of the largest heists occurred in August of 2014 when 850,000 bitcoins worth $450 million at the time was stolen from the wallets managed by Mt. Gox, the largest Bitcoin exchange at the time. It's important to understand that such heists have not breeched the blockchain itself. These heists happen outside the blockchain – that is in the vulnerable access points to a blockchain.

We've explained all the component parts of a blockchain application but what's usually asked next is: How is a blockchain's distributed ledger different from a traditional distributed database?

2.5. Distributed ledger vs. traditional distributed databases

"In short: the difference is decentralized control."

Shaan Ray, Blockchain Pundit[45]

"Blockchain are really developing not only as a place to secure data, but also through the smart contract, blockchains are an interesting way to create links between companies without going through the formal process that you normally would with databases."

Founder of a Consortium[46]

"Blockchains are not just Distributed Ledger Technology... Blockchains are about guarantee of execution."

Henning Diedrich[47]
Author of Ethereum: Blockchains, Digital Assets, Smart Contracts, DAOs

'Distributed databases' is an umbrella term that encompasses many different architectural designs where data is stored in multiple places and where agreement is maintained through computer algorithms that lock and time stamp records. Given that definition, we see that ***blockchains are distributed database systems, just of a special kind***. Whereas traditional distributed databases are centrally controlled so that a single organization can decide to alter records or access rules, blockchains are distributed – no one entity has the power to roll back or alter history.

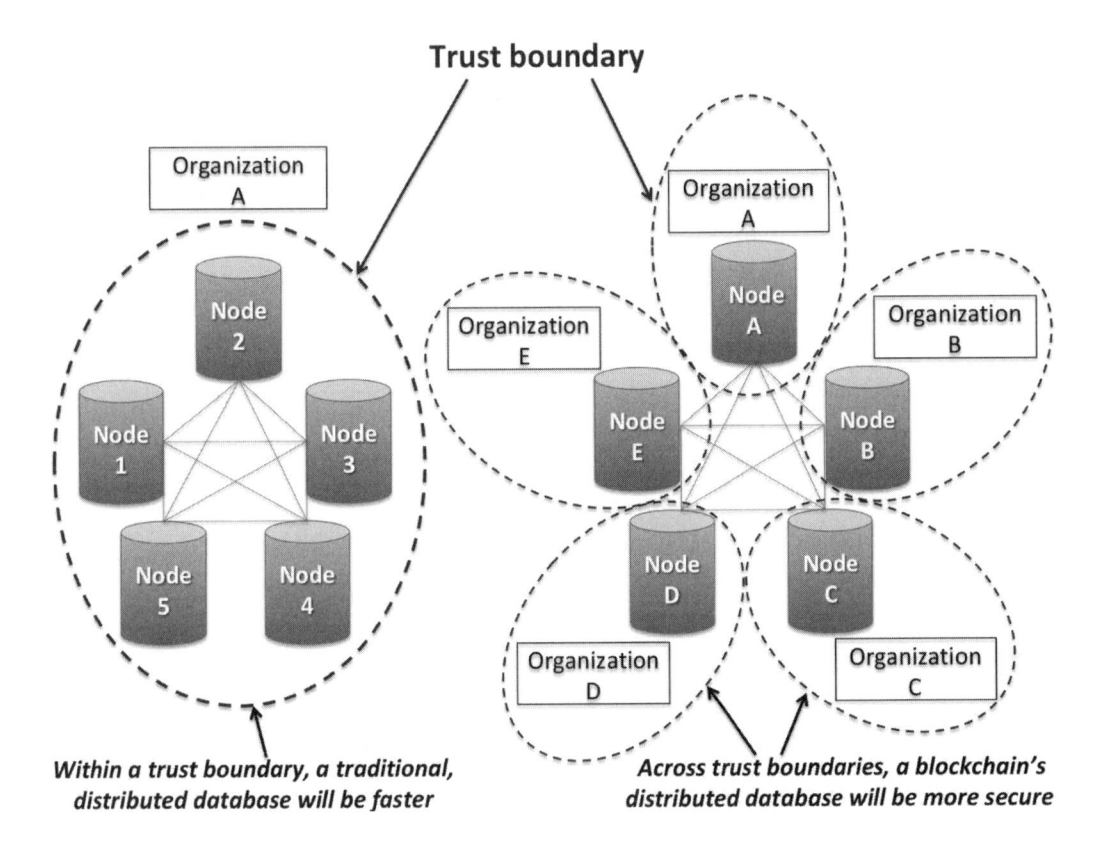

Trust boundary

Within a trust boundary, a traditional, distributed database will be faster

Across trust boundaries, a blockchain's distributed database will be more secure

Figure 2.10: The 'trust boundary' as the distinguishing difference
Source: Adapted from Richard Gendal Brown[50]

Under what circumstances is the distributed control of blockchains preferable to the centralized control of traditional databases? Some pundits argue that the answer depends on the 'trust boundary' (see Figure 2.10). Those with this view recognize that all the nodes in a traditional distributed database environment trust each other, and therefore fewer verifications are required.[48] Trust is not presumed among nodes in a blockchain distributed ledger, so every event must be checked and rechecked – which is one reason why traditional distributed databases are magnitudes faster than blockchains.[49] Other experts also point to the inclusion of smart contracts as a distinguishing feature, and advantage, of blockchains over distributed database systems.

Hopefully by now, readers are comfortable with the notions of blockchains' protocols, code bases, use cases and application interfaces. We've learned that blockchains are appropriate for contexts where trading partners do not want any one entity in charge of validating and maintaining their shared records. Armed with the knowledge of these concepts, we will revisit Bitcoin and see how it is, indeed, just one type of blockchain application. We are now ready to map Bitcoin to the blockchain application framework introduced in Figure 2.2.

2.6. Mapping bitcoin to the blockchain application framework

Like all blockchain applications, Bitcoin has its own protocols, code base, use case, and access points, which are mapped to the blockchain application framework in Figure 2.11. Beginning at the bottom of the figure, Bitcoin is based on a **permissionless blockchain protocol**; anyone with access to the Internet can view every transaction that has ever occurred on the blockchain. Bitcoin's *distributed ledger* is structured as a chain of blocks. Bitcoin's *native digital asset* is a bitcoin. Bitcoin uses digital signatures (and other sophisticated *cryptographic* techniques) to authenticate asset ownership and to secure transactions. Bitcoin uses proof-of-work as its mechanism to ensure *consensus* across nodes in the network. One will note, from Figure 2.11, that Bitcoin does not have what is called a 'Turing Complete' (see Glossary)[51] smart contracting component – that innovation came later, with Ethereum.

Moving up the framework diagram in Figure 2.11, the *code base* is called Bitcoin Core, and is maintained and supported by an open source community. Anyone may download the code base from GitHub (https://github.com/). As of 2017, there were about 5,000 nodes running the full Bitcoin source code, which means any of them could be competing for mining rewards.

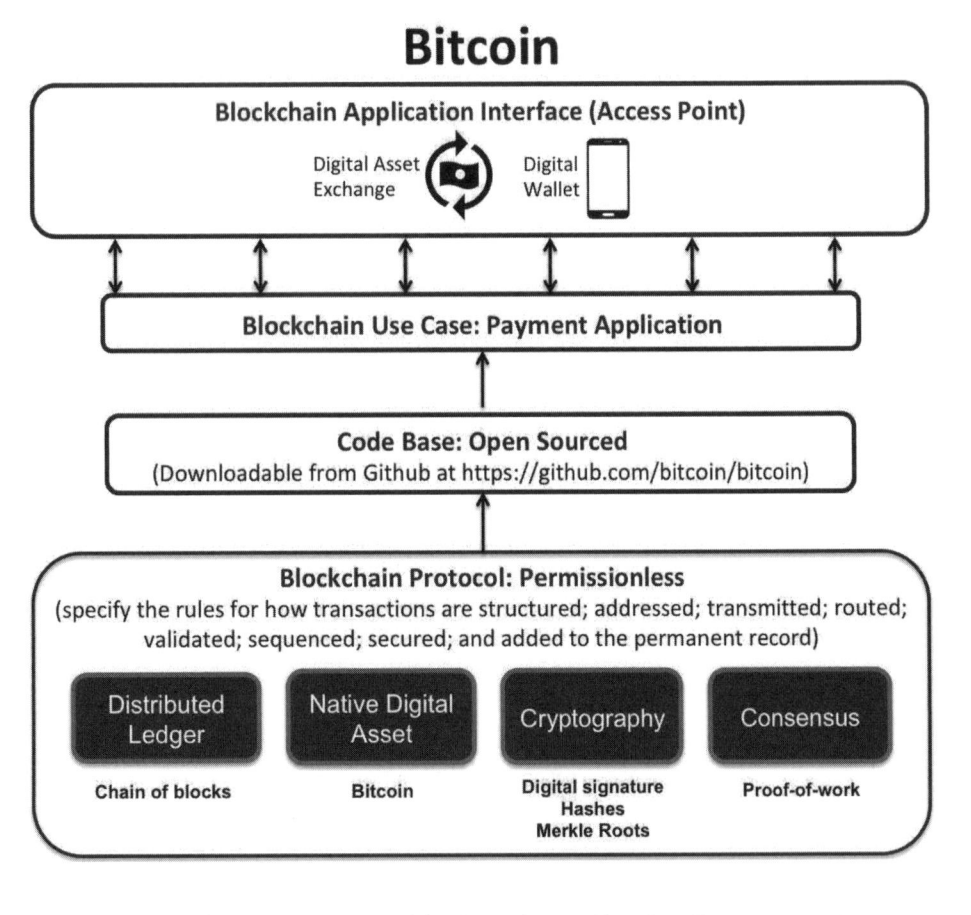

Figure 2.11: Bitcoin is a blockchain application for payments

Bitcoin's *use case* is a payment application system; it is used to settle and store transfers of value on the distributed ledger. The *interface* to Bitcoin requires wallet software that stores the user's private keys off the blockchain. Wallet software makes it easy for users to buy and sell bitcoins (see Figure 2.12).

To get a better understanding of Bitcoin's transparency, immutability and anonymity, one may visit https://blockexplorer.com to see the most recent blocks (see Figure 2.13). One can also search the entire history of the blockchain by block number (called block 'height'), transaction ID or address (i.e. a version of the public key).

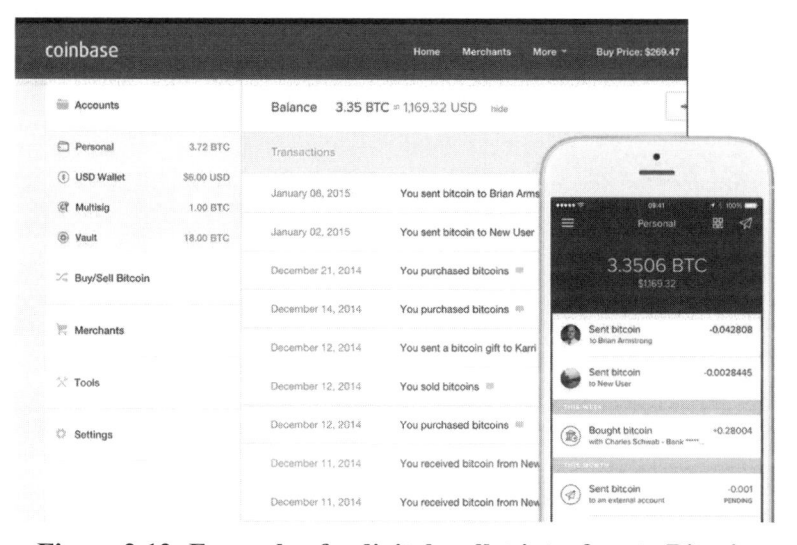

Figure 2.12: Example of a digital wallet interface to Bitcoin

Source: https://www.coinbase.com/assets/home/global3-
f9646244d66dd7c26191f091585db0f4feda2af3cad7cfe63b0de080d1cd36c5.png

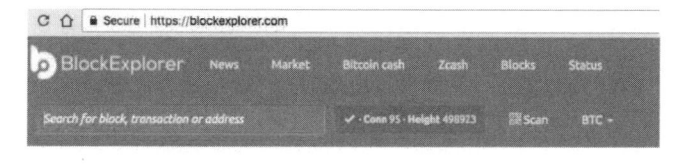

Latest Blocks

Height	Age	Transactions	Mined by	Size
498923	38 minutes ago	2229		976466
498922	41 minutes ago	2853		979790
498921	44 minutes ago	2950	AntMiner	970384
498920	an hour ago	2176	AntMiner	982828
498919	an hour ago	3031		980865

See all blocks

Latest Transactions

Hash	Value Out
27f85e893db7be2959ed5d0ed806d008c588294976...	0.13353399 BTC
deffac7028bb2cc2aa58f0c264a6a09fffeabb1dbdc20...	0.043186 BTC

Figure 2.13: A screenshot of a website to view Bitcoin's blockchain

Block 498923 was the 'latest block' on this date and time. It contained 2,229 transactions.

2.7. Conclusion

In this chapter, we have learned that a blockchain application comprises protocols, code bases, use cases, and application interfaces. We've invested some time understanding the differences between permissioned and permissionless protocols, and took a closer look at the protocols associated with distributed ledgers, native digital assets, cryptography, consensus and smart contracts. Hopefully, readers can now comprehend the definition that opened this chapter:

> A ***blockchain application*** is a distributed, peer-to-peer system for validating, time-stamping, and permanently storing transactions on a ***distributed ledger*** that uses ***cryptography*** to authenticate ***digital asset ownership*** and asset authenticity, and consensus algorithms to add validated transactions to the ledger and to ensure the ongoing integrity of the ledger's complete history. Enterprise blockchains also use ***smart contracts*** that apply rules to automatically execute transactions based upon pre-agreed conditions.

From a business perspective, managers need to see more examples of blockchain applications besides Bitcoin – the topic of the next chapter.

Citations

1. Diedrich, H. (2016), *Ethereum: blockchains, digital assets, smart contracts, decentralized autonomous organizations,* Wildfire publishing.

2. World Economic Forum (August 2016), *The Future of Financial Infrastructure: An Ambitious Look at How Blockchain Can Reshape Financial Services*, http://www3.weforum.org/docs/WEF_The_ future_of_financial_infrastructure.pdf

3. European Central Bank (September 1999), *Improving Cross-border Retail Payment Services: The Eurosystem's view,* https://www.ecb.europa.eu/pub/pdf/other/retailpsen.pdf

4. McKinsey (2015), Global Payments 2015: *A Healthy Industry Confront Disruption*, http:// www.mckinsey.com/~/media/mckinsey/dotcom/client_service/financial services/latest thinking/ payments/global_payments_2015_a_healthy_industry_confronts_disruption.ashx

5. *Navigating the world of cross-border payments*, http://www.iqpc.com/media/1003982/57107.pdf

6. Rawson, R. (August 2nd 2013), *Crazy High Currency Exchange Fees: How to Stop the Banks from Taking Advantage of You*, https://biz30.timedoctor.com/crazy-high-currency-exchange-fees-how-to-stop-the-banks-from-taking-advantage-of-you

7. Catalini, C., and Gans, J. (2016), Some Simple Economics of the Blockchain, *MIT Sloan School of Management Working Paper* 5191-16.

8. Ross, A., *11 data breaches that stung US consumers*, bankrate.com: http://www.bankrate.com/finance/banking/us-data-breaches-1.aspx

9. Quotes are from the website, Best Bitcoin Quotes, https://www.weusecoins.com/best-bitcoin-quotes/

10. Quotes are from the website, Best Bitcoin Quotes, https://www.weusecoins.com/best-bitcoin-quotes/

11. Loop, J. (July 23rd 2016), *Bitcoin: The Trust Anchor in a Sea of Blockchains,* Coindesk, https://www.coindesk.com/bitcoin-the-trust-anchor-in-a-sea-of-blockchains/

12. Nakamoto, S. (2008), *Bitcoin: A Peer-to-Peer Electronic Cash System*, https://bitcoin.org/bitcoin.pdf

13. Diedrich, H. (2016), *Ethereum: blockchains, digital assets, smart contracts, decentralized autonomous organizations*, Wildfire publishing

14. Chaum, D. (1982), *Computer Systems Established, Maintained and Trusted by Mutually Suspicious Groups*, University of California, Berkeley.

15. Popper, N. (2015), *Digital Gold: Bitcoin and the Inside History of the Misfits and Millionaires Trying to Reinvent Money*, Harper, New York.

16. As terms are evolving, some people equate 'permissionless to public' and 'permissioned to private' blockchains. Other authors consider permissionless/permissioned and public/private as distinctive dimensions

17. Jayachandran, P. (May 31st 2017), *The difference between public and private blockchain,* https://www.ibm.com/blogs/blockchain/2017/05/the-difference-between-public-and-private-blockchain/

18. For example, Bitcoin's original white paper describes the incentives as follows:

    "If a greedy attacker is able to assemble more CPU power than all the honest nodes, he would have to choose between using it to defraud people by stealing back his payments, or using it to generate new coins. He ought to find it more profitable to play by the rules, such rules that favour him with more new coins than everyone else combined, than to undermine the system and the validity of his own wealth." Nakamoto, S. (2008), Bitcoin: A Peer-to-Peer Electronic Cash System, https://bitcoin.org/bitcoin.pdf

19. Associated Press (June 28th 2015), *The Latest: Strict limits on bank withdrawals will not apply to foreign credit cards*, US News, https://www.usnews.com/news/business/articles/2015/06/28/the-latest-greece-wants-ecb-to-keep-giving-emergency-help

20. Quoted in CoreDump post (January 10th 2017), *Blockchain – What is Permissioned vs Permissionless?*, https://bornonjuly4.me/2017/01/10/blockchain-what-is-permissioned-vs-permissionless/

21. Wisselink, B. (January 31st 2017), P*ermissioned Blockchains: Why they are silly*, https://baswisselink.com/articles/permissioned-blockchains-why-they-are-silly/

22. Allaby, D. (October 27th 2016), *The Trust Trade-Off: Permissioned vs. Permissionless Blockchains*, https://www.fjordnet.com/conversations/the-trust-trade-off-permissioned-vs-permissionless-blockchains/

23. Popov, S. (2017), *The Tangle, IOTA whitepaper*, https://iota.org/IOTA_Whitepaper.pdf

24. Popov, S. (2017), *The Tangle, IOTA whitepaper*, https://iota.org/IOTA_Whitepaper.pdf

25. https://coinmarketcap.com/all/views/all/

26. Xie, L. (May 22nd 2017), *A beginner's guide to Ethereum tokens*, https://blog.coinbase.com/a-beginners-guide-to-ethereum-tokens-fbd5611fe30b

27. Beck, A. (2002), *Hashcash - A Denial of Service Counter-Measure*, white paper, http://www.hashcash.org/papers/hashcash.pdf

28. Baliga, A. (April 2017), *Understanding Blockchain Consensus Models*, https://www.persistent.com/wp-content/uploads/2017/04/WP-Understanding-Blockchain-Consensus-Models.pdf

29. '*Proof-of-Elapsed-Time (PoET)*' was created by the Hyperledger Sawtooth project, https://www.hyperledger.org/projects

30. Chan, R. (May 2nd 2016), *Consensus mechanisms used in blockchains*, https://www.linkedin.com/pulse/consensus-mechanisms-used-blockchain-ronald-chan

31. Castor, A. (March 4th 2017), *A Guide to Blockchain Consensus Protocols*, Coindesk, https://www.coindesk.com/short-guide-blockchain-consensus-protocols/

32. King, S. and Nadal, S. (2012), *PPCoin: Peer-to-Peer Crypto-Currency with Proof-of-Stake*, PeerCoin White Paper, https://peercoin.net/assets/paper/peercoin-paper.pdf

33. NXT White Paper (2014), *NXT Community*, https://bravenewcoin.com/assets/Whitepapers/NxtWhitepaper-v122-rev4.pdf

34. Castro, M., and Liskov, B. (1999), *Practical Byzantine Fault Tolerance, proceedings of the Third Symposium on Operating Systems Design and Implementation*, New Orleans, http://pmg.csail.mit.edu/papers/osdi99.pdf

35. Castro, M., and Liskov, B. (1999), *Practical Byzantine Fault Tolerance, proceedings of the Third Symposium on Operating Systems Design and Implementation*, New Orleans, http://pmg.csail.mit.edu/papers/osdi99.pdf

36. *The Future of Blockchains: Smart Contracts,* Technode, http://technode.com/2016/11/14/the-future-of-blockchain-technology-smart-contracts/

37. This website tracks contract accounts running on Ethereum, https://etherscan.io/contractsVerified

38. Diedrich, H. (2016), *Ethereum: blockchains, digital assets, smart contracts, decentralized autonomous organizations*, Wildfire publishing.

39. See Gupta, S. and Mondal, T. (2017), *HfS Blueprint Report: Enterprise Blockchain Services*

40. Source: Questions & Answers posted on Monero: *How many lines of source code does Monero have? How does that number compare with the amount of Bitcoin source code?*, https://monero.stackexchange.com/questions/1113/how-many-lines-of-source-code-does-monero-have

41. Source: http://www.visualcapitalist.com/millions-lines-of-code/

42. Source: https://code.org/loc

43. Lacity, M. and Willcocks, L. (2018), *Robotic Process and Cognitive Automation,* SB Publishing, UK

44. Source: http://minetopics.blogspot.com/2013/01/hiding-bitcoins-in-your-brain.html

45. Shaan Ray (November 5th 2017), *Blockchain versus traditional databases*, Hackernoon, https://hackernoon.com/blockchains-versus-traditional-databases-c1a728159f79

46. Personal Interview with Mary Lacity in 2018

47. Diedrich, H. (2016), *Ethereum: blockchains, digital assets, smart contracts, decentralized autonomous organizations*, Wildfire publishing.

48. Brown, R. (November 8th 2016), *On distributed databases and distributed ledgers*, https://gendal.me/2016/11/08/on-distributed-databases-and-distributed-ledgers/

49. Diedrich, H. (2016), *Ethereum: blockchains, digital assets, smart contracts, decentralized autonomous organizations*, Wildfire publishing.

50. Brown, R. (November 8th 2016), *On distributed databases and distributed ledgers,* https://gendal.me/2016/11/08/on-distributed-databases-and-distributed-ledgers/

51. In layman's terms, 'Turing Complete' means a programming language has a comprehensive instruction set; Bitcoin's scripting tool is not 'Turing Complete' because it has no way to program logic loops, among other missing features. (See https://en.bitcoin.it/wiki/Script for Bitcoins command set)

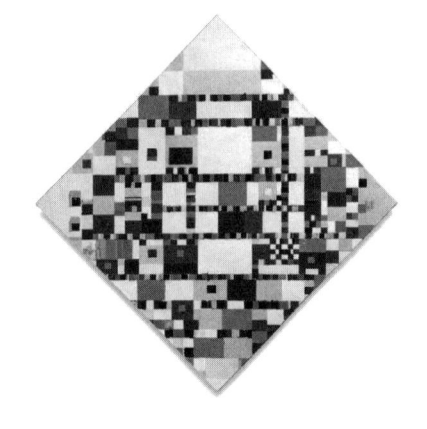

Chapter 3

Business Application Examples

"We don't want [centralized databases], because when you are the center of the universe, you can play God and change history in destructive ways, and control who gets to write and not write in ways that are hard to detect. Instead, we want records to be tracked, verifiable and distributed among a crowd – not just for cryptocurrency but also for supply chains, provenance tracking and finance... We want to know what to audit and where information has flowed. This goes for education records, prison records, births, property titles and other ecosystems that act as central registries. There are other situations too where registries are not yet centralized, and rather than create an eBay or an Uber, you want something more distributed. This is what blockchain [technology] is uniquely positioned to support."

Brian Behlendorf, Executive Director, Hyperledger Project[1]

3.1. Introduction

Thus far in this guide, Bitcoin has served as our most visible example of a functioning blockchain application. Bitcoin rightly deserves attention because it's been successfully running since 2009. For managers, Bitcoin is most intriguing because it proves that an anonymous crowd can securely maintain a completely distributed application – no one entity owns it or controls it. We've learned that Bitcoin is just one type of blockchain application – it's a payment system – but the same underlying technology has thousands of potential use cases. Blockchains are thus a completely new form of software that enables new forms of organization. However, managers need more examples beyond Bitcoin to envision how blockchains might be used in their enterprises and how they might affect their business models.

Sector	Enterprise	Enterprise Type	Blockchain Application	Status as of start of 2018
Financial Services	Ripple	Private startup	Global payments; targets institutions	Ripple provides an open-sourced network that enterprise adopters access through gateways. The network has been running 'without incident' since 2014
	Stellar	Non-profit startup	Global payments; targets the underserved	Stellar provides an open-sourced network upon which enterprise adopters build applications. The network has been running since 2015
	BNP Paribas	Traditional bank	Global payments for customers	The private blockchain was tested internally with corporate clients in 2017 and is scheduled to go live in 2018
	Australian Securities Exchange (ASX)	Entity overseen by a government	Post-trade settlements	ASX plans to replace its existing post-trade settlement system with a blockchain application – perhaps in the later part of 2018
Energy	LO3 Energy	Private startup	Peer-to-peer marketplace for electricity generated from neighbor's solar panels	The Brooklyn Microgrid, one of LO3's projects, was running in a shadow market of 60 prosumers and around 500 consumers by year-end 2017. Live transactions will occur once required licenses from regulators are obtained, estimated to be in first or second quarter of 2018
	Share & Charge	Innogy spinoff	Peer-to-peer marketplace for charging electric cars	Over 1,000 blockchain-enabled charging stations installed around Germany and mobile app available since April 2017
Supply Chain	IBM	Partnerships	3-mini cases with Everledger, Maersk and Wal-Mart	Everledger is in production; Other blockchain POCs are moving from trials to market through joint ventures and alliances
	Provenance	Private startup	A platform for transparent supply chains	Successful trial tracked sustainably caught tuna from sea to store
	Moog Aircraft	Traditional manufacturer	Trading platform for 3-D printed parts	Actively working with partners and regulators to move the platform to market in 2019
	Center for Supply Chain Studies	Non-profit	Trace for pharmaceuticals	Finished the first study; two more studies underway

Table 3.1: Blockchain Application Examples

In this chapter, we examine a cross-section of use cases from three sectors – financial services, energy, and supply chain (see Table 3.1). We sample a variety of organizations leading these efforts, including: traditional enterprises; spinoffs from traditional enterprises; partnerships; private startups; non-profits; and industry consortia. Some blockchain applications were already live in 2018, some were quite close to deployment, and some were still in design or pilot mode, but aimed to make significant progress in 2018.

From the cases, we gain a deeper appreciation for the technical and business challenges of moving blockchain applications from innovation labs to market. Within these cases, we meet visionary leaders who are not just waiting for blockchains to mature – they are actively working to ripen the technology, define industry standards, create new models of shared governance, and lobby for new laws and regulations. These leaders remain resolute during the long implementation journeys.

3.2. Blockchain applications in financial services

"In the international trade finance case, it's a very old legacy process with a lot of paper documents. It was perceived that there could be value and the banks would be able to introduce a more efficient process through this technology."

Lead Digital Architect for a large global bank[2]

"It's a myth that Blockchain equals Bitcoin or Bitcoin equals Blockchain. Initially, the payment people paid attention to cryptocurrency and it was appropriate for them to watch over this new phenomenon. Sometime in the mid 2015 timeframe, the entire financial services industry – ourselves included – became enlightened that this was far more broadly applicable than cryptocurrency."

Blockchain Architect for a large global bank[3]

Enterprises in the financial services sector have been among the first players to recognize the threats and opportunities afforded by Bitcoin's blockchain underbelly. Incumbent enterprises, including banks like Barclays, State Street, and Wells Fargo that have been in continuous operation for hundreds of years, are among the early explorers of blockchain technologies. Industry consortia like R3, founded in 2014, were started to help incumbent enterprises create standards, write code bases, and bring blockchain financial services applications to life. Over 250 FinTechs[4] have entered the space – such as Axoni, BitPesa, and Digital Asset Holdings. These enterprises have developed proof-of-concepts (POCs) for a dizzying array of financial services: Anti Money Laundering (AML); betting & prediction markets; bond issuance; collateral management; compliance reporting; commodities pricing; cross-border payments; crowd-funding; currency exchange; deal origination; derivatives trading; equities; fixed income; Know Your Customer (KYC); mutual funds markets; payments; peer-to-peer lending; purchase orders for new securities; settlements; Total Return Swaps (TRS); trade finance; and trade reporting.

In this section, we provide four examples of financial services blockchain applications developed by Ripple, Stellar, BNP Paribas, and Australian Securities Exchange (ASX). Interestingly, the first three are examples of global payments applications for currency exchanges and remittances. In a way, global payments – also called 'cross-border' payments – are the poster child of enterprise blockchain applications. Its primary use case is an enterprise version of Bitcoin that realizes blockchain's promises of peer-to-peer trading; instant track and trace; rapid settlement times; low transaction costs; guarantee of execution; and heightened security, but uses fiat currencies and abides by regulations. We'll see that Ripple and Stellar do have native digital assets – which grab much of the attention, because both cryptocurrencies are typically among the top ten cryptocurrencies by market capitalization – but our focus is on the business uses of their global payments blockchain applications. Ripple and Stellar serve as examples of new enterprises that have already deployed operational applications – Ripple was founded in 2012 and Stellar was founded and launched in 2015. BNP Paribas serves as a model for how an incumbent player might explore blockchain applications within the walls of its own organization to benefit their own customers. BNP Paribas's cross-border application was nearly production-ready as of year-end 2017. Moving from global payments to trade settlement, the ASX application is scheduled to go live in 2018. ASX is an example of a government-owned company seeking to replace its existing system with a new blockchain application.

We need to understand better the pain points in today's financial services in order to appreciate the aims of these blockchain applications. Let's first begin by understanding how global payments work today.

3.2.1. Global payments before blockchains

"Around 2 billion people don't use formal financial services and more than 50% of adults in the poorest households are unbanked. Financial inclusion is a key enabler to reducing poverty and boosting prosperity."

Jim Yong Kim, President of the World Bank[5]

According to McKinsey, the world sends more than $135 trillion dollars across borders each year.[6] Third-party intermediaries collect about $2.2 trillion in revenue to facilitate these transactions. Money may move around the world in several ways using a variety of services, but we'll focus on a simplified version of the process. In today's global financial systems, each country has its own national payment system and uses its own sovereign currency.[7] A bank must be licensed to use its country's national payment system. International transactions often rely on the cooperation between banks in different countries, creating a messy web of correspondent bank relationships (see Figure 3.1 for a simplified depiction).[8] With a cross-border payment in today's global financial system, the sending and receiving parties' financial institutions, national payment systems, and corresponding banks process the transaction. Parties to an exchange have no access to the status of the transaction, the fees being charged, or even which institution controls a transaction as it works its way through the system. Fees accumulate with each step in the process. Trading partners do not always know the fees in advance, which can become quite substantial. As we learned in Chapter 2, sending remittances cost an average of 7.99 percent of the amount sent[9], and takes between three to five business days to settle.[10]

Because of the high transaction costs, financial intuitions cannot offer reasonably priced services for low-income people. On average, American banks incur costs of $349 a year per checking account and recover only $268 in transaction fees.[11] In short, banks lose money on checking accounts, so they have few financial incentives to service low-income people. Consequently, over a quarter of the world's population doesn't have access to financial services – they rely solely on cash. According to research by McKinsey[12], everyone will benefit from larger financial inclusion. If 1.6 billion more people are included, McKinsey estimated they would generate:

- $3.7 trillion to GDP by 2025
- 95 million new jobs
- $2.1 trillion in new credit
- $4.2 trillion in new deposits

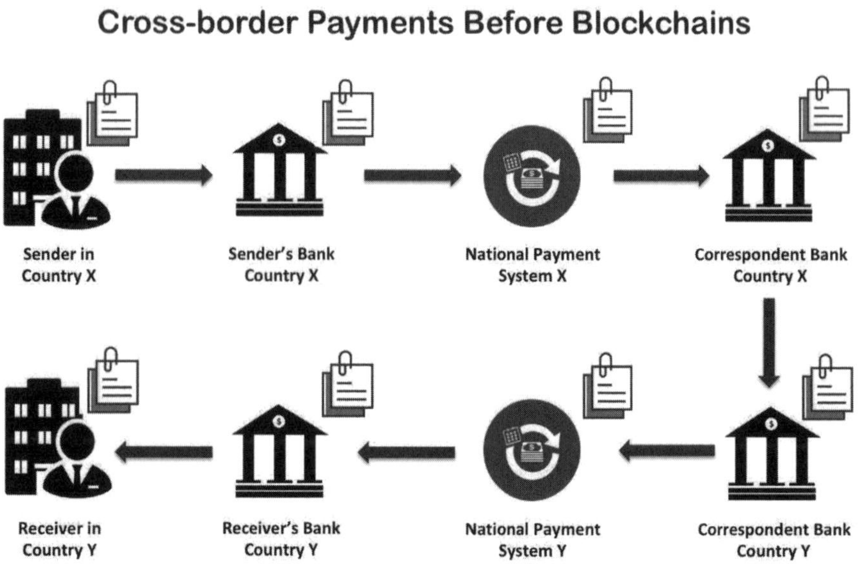

Cross-border Payments Before Blockchains

Figure 3.1: A simplified example of cross-border payments before blockchains

Experts generally agree that banks and governments need to be part of the solution.[13] The poor cannot simply adopt cryptocurrencies to solve all their financial needs. They need access to fiat currencies for credit and payments. The Financial Services for the Poor Program, funded by the Bill & Melinda Gates Foundation, defined the minimum requirements for a globally inclusive mobile payments platform: The platform must run on inexpensive mobiles phones;[14] it must support national currencies; governments must set regulations to deter fraud, money laundering and cyberterrorism; transactions must settle quickly for small merchants, and it must be interoperable with other systems.[15] So far, there are about 150 mobile payment platforms (like bKash[16] and M-pesa[17]), but they operate in islands. So how might blockchains help?

Alin Dragos, a member of the MIT Digital Currency Initiative, believes banks can increase financial inclusion if they adopt blockchains to radically reduce their back office costs. He estimates banks could get their average costs per account down to $100 per year. A more ambitious bank might build a blockchain centric bank, which might reduce costs to $50 a year. [18] Additionally, blockchains for identities could help the more than 230 million undocumented migrants worldwide gain access to financial services and employment.[19]

So, there are plenty of problems to tackle in the global payments arena. As one of the first blockchain applications for business, many people recognized that blockchain applications for cross-border payments could alleviate many of the pain points.[20] Bitcoin provided the baseline model, but its user anonymity, low scalability, and massive resource consumption could not meet the needs of trading partners in the highly regulated world of financial services. Ripple, Stellar and BNP Paribas each built global payments applications that overcome Bitcoin's limitations while still delivering rapid settlement times and low transaction costs. They are each interesting in that they target different markets. Ripple targets institutional customers; Stellar aims to expand access to financial services for those excluded today; BNP Paribas aims to provide better services to its global customers. After their stories are told, we'll move to another financial services context, namely post trade settlements at the Australian Securities Exchange.

3.2.2. Ripple

"Banks join Ripple's global settlement network to send cross-border payments in real time. Ripple eliminates time delays and ensures certainty of settlement, resulting in new revenue opportunities and lower transaction costs for banks and their customers."

Ripple website[21]

"Digital currencies were born out of the necessity for a monetary form that was not controlled by a central bank and cannot be manipulated by politics… Ripple is the first currency exchange that allows trading in all currencies or any unit that has value like frequent flier miles, virtual currencies, and mobile minutes."

Elliott Branson, author of *Ripple: The Ultimate Guide to Understanding Ripple Currency*[22]

Ripple was founded by Chris Larsen and Jeb McCaleb in 2012 to build upon Ryan Fugger's idea for a decentralized, real-time settlement system. Headquartered in San Francisco, Brad Garlinghouse is its current CEO.[23] By 2016, Ripple employed 150 people.[24] Ripple received Angel funding in 2013, Series A funding in 2015 and Series B funding in 2016. Investors include Accenture; Andreessen Horowitz; CME Ventures; Google Ventures; SBI Group; Santander InnoVentures; and Standard Chartered.[25]

Ripple aimed to overcome Bitcoin's relatively slow settlement times, inability to trade other currencies, and massive electricity consumption, while still being inexpensive, transparent, private, and secure. According to Ripple's website, its network handles 1,500 transactions per second (TPS), operates 24x7, and can scale to 50,000 TPS. It also claims a five-year track record of its distributed ledger closing without incident.[26]

Ripple's target customers are primarily institutional enterprises like banks, corporates, payment providers and exchanges. As of 2018, Ripple offered three integrated services that ran on its RippleNet platform: *xCurrent* to process payments, *xRapid* to source liquidity, and *xVia* to send payments. For banking customers, Ripple promises that banks will capture new revenue by booking new corporate and consumer clients, reduce their transaction costs, and provide one integration point and a consistent experience for rules, standards and governance.[27] For corporates, Ripple promises on-demand payment with tracking and delivery confirmation and richer data transfers such as appending invoices to payment transfers.[28]

Germany's online bank, Fidor, was Ripple's first intuitional customer, which announced the partnership in early 2014. As of 2017, Ripple claims over 100 customers – including such powerhouses as Bank of America; The Bank of Tokyo; Royal Bank of Canada; SEB; Standard Chartered; and UBS[29] – but it is unclear the extent to which institutions are using the network for live transactions versus investigating its potential. Ripple's website does include case studies, such as SBI Remit, which enables Thai nationals living in Japan to send money directly to their accounts in Thailand. Prior to this service, Thai nationals living in Japan had to hire agents and use cash for transfers.[30] *Fortune Magazine* covered a story about American Express using Ripple for its US-based corporate customers to send funds to their UK-based accounts at Santander Bank. According to this article, some customers were actually using the service in November 2017, so it was not merely a POC.[31]

Institutional customers use an API to connect to the Ripple network via a Ripple Gateway (see Figure 3.2). Gateways can establish trust lines up to certain amounts with other gateways. Two gateways that trust each other can transact directly. However, if the sending gateway does not have a direct trust line with the receiving gateway, the network protocol will find a path of trust, thus transactions will 'ripple' through the network. One may think of this path as appropriating other people's trust. If Sally wants to send money to Sam without really trusting Sam, Sally could send money to someone she trusts, say John; John then sends the money to someone he trusts, say Sue; Sue sends the money to Sam, whom she trusts. If no path of trust can be found, the value can be transferred using Ripple's native digital asset called 'Ripple' (symbol XRP). In this way, XRP can be used as a bridge currency if no paths of trust exist between trading partners. The protocol searches for the best possible exchange rates and makes the currency exchanges in seconds, costing just a few cents worth of fees.[32]

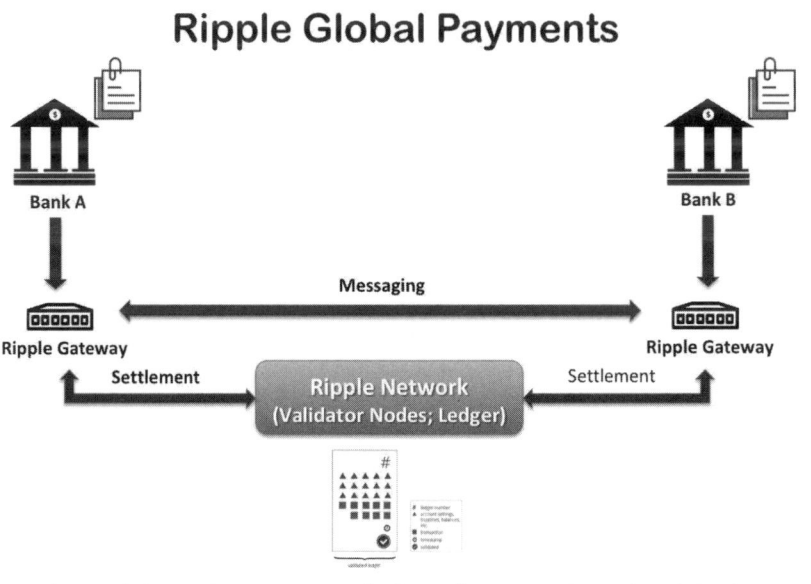

Ripple Global Payments

Figure 3.2: A high-level depiction of two banks using Ripple

So what's happening with the ledger? Ripple's ledger stores issuances, i.e. digital balances that represent currency or assets of value held by an issuer. Here's how it works:

*When a customer sends money **into** the XRP Ledger, a gateway takes custody of those assets outside of Ripple, and sends issuances in the XRP Ledger to the customer's address. When a customer sends money **out** of the XRP Ledger, she makes an XRP Ledger payment to the gateway, and the gateway credits the customer in its own system of record, or in some other account. Like issuances, XRP can be freely sent and exchanged among XRP Ledger addresses. But unlike issuances, XRP is not tied to an accounting relationship – XRP can be sent directly from any XRP Ledger address to any other, without going through a gateway or liquidity provider.[33]*

Figure 3.3 maps Ripple to the blockchain application framework which we developed in Chapter 2. Beginning with the protocols, Ripple defined a new distributed ledger protocol, called the Ripple Transaction Protocol (RTXP).[34] The protocol is sometimes referred to as 'semi-permissioned' in that XRPs can be sent to anyone (permissionless), but also features trust lines where transactions can only ripple through the network on approved paths (permissioned).

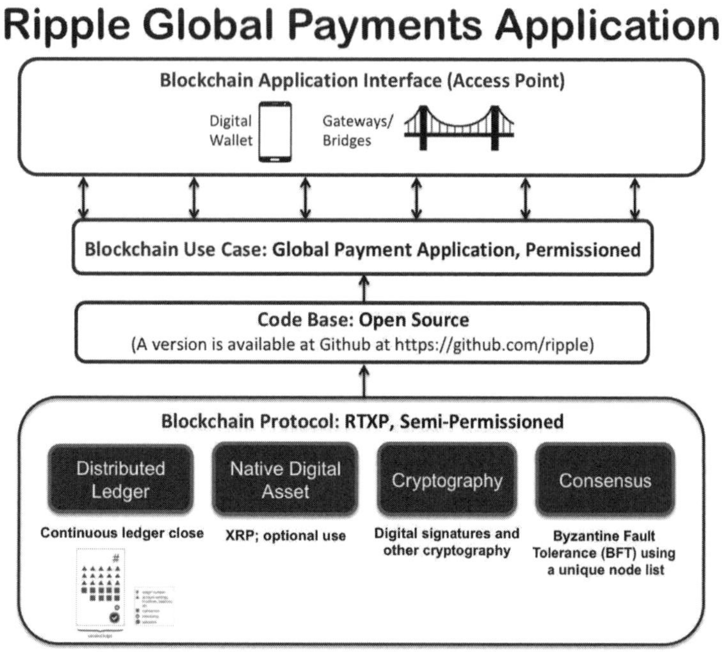

Ripple Global Payments Application

Figure 3.3: Ripple mapped to the blockchain application framework

Distributed Ledger. Ripple does not structure transactions as a chain of blocks. It structures the ledger as a long list of sequenced transactions and account settings/balances that gets closed every few seconds.[35] The ledger also stores buy and sell offers for different currencies. Every version of the ledger has a unique ID and time stamp. Like Bitcoin, Ripple transactions are permanently stored on Ripple's distributed ledger and are irreversible.

Native Cryptocurrency. Ripple's native cryptocurrency, called 'ripples' (XRP), serves several purposes. As noted above, XRP can be used as a bridge currency if no path of trust can be found between trading partners. XRP is also a way to pay gateways, as each may establish fees in the form of XRP for using the gateway. If trading partners transact directly without using gateways, senders of ripple transactions pay a small amount of ripples so that attackers won't spam the system with millions of transactions, as the attackers would run out of XRP.[36] Designed to be a scarce asset, the XRP money supply is exactly 100 billion ripples and was issued at the launch of the protocol, rather than released through the process of mining as Bitcoin does.[37] Ripple is a deflationary currency – once ripples have been used to pay for transactions, they are destroyed. Participants are not required to use ripples; they can transact directly with other currencies.[38]

Consensus Protocol. Ripple uses a different consensus protocol than Bitcoin. Whereas Bitcoin uses proof-of-work, Ripple uses a Byzantine Fault Tolerance (BFT) consensus protocol. In this consensus system, transactions for which the majority of computers on the network agree upon get recorded in the ledger.[39] (See Chapter 2 for a longer explanation). A Ripple transaction is considered 'safe' after it has been validated by 80 percent of the nodes.[40]

When institutions or consumers join the ripple network, they can select which nodes they want to perform validation checks, which is called a Unique Node List (UNL), or they can accept the default list maintained by Ripple. Ripple maintains its own validator nodes around the world and also has CGI, MIT and Microsoft as transaction validators.[41] Without the incentives of mining, Ripple asks intuitions to run a validator node when they join the system to help secure the network.

Compared to Bitcoin, the costs of performing the validator role are near zero dollars.[42] It only takes a few seconds for transactions to settle, and uses much less electricity than Bitcoin – about as much electricity as it costs to run an email server.[43]

Smart Contracts. In July 2014, Ripple Labs proposed a project to add smart contracts to Ripple. Just a year later, Ripple abandoned the project, saying it was not needed.[45]

Code Base. Ripple's code base is open source and may be downloaded from Github.

Application Interface. Users may transact directly with the Ripple network using a Ripple wallet, but it requires a minimum balance of 20 XRPs.[46] Most customers use Ripple gateways operated by cryptocurrency exchanges or financial intuitions.[47] Ripple has bridge protocols that allow payments to and from external networks. For example, Ripple has a Bitcoin bridge protocol that allows users to send ripples to bitcoin addresses.[48]

Issues with Ripple. Like all new startups, Ripple has faced some challenges around trust, hacks, and regulatory compliance. Regarding trust, some people worried that Ripple's owners had too much control over the money stock and network nodes. Ripple's owners retained 20 billion ripples at launch and gifted the rest to Ripple – charged with distribution to gateways, market makers, and charitable organizations.[49] The worry was this: What prevents owners from cashing in and thus devaluing the currency? After years of concern, Ripple's owners promised, in May 2017, to put 55 billion ripples into escrow and release about 1 billion into the market each month.[50]

Blockchains, in principle, are not supposed to rely on trusted third-party institutions. In practice, network participants typically accept Ripple's default list of nodes rather than pick their own nodes, thus giving Ripple centralized power. David Mazières of the Stellar Foundation wrote:

> *"Generally, membership in Byzantine agreement systems is set by a central authority or closed negotiation. Prior attempts to decentralize admission have given up some of the benefits. One approach, taken by Ripple, is to publish a 'starter' membership list that participants can edit for themselves, hoping people's edits are either inconsequential or reproduced by an overwhelming fraction of participants. Unfortunately, because divergent lists invalidate safety guarantees, users are reluctant to edit the list in practice and a great deal of power ends up concentrated in the maintainer of the starter list."[51]*

Ripple advises users to pick 1,000 validator nodes across continents and across industries where collusion is unlikely, such as selecting merchants, financial firms, non-profits, political parties, and religious groups from North America, South America, Europe, Asia, and Australia.[52] This advice is difficult to reconcile with reports that there were fewer than 400 active nodes as of January 3, 2018.[53,54]

Ripple was hacked in October 2014. Due to a weakness in the code, a hacker was able to send 1000 bitcoins from an address that had only .0001 bitcoins in funding. Ripple reported fixing the bug a few days later and the network has operated without incident since.[55]

In summary, Ripple is an important blockchain application – it's running, it's working, and it's adoption rate by institutional customers is increasing. The next example focuses on solving the problem of financial exclusion.

3.2.3. Stellar

"Our mission is to connect people to low-cost financial services to fight poverty and maximize individual potential."

Stellar Development Foundation[56]

"Our goal is to make global payments as open as the Internet, so that anyone can send money around the world easily, regardless of what financial institutions they are using. Payments should move like email and should all be interoperable."

Jed McCaleb, Cofounder and CTO of Stellar Development Foundation[57]

Jed McCaleb and Joyce Kim co-founded the Stellar Development Foundation (SDF) – a US-based, non-profit organization – in 2014. Stellar's mission is to expand financial access and literacy worldwide.[58] The white paper for the Stellar protocol[59] was released in April of 2015 and the network went live in November of that year.[60] Stellar's network for global payments settles transactions in two to five seconds at a very low transaction fee of one lumen (Stellar's native digital asset) for 100,000 transactions. Stellar can process over 1,000 operations per second. By the end of 2017, SDF employed 15 people and had secured $3 million in funding.[61]

SDF does not have direct contact with users. Instead, SDF aims to have other intuitions develop business models and use the Stellar code base to develop applications for services such as remittances, micropayments, mobile branches, mobile money, and other services for the under-banked. Stellar does not charge institutions or individuals any fees to use the Stellar network, beyond the modest per-transaction fee. Its network is based on open source code that is supported by the foundation, but adopters are free to develop commercial applications, modify or distribute the source code. As of January 2018, several companies were using the Stellar network for real payments.

Stellar has been adopted by Deloitte, the Parkway Project, Tempo, ICICI Bank, and IBM/ KlickEx – all seeking to realize SDF's mission to bring financial services to the poor.[62] For example, Deloitte built an application for affordable micropayments based on Stellar where people can use their mobile phones to make cross-border payments in seconds with low fees.[63] Tempo adopted Stellar for cross-border payments for customers to pay utility bills.[64] As of 2018, Tempo helps customers from Europe – mostly based in France and Germany – to transfer payments to Coins.ph, their company based in the Philippines.[65] Jed McCaleb said:

> *"Tempo is pretty awesome; there's real money flowing across the live network."*[66]

The Parkway Project involved Oradian, an Africa-focused FinTech, which aimed to bring financial services to 300,000 unbanked people in rural Nigeria, 90 percent of whom are women.[67] The project was halted for a while when the Nigerian Central Bank stopped all remittance companies from operating in Nigeria except Western Union and MoneyGram. The project will re-launch in 2018 with Flutterwave,[68] a startup founded in San Francisco in 2016 with offices in Lagos, Nigeria, Accra, and Johannesburg.[69]

ICICI Bank, based in India, is another Stellar adopter. It plans to allow its customers in India to transfer money over the Stellar network using a free mobile wallet. As of August 2017, it was piloting the service at a few universities, and the wallet is live on the Stellar network.[70]

IBM is Stellar's most notable institutional adopter so far. In October of 2017, IBM and KlickEx – a Polynesian-based payments system for low value electronic foreign exchange – announced it would use Stellar for cross-border payments. The partners aim to process 60 percent of all cross-border payments in the South Pacific by 2018 in such places as Fiji and Tonga.[71] Jed McCaleb said:

> *"IBM is using Hyperledger Fabric for some parts of the project, and they're using Stellar to do the cross-border payments."*[72]

Institutional users that connect to the Stellar network as anchors, are responsible for being licensed and for complying with regulations.[73] Jed McCaleb explained:

> *"The Stellar foundation is never in the flow of funds; we don't have customers. We provide the software and financial institutions deploy it. The burden of regulatory compliance lays on the anchor – the financial institutions – using the network because they still have the relationship with the person who's sending the money and the person who's receiving the money."*[74]

Figure 3.4 maps Stellar to the blockchain application framework developed in Chapter 2. As noted above, McCaleb was also cofounder of Ripple, which he left to start Stellar.[75] Due to the common history, Stellar's protocol was based on the Ripple protocol, so they are similar in terms of its distributed ledger process. Both networks also make use of APIs to connect organizations to the networks, but Stellar uses the term 'anchors' whereas Ripple calls them trust lines between 'gateways'. Stellar, as we shall see, uses a different consensus algorithm than Ripple and aims to be more decentralized.

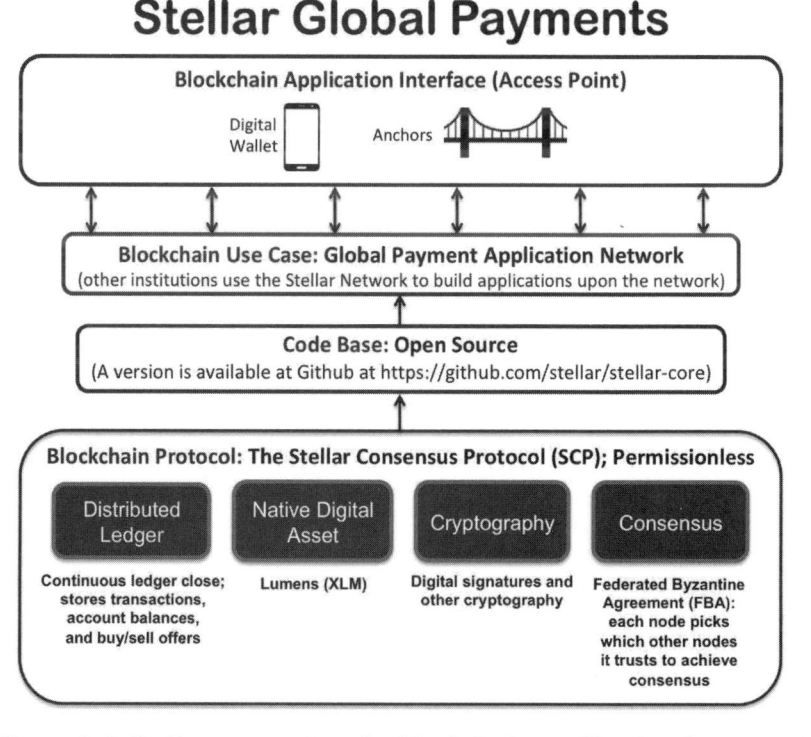

Figure 3.4: Stellar mapped to the blockchain application framework

Distributed Ledger. Like Ripple, Stellar does not structure transactions as a chain of blocks. Transactions are added to the ledger after they are validated. It structures the ledger as a long list of sequenced transactions and account balances that get closed every few seconds. The ledger also stores the current order books, which records the buy and sell offers for different currencies. Stellar's transactions are permanently stored on the distributed ledger and are irreversible. However, Stellar users may freeze funds on the ledger so that they cannot be spent in instances of disputed or mistaken transactions.[76]

Native Cryptocurrency. Stellar's native digital asset, lumens (XLM), serves several purposes.

First, lumens are used to fund the operations of the SDF. Stellar released 100 billion lumens in 2014, retaining five percent for the foundation to operate, and holding the rest in reserve. XLM is an inflationary currency – new lumens are added to the network at the rate of one percent of the money supply each year.[77] The foundation aims to distribute lumens to a broad range of individuals and organizations, including 50 percent to individuals, 25 percent for non-profits aiming to reach underserved populations, and 20 percent to bitcoin holders.[78] To reach individuals, the foundation releases lumens for auctions on exchanges like Kraken. People and institutions may also apply to the SDF for lumens to fund projects. In order to provide additional stability to the system, employees of the foundation are not allowed to buy lumens at auctions, and Stellar's owners agreed not to sell any of the lumens initially for at least five years.[79,80] As of January 2018, over 8 billion lumens had been distributed. (See https://dashboard.stellar.org/ for current distribution numbers.)

Second, lumens can be used as a bridge currency within the Stellar network if no direct markets exist between trading partners. Jed McCaleb offered this example:

> *"If you imagine somebody wants to send money from Thailand to Brazil, there's probably not a good liquid market between those two currencies. So you would go to some bridge currency in the middle. Maybe you would go Thai baht to US dollars, US dollars to Brazilian real. But you could also go to the lumens in the middle, or bitcoins. You can go through multiple hops to get the best rates."*[81]

Finally, lumens are used to prevent Denial of Service (DoS) attacks. Each Stellar transaction requires a minor fee of 0.00001 lumens: *'This fee prevents users with malicious intentions from flooding the network (otherwise known as a DoS attack). Lumens work as a security token, mitigating DoS attacks that attempt to generate large numbers of transactions or consume large amounts of space in the ledger.'*[82]

Consensus Protocol. Stellar's protocol is called the Stellar Consensus Protocol (SCP).[83] Its main innovation is a new model for consensus called Federated Byzantine Agreement (FBA). FBA distinguishes between a network-level *quorum* of nodes that need to agree, and a *quorum slice* that a particular node chooses to rely upon to validate transactions. This protocol ensures that the Stellar network remains permissionless in that anyone may join, but empowers each participant operating a node to decide which other nodes it will trust to validate transactions and add them to the ledger.[84]

About 20 validator nodes were operating as of January 2018, of which SDF operated three[85], IBM operated eight[86], and other enterprise adopters, such as Tempo and ICICI Bank, and universities, were running other nodes. Nodes are distributed globally, in such counties as Australia, Brazil, Canada, Norway, Italy, India, and the US.[87] When asked how quorum slice selection works in practice, given that Stellar had just 20 nodes in 2018, Jed McCaleb explained that people select a diverse set of nodes where collusion behind the scenes would be highly unlikely. He said:

> *"Nodes are advertised on each company's website. It would be very unlikely for IBM, Tempo and a university to collude, so while there is no magical answer, people can make sound judgments."*

Smart Contract. Stellar does not contain a Turing complete smart contracting feature.[88]

Code Base. Stellar's code base is open source and may be downloaded from Github, (https://github.com/stellar/stellar-core).

Application Interface. Users may transact directly with the Stellar network using a digital wallet, but it requires a minimum balance of 20 XLMs to ensure that accounts are authentic.[89] Stellar does not own or operate any digital wallets, but maintains a list of organizations that do (see https://www.stellar.org/lumens/wallets/). Users may also access the Stellar network through anchors institutions like Tempo and ICICI Bank who built services on top of the network. Anchors take deposits from their customers and issue credits to addresses stored on the distributed ledger.

What's next? The Stellar Foundation is quite small, with just 15 employees as of 2018. The foundation does not have the capacity to help institutions develop applications using the Stellar network, although there is a strong demand for such services.

To meet this need, Jed McCaleb founded Lightyear.io in May 2017. He explained:

> *"When we talk to financial institutions, they want somebody to provide service and support, and they want someone to help them with integration. SDF is not set up to do that. Pretty quickly, we realized that there's a need for a for-profit institute. So essentially you can think of SDF as the Linux and Lightyear as the RedHat."*

91

The SDF website posted a clear explanation of the separation of duties between SDF and Lightyear.[90]

In summary, Stellar is an important blockchain network – it's running, it's working, and its adoption rate is increasing. The next case provides an example of a traditional bank building a blockchain application to remove paint points with cross-border transfers for its institutional customers.

3.2.4. BNP Paribas[(i)]

> *"There's a lot of uncertainty and inefficiency in making a cross-border payment, even when it is between your own two accounts within the same bank. A transaction can take either a couple of hours or a couple of days and can cost a few cents or tens of dollars."*
>
> **Jacques Levet, Head of Transaction Banking, EMEA at BNP Paribas CIB**[91]

> *"Success depends on the value proposition for our clients – which will drive their interest and approval – and for the bank. We see that clients are very eager to get involved."*
>
> **Alain Verschueren, Head of Distributed Ledger Technology for Trade and Treasury Solutions BNP Paribas**[92]

The culmination of two centuries of banking, the BNP Paribas Group (BNP Paribas) was formed in 2000 from the merger of BNP (Banque Nationale de Paris) and Paribas (Banque de Paris et des Pays-Bas), each already the product of earlier mergers.[93] In 2017, BNP Paribas was the second largest bank in the Eurozone and among the ten largest banks worldwide.[94] It operated in seventy-four countries and '*had more than 192,000 employees worldwide,*[95] *serving nearly 32 million individual customers, and 850,000 professionals, entrepreneurs, small and medium-sized enterprises, and large corporate clients*'.[96] Jean-Laurent Bonnafé had been chief executive officer since 2011. The bank was organized into three divisions: Domestic Markets, International Financial Services, and Corporate and Intuitional Banking.

(i) This excerpt is based on Lacity, M., Moloney, K., and Ross, J. (2018), *Blockchain at BNP Paribas: The Power of Co-Creation*, Center For Information Systems Research (CISR), MIT Sloan School of Management.

BNP Paribas had been thinking about blockchain since 2011, but 2015 marked the year it accelerated its blockchain activity. In its 2015 annual report to shareholders, the bank indicated that blockchain was one of the technological innovations in which it was investing, along with artificial intelligence and big data. The report emphasized the important role customers were playing in building the bank of the future: *'The best partners to build the bank of tomorrow with are clients themselves. We're entering into a natural phase of co-creation with clients. This represents a fundamental change in our practices....'*[97] In addition to defining blockchain, the report outlined a vision for exploring blockchains: *'This new way of managing and authenticating transactions is an opportunity to imagine radically innovative services and to enhance the customer experience and efficiency of the bank's services.'*[98]

BNP Paribas cemented its commitment to blockchain in 2015 by investing in Digital Asset Holdings, LLC, a New York-based FinTech start-up specializing in blockchains for the financial services industry.[99] Blythe Masters, the chief executive officer of Digital Asset Holdings, was well known in the financial services sector, in part for the credit default swap for which she had been accredited while working at J.P. Morgan.[100]

In November 2015, BNP Paribas joined the R3 consortium.[101,102] The next month, an initiative launched by the Caisse des Dépôts Group (CDC),[103] a public policy group based in France that aimed to develop economic policies that served the public interest, included BNP Paribas among eleven collaborators pooling research on blockchain.[104]

Beyond participation in these externally focused groups, BNP Paribas launched a number of internal blockchain proofs of concept (POCs) in partnership with the bank's customers. Blockchain POCs were led by decentralized units within the bank, supported by a centralized blockchain lab based in Paris. This lab oversaw the bank's blockchain toolkits and served as a central repository and source of knowledge for the business units.

A POC for a project in BNP Paribas's Transaction Banking division – called Cash Without Borders – proposed to use a blockchain to improve the existing trans-border transaction process. At the time, each country had its own payment system in its local currency (the exception being the European Union, whose members used the Single Euro Payments Area, or SEPA, to manage bank transfers of money).[105] For the trans-border transaction process, a bank had to be licensed to use its country's payment system. International transactions often relied on cooperation between banks in different countries (see Figure 3.1 for a simplified depiction).[106] The Cash Without Borders blockchain project proposed to intercept requests for trans-border payments between two BNP Paribas accounts and pass the requests to the internal blockchain. The blockchain would interact with the bank's systems of record to do the transfer. The customer interface and the bank's legacy systems of record would not be modified. The entire transfer would remain internal to BNP Paribas (see Figure 3.5).

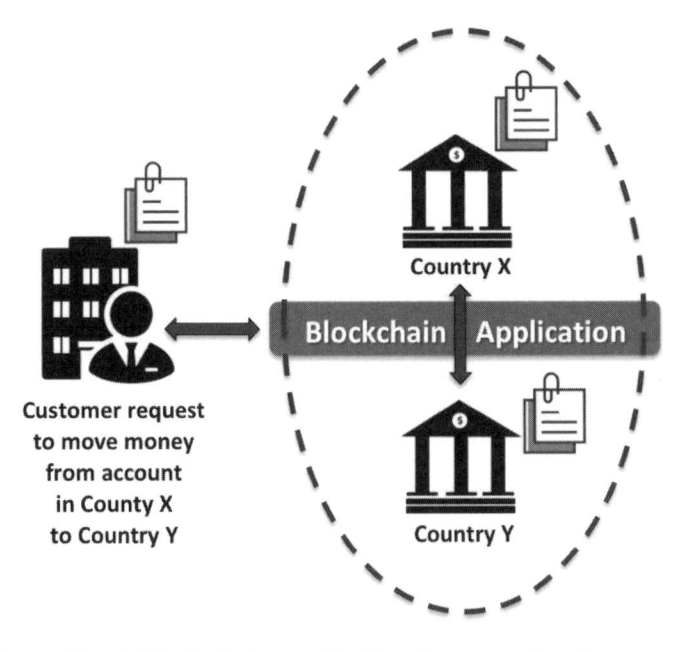

Figure 3.5: A blockchain application for cross-border payments

The customer uses the normal web-portal to request transfer from an account in Country X to an account in Country Y. The blockchain application intercepts the request, then inserts liquidity onto the blockchain. Transfer is made and the systems of record are updated in both countries; liquidity is extracted from the blockchain. The customer views the successful transfer of funds via his or her normal web-portal.

The blockchain project team was composed of BNP Paribas employees and customers. BNP Paribas's members comprised two blockchain coders plus six bank employees that had volunteered to work on the project in addition to their regular jobs. Volunteers from two institutional customers of the bank joined them. While financed by BNP Paribas, the POC required a direct cash outlay of only about €50,000. The bank built the system using Nxt protocols, mostly because it was the platform the team members knew best at the time.[107]

The POC was a success. The blockchain piece of the entire transaction occurred in sub-second time, and the entire process through the bank's legacy systems took less than two hours. The POC demonstrated that, for blockchain transactions internal to BNP Paribas, customers would know the price beforehand.

BNP Paribas planned to deploy Cash Without Borders in five countries – the United States, Belgium, the United Kingdom, Germany, and the Netherlands – by the end of 2017 or early 2018, with other countries to follow.

There are three notable things about this use case:

- First, while the firm participates in industry consortia to define standards for global cross-border payment blockchain applications, it did not wait to solve the pain-points within its own global organization.
- Second, the enterprise did the POC with two of their institutional customers, believing that all innovations should be co-created with customers.
- Third, the POC required a direct cash outlay of only about €50,000 because the bank began by adapting an open-source code base to build its private blockchain.

The next case provides an example of how an entity overseen by a government is building a blockchain to replace its current system.

3.2.5. Australian Securities Exchange (ASX)[108]

ASX is a public company governed by the Australian Securities and Investments (ASIC) and the Reserve Bank of Australia (RBA). ASX plans to replace its existing post-trade settlement system, called Clearing House Electronic Subregister System (CHESS), with a blockchain application perhaps in the later part of 2018.[109]

CHESS clears and settles transactions as well as registers assets. Overall, CHESS seems to perform quite well, with the ASX reporting 99.99 percent availability and an average T+2 settlement cycle, meaning most securities transactions settle within two business days. However, it has had issues. In September 2016, a hardware failure in the main database used by the system caused the exchange to shut down.[110] Why replace the system? According to ASX's website, the new blockchain application will *'provide a broader range of benefits to a wider cross section of the market.'*[11] The new blockchain application aims to benefit both investors and traders by providing more control over their transactions and enabling faster and less costly settlements. According to Dominic Stevens, CEO, the strategic move aims to put *'Australia at the forefront of innovation in financial markets.'*[112]

ASX partnered with the Digital Asset Holdings in 2016 to produce a permissioned blockchain POC for the cash equities market. The POC was completed in 2016. ASX spent the next year and a half on extensive testing and change management. It hired third-party security reviews; sought broad stakeholder inputs on desired system features; tested the system for scalability, security, and performance; and assessed privacy, security, and compliance risks. At the end of 2016, the ASX established six working groups to focus on :

(1) Account structures and participant models
(2) Corporate actions
(3) Transfers and conversions
(4) Settlement enhancements
(5) Data storage and delivery
(6) Reporting and non-functional requirements

Their work identified 45 business requirements by November 2017. The ASX's blockchain application is based on a private, permissioned ledger that promises to be based on an enhanced database architecture (see Figure 3.6). As of the beginning of 2018, ASX had not announced a specific target date for live deployment, but it planned to release a public migration plan in March of 2018.[113]

Overall, ASX's proposed blockchain application has garnered worldwide media attention; if it can pull off a successful implementation, it will be heralded as one of blockchain's bellwether events.

In summary, Ripple, Stellar, BNP Paribas and ASX represent a variety of organizations exploring blockchain applications to solve problems in today's financial systems. Next, we'll explore blockchains in the energy sector.

ASX Private Permissioned Ledger
Similar to today, but an enhanced database architecture

• Highly regulated market
    – Infrastructure providers with licences to operate
    – Rule book defines market operation
    – Participants identified and meet regulatory standards
     (e.g. KYC and AML)
 	
• Operated on a system within a private network
    – Technology controls retained
    – Securities exist digitally only within the ASX register
    – Cash remains within banking system
 	
• Enhanced data integrity
    – Equivalent or better security of data (cryptography)
    – Multiparty authentication and authorisation
    – Creates a secure single source of truth
    – Could provide significant benefits to the industry

Figure 3.6: Attributes of ASX's proposed blockchain application

Source: ASX Consultation Paper[114]

3.3. Blockchain applications in the energy sector

The world over, large electric utilities are the primary suppliers of electricity. These large, centrally-managed organizations have been operating with the same business models for a 100 years or more and they are markedly energy inefficient. According to Lawrence Livermore National Laboratory, only 32 percent of electric energy generated in the US is actually 'useable energy', called 'exergy'.[115] That means most of the electric energy generated by utilities is wasted through the processes of conversion, transportation and consumption.[116]

Consumers are increasingly concerned about the waste, expense, and lack of control over their power supply. Consequently, many households have installed solar panels on their properties. US solar power installations doubled from 2015 to 2016,[117] and more than 1 million US households had solar power by 2016.[118] Consumer adoption of solar panels is prompted by many factors besides lower electric bills; consumers want energy independence, increased property values and reduced carbon footprints. Pertaining to this last point, Energysage – a company that helps consumers find solar solutions – claims *'typical residential solar panel system will eliminate three to four tons of carbon emissions each year – the equivalent of planting over 100 trees annually.'*[119] However, US consumers with solar panels are still connected to, and reliant upon, their major electric utility providers. Any excess capacity generated from a household solar panel is put right back into the traditional electric grid and the utility provider credits the consumer's bill; the 'prosumers' – households that produce excess energy – have no market to sell excess capacity to besides the utility provider. That is, until now. Lawrence Orsini, founder and CEO of LO3 Energy, aimed to create a way for neighbors to buy and sell excess electric capacity directly from each other. Like other examples in this chapter, his company is building the technology platform to create peer-to-peer markets for the sharing economy. So his story begins…

3.3.1. LO3 Energy's Microgrid

"With the Microgrid, there is no need for a utility company to act as an intermediary, leaving residents in control of their own power."

LO3 Energy News story[120]

"We're really providing choice. More choice for the community, more choice for what types of energy they can buy, who they can buy it from, what they can do with the money that they were spending on energy."

Lawrence Orsini, Founder and CEO of LO3 Energy[121]

"The next time a superstorm comes through and knocks out all of the power, Brooklyn Microgrid will make sure the power stays on in critical areas so you have a safe place to charge your phone, get food or send out emails to let people know you are okay."

Neighbor featured on Brooklyn Microgrid Introduction[122]

LO3 Energy founded. Lawrence Orsini spent years in the energy sector – before founding LO3 Energy in 2012 in Brooklyn New York, he worked for PECI, a non-profit organization based in Portland Oregon that helps utilities, governments and other clients to become more energy efficient.[123] He was also Director of New Products at CLEAResults, an Austin Texas-based company that helps utilities, businesses, and consumers to become more energy efficient.[124] This position brought him to New York City.

Orsini envisioned a future of energy production and consumption that is sustainable, local, reliable, efficient, and self-governing. He wanted to build the platform where prosumers sell excess energy capacity from their solar panels directly to neighbors using a mobile app. His idea became even more pertinent in the aftermath of Hurricane Sandy, which hit New York City in October of 2012. It was the largest hurricane on record – a whopping 1,100 miles in diameter. As Hurricane Sandy flooded the streets of New York City, power went out to over 800,000 residences and businesses and stayed off for days.[125] Even residents with solar panels could not use their own power because the photovoltaic panels (PV) that connected them to the utility grid were shut off. The pain and aftermath of Hurricane Sandy awakened consumers and made them receptive to LO3 Energy's value proposition.

Exergy – a transactive energy platform. To accomplish Orsini's vision, LO3 Energy is building both the hardware and software to create what is called a 'transactive energy platform', they branded 'Exergy'. The platform comprises hardware such as smart meters, switches, and controllers. The software is based on a proprietary blockchain-based application with a customizable, mobile user interface (see Figure 3.7).

Hardware. The IoT smart meters are installed on the prosumers' properties (typically basements) to measure production and consumption of electricity. The control system, which was still being built in 2017, will be able to isolate a part of the existing, physical electric grid so that it can be re-routed, say to hospitals or community shelters, in the case of a blackout.[126] (See Figure 3.8 for a first generation hardware installation). The hardware feeds data to the proprietary and patented blockchain-based application every second. Only the prosumers need the specialized hardware installed; consumers interact with the platform through a mobile or desktop app.

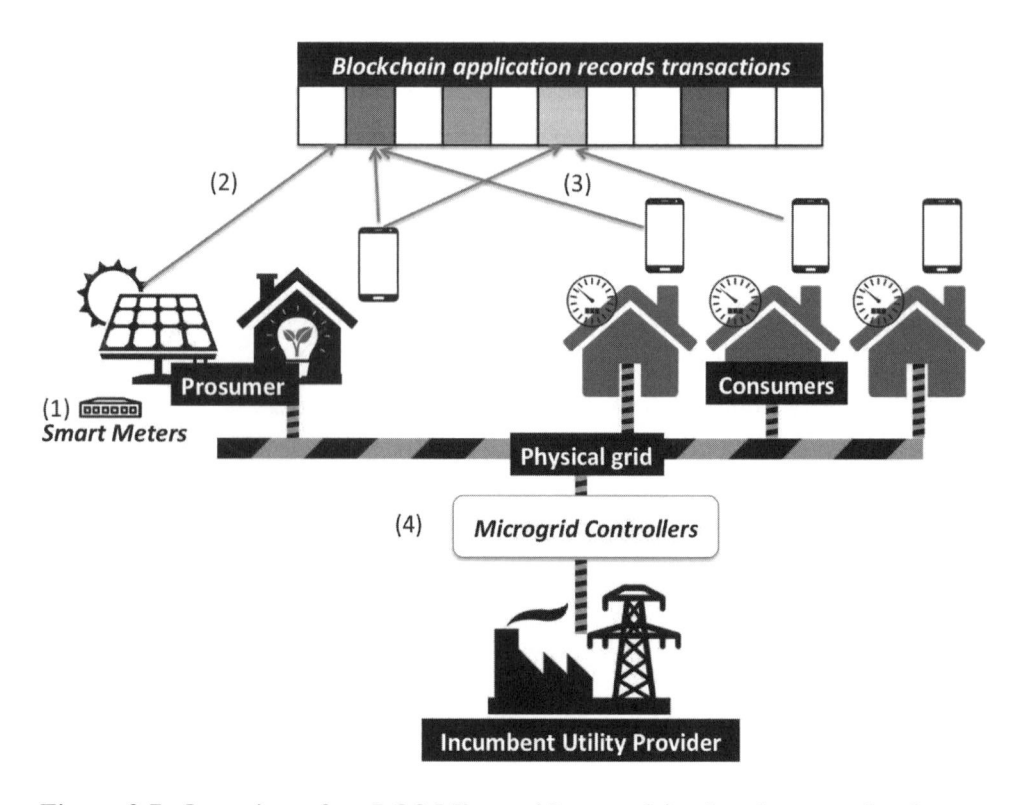

Figure 3.7: Overview of an LO3 Microgrid comprising hardware and software
Source: Adapted from LO3 Video and LO3 white papers[127]

(1) Prosumers install IoT smart meters (2) that record production each second on a hardware-embedded blockchain. Each smart meter becomes a node in the blockchain network for validation and consensus. (3) Prosumers and consumers transact based on the data stored on the propriety blockchain application using a mobile application. (4) Controllers will create a separate, physical microgrid from the main grid that can run on its own in times of need.

Software. The blockchain application is actually embedded within the hardware. It records information collected from the smart meters onto the blockchain ledger about the state of the grid, the time and location of production, the consumption requirements, and the buy and sell offers of market participants. Lawrence Orsini explained the suitability of a blockchain for the platform as follows:

"The architecture is very well aligned with our decentralized infrastructure. So the ledger needs to be on the grid; it needs to be distributed amongst the grid. If you're going to run a physical microgrid, or even a virtual microgrid, and you're incorporating a resiliency plan, then you can't have cloud hosting – because when the grid goes down, you have no communication." [128]

Figure 3.8: Example of LO3 Hardware

Sources: Left Photo Credit: Emma Foehringer Merchant;[129] Right: Photo Credit: LO3 Energy

The mobile application connects neighbors to the blockchain to allow peer-to-peer transactions; neighbors use the app to place and execute buy and sell orders. Essentially, prosumers are selling their excess capacity credits to neighbors rather than back to the utility. The mobile application is a white-label product that other companies can rebrand. (See Figure 3.9 for an example of the user interface for the Brooklyn Microgrid project.)

LO3 is building the components through partnerships with Siemens, contractors, and other parties. For example, LO3 is working with Siemens to build the physical grid that will separate from the main utility grid so that locally-generated power can be re-routed to critical locations in time of need.[130]

The Brooklyn Microgrid Project. As LO3 continues to build and improve upon the platform, it is conducting live tests through a project called the Brooklyn Microgrid project. In 2016, LO3 tested the microgrid concept in one residential neighborhood on President Street in Brooklyn New York (see Figure 3.10). It chose this street for the proof-of-concept (POC) because it had a high concentration of solar adopters on one side of the street and a high concentration of neighbors interested in green energy on the other side. Orsini said:

"It was an obvious choice. These are neighbors across the street from each other, they had good relationships."[131]

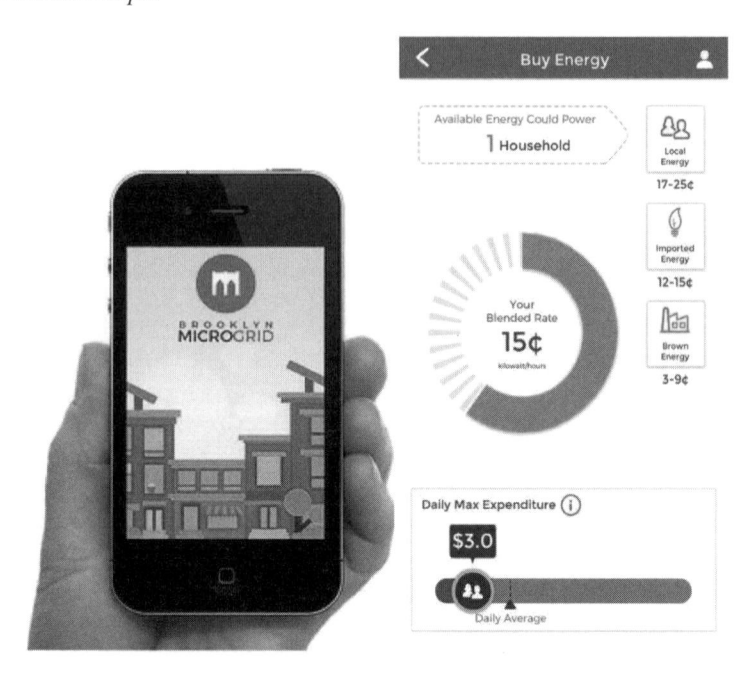

Figure 3.9: Example of mobile app interface for Brooklyn Microgrid project
Consumers can set the maximum daily rates and buy energy from neighbors, clean energy, or brown energy sources.

Sources: Left: https://www.sacramento.energy/video-gallery
Right: Author's mobile app screenshot on February 24th 2018

The POC proved that the smart meters could successfully count the electrons generated from solar panels, could record data on the prototype blockchain (initially built on Ethereum) and could make data accessible to prosumers and consumers.[132] This test also proved that consumers were willing to pay a little bit more for electricity produced by their neighbors. Orsini explained:

"What we are doing is enabling consumer choice. Many consumers don't want cheap, they want theirs. Just like many consumers are willing to pay more for locally produced food, many are willing to pay more for locally produced electrons – and we empower them to do that. If they're looking for cheap, then they will have access to cheap as well. Our model has everything to do with providing choice."[133]

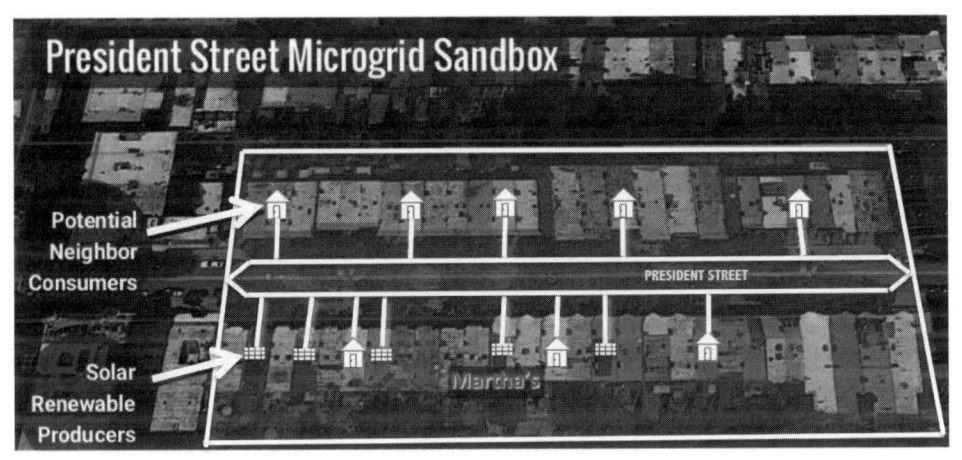

Figure 3.10: Site of proof-of-concept test on President Street in Brooklyn, New York

Source: Microgrid media[134]

After the successful POC, LO3 was ready to scout for a location to expand the Brooklyn Microgrid project to a full-scale, live test of the business model and platform. The search was on for a location that would test the business model across social strata. After six months of searching, LO3 decided on Brooklyn's Gowanus and Park Slope neighborhoods (see Figure 3.11). Orsini explained:

> *"This neighborhood was the right place to do it. So, from a social strata perspective, we've got some of the poorest of the poor in New York living here in Brooklyn, all the way up to some of the most expensive properties in the city, right along the park. Mayor De Blasio (mayor of New York City) and Chuck Schumer (US Senator from New York State) live in Park Slope. From the business perspective, the strata covers manufacturing, light industrial, and local retail all the way up to the highest-end retail businesses. So, that's why we chose this location."[135]*

By December 2017, LO3 had installed 60 smart meters in the neighborhood and 500 consumers had downloaded the mobile application. The grid is operating in a shadow market until all the regulatory requirements are met. As of December 2017, LO3 was quite close to getting regulatory permission to operate in New York State.[136]

Since inception, LO3 Energy has worked very closely with New York regulators and policy makers. LO3 has also met with the US Federal Energy Regulatory Commission. Orsini said:

"We have a very good relationship with the regulators. The regulators in New York are pretty excited about and engaged in what we're doing, particularly for the transactive energy platform."[138]

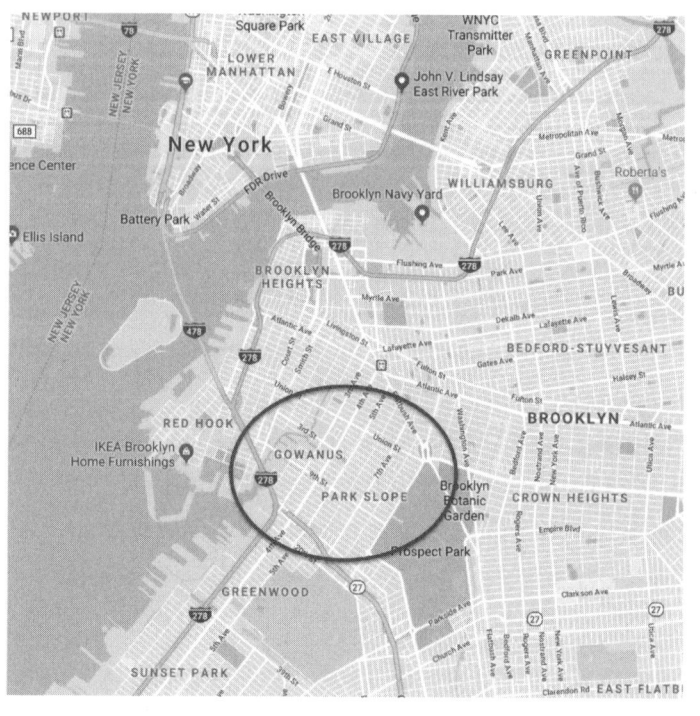

Figure 3.11: Gowanus and Park Slope neighborhoods of Brooklyn, New York

Source: Googlemaps[137]

The same regulatory permission process will need to be repeated as communities adopt the Exergy platform in other US jurisdictions and beyond to other countries. Orsini had already met with regulators from Australia and Europe[139], but as a business model, it would be untenable for LO3 to lead the efforts for subsequent adoptions. Therefore, going forward beyond the Brooklyn Microgrid project, LO3 Energy will sell its transactive energy platform, Exergy, directly to other communities or institutions interested in adoption, but it will not own the projects. Local adopters are in the best position to rally neighbors, educate users and secure local regulatory permissions. Several other community-based projects are underway, including projects in Sacramento California,[140] South Australia,[141] Germany[142] and across Europe.[143] Orsini said that hundreds of interested communities have approached LO3 about participation.[144]

What's next for LO3? Well, a new not-for-profit foundation, the 'Exergy Foundation', is set to launch and manage a digital token.

Exergy Foundation. In 2018, a non-profit called the Exergy Foundation will launch the sale of its blockchain's token, called Exergy (symbol XRG).[145] The token will facilitate the use of data about the current state of the grid, the time and location of production, and multi-party consumption requirements (see Figure 3.12).[146]

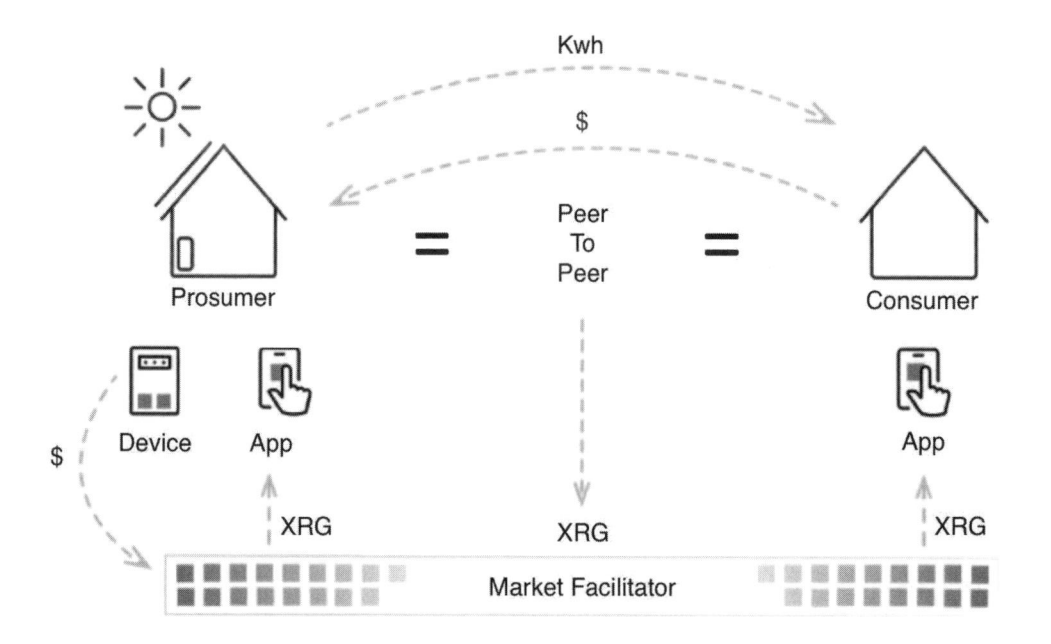

Figure 3.12: Flow of tokens and dollars in Exergy blockchain application
Source: Exergy Business White Paper[147]

A prosumer buys and installs an Exergy-compliant smart meter, downloads the mobile app and stakes XRG tokens, which are tied to his or her meter. A consumer downloads the app, stakes XRG tokens to his or her account. The blockchain-based application facilitates transactions; the XRG tokens indicate that a certain amount of energy was produced from a smart meter and can be transacted on the blockchain to transfer value from one wallet to another. Real dollars are exchanged between buyers and sellers.

Orsini is well on his way to realizing his vision for energy production and consumption that is sustainable, local, reliable, efficient, and self-governing. LO3 energy is ahead of other players in the space because Orsini and his team knew that they needed to do more than just build a great platform – they needed to prove they could get the platform legally and socially embedded into a real community. To scale globally, they also needed to show that its platform could attract other partners to build new business models on top of it.

The next case addresses a business model innovation for electric car charging.

3.3.2. Share&Charge

> *"The idea is to solve the lack of public charging infrastructure in Germany by integrating private charging stations. We are enabling people with our app to share their charging stations."*

> **Dietrich Sümmermann, Innogy Innovation Hub and Co-founder of**
> **Share&Charge**[148]

Innogy, a subsidiary of the Germany-based electric utility RWE, was established in 2016 to focus on renewable energy solutions. Innogy's Innovation Hub aims to create or collaborate with start-ups to bring new energy solutions based on 'ethical machines' to market.[149] One of its projects is 'Share&Charge', a startup venture to create a peer-to-peer marketplace for electric car charging. Innogy wanted to expand Germany's infrastructure by enabling 60,000 private charging stations to join Germany's 6,500 public charging stations.

Working with the partners TÜV Rheinland and MotionWerk, Share&Charge installed over 1,000 blockchain-enabled electric charging stations around Germany (see Figure 3.13).[150] Owners of a charging station can set their own flat rate, time-based, or kilowatt hour-based fees. The fees can also be discounted for family, friends, or charities. Using a mobile app, drivers can search for nearby charging stations, charge their electric cars at any of the authorized stations and pay for the charges using Share&Charge's native digital asset called a 'Mobility Token'.[151]

The application is built on Etherum using three smart contracts: MobilityToken, ChargingPoles, and LibManager. MobilityToken is the token contract that holds balances and enforces rules; each token is backed by a real Euro and complies with German regulations. ChargingPoles registers all the charging pole stations and executes the operations at the charging stations, such as the start and stop meter functions. LibManager is a library of contracts that will allow Share&Charge to update smart contracts or fix programming errors in the future.[152]

Share&Charge has been available since April of 2017, but it still has a long journey ahead as far as gaining a critical mass of adopters within Germany and beyond.

Figure 3.13: Innogy charging station with embedded Etherum node
Source: https://cdn-images-1.medium.com/max/1600/1*aZuXOx0TiiXEry3QoZMDjw.jpeg

3.4. Blockchain applications in supply chains

"Consumers increasingly want to know that the ethical claims companies make about their products are real. Distributed ledgers provide easy ways to certify that the backstories of the things we buy are genuine. Transparency comes with blockchain-based time-stamping of a date and location – on ethical diamonds, for instance – that corresponds to a product number."

Blockgeeks[153]

"In the international trade finance case, it's a very old legacy process with a lot of paper documents. It was perceived that there could be value and the banks would be able to introduce a more efficient process through this technology."

Lead Digital Architect for a large global bank[154]

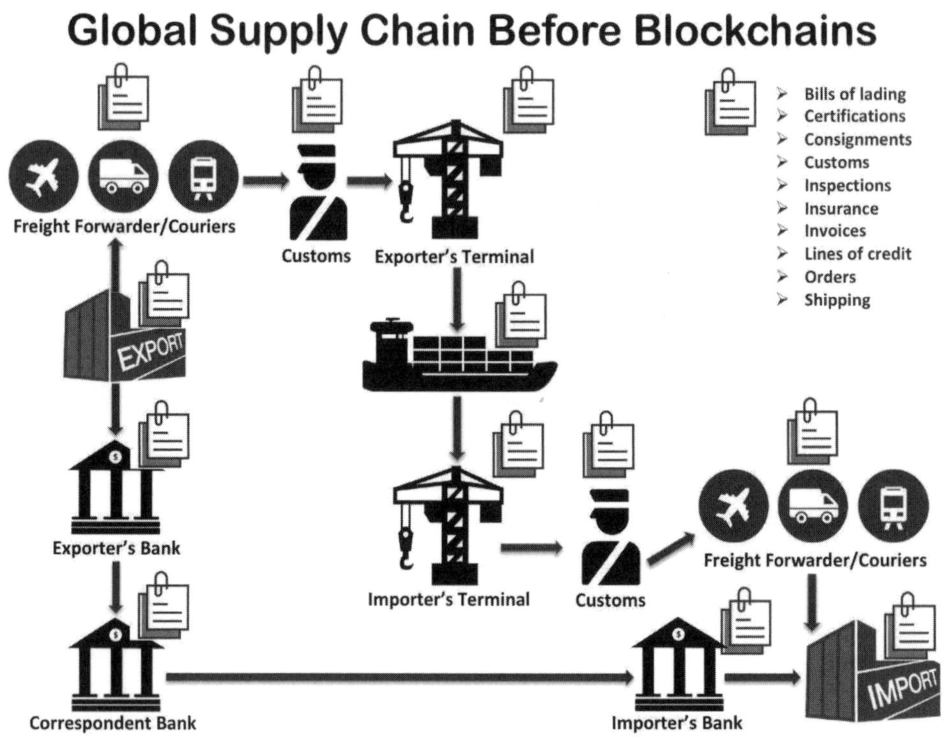

Figure 3.14: Global supply chains before a blockchain application

While manufacturers; exporters; couriers; freight forwarders; customs; inspectors; exporters; shippers, and importers, move physical goods through the global supply chain, they are also creating data about those movements with bills of lading; certifications; consignments; customs forms; inspections data; insurance forms; invoices; lines of credit; purchase orders; shipping manifestos; and receiving documents.

Today's global supply chains are a complex web of trading partners and trusted third-parties. Each party maintains its own centralized systems and subsequently partners face significant challenges trying to synchronize the data about the flow of physical goods and services, with the actual flow of goods and services (see Figure 3.14). While manufacturers, exporters, couriers, freight forwarders, customs, inspectors, exporters, shippers, and importers are moving physical goods, they are also creating data about those movements with bills of lading; certifications; consignments; customs forms inspections data; insurance forms; invoices; lines of credit; purchase orders; shipping manifestos; and receiving documents, to name just a few.

As a consequence of so many players with their own centralized systems, and so much paperwork: assets get lost; shipping containers get delayed in ports because of missing paperwork; inconsistent records across trading partners trigger disputes; and counterfeit products slip through supply chains, to highlight some of the many challenges. Consequently, consumers often have no way of confidently knowing the sources of the products they purchase.

Blockchains have the potential to solve many of these challenges. Blockchains can provide a trusted shared record of data provenance from the asset's origin to a time-stamped history of events related to that asset. Given all the potential benefits, it's no wonder that so many enterprises have experimented with supply chain blockchain applications. Four mini-cases and one larger case at Moog Aircraft show the possibilities.

3.4.1. IBM's blockchain partnerships

IBM has been a major player in this space. Its strategy is to work with anchor tenants – powerful supply chain leaders like Maersk and Wal-Mart – to attract other suppliers and partners within each market.[155] IBM also works with promising startups like Everledger. All of these projects are based on Hyperledger Fabric – the open source code base for which IBM provided much of the code.

Everledger. Everledger tracks diamonds from mines to retail stores. Founded in 2015 by Leanne Kemp, she aimed to help stop 'blood diamonds' – diamonds mined to finance conflicts in such places as Sierra Leone, Liberia, Angola, and the Ivory Coast – by better tracking the warranties associated with fair trade practices established by the United Nations. The United Nations created the World Diamond Congress to define the standards, which it subsequently passed in 2003. Known as the 'Kimberly Process Certification', the process requires sellers of rough and polished diamonds to insert a warranty declaration on invoices that reads, *The diamonds herein invoiced have been purchased from legitimate sources not involved in funding conflict and in compliance with United Nations resolutions. The seller hereby guarantees that these diamonds are conflict free, based on personal knowledge and/or written guarantees provided by the supplier of these diamonds.'*[156]

Everledger tracks diamonds by creating a unique digital version of the physical diamond by specifying 40 meta data points using high resolution photographs (see Figure 3.15). Everledger worked with IBM to build the blockchain application on Hyperledger Fabric. Over 1 million diamonds were represented on the ledger as of March 2017.[157] Everledger has since expanded its business model to track and trace other valuable assets such as art, wine, and antiquities.

Maersk. IBM and Maersk – the world's largest shipping firm – began working on a blockchain application in 2014 to track and trace containers of perishables through a global supply chain. The partners first had to map the process, which comprises over 200 transactions and 30 partners, then digitize documents to feed into the blockchain application. The blockchain application, based on Hyperledger Fabric, was tested in 2016 and 2017 with numerous partners. One test tracked a container from the Port of Rotterdam across the Atlantic Ocean to the Port of Newark in partnership with Schneider Electric, customs administrations from the Netherlands and the US, and the US Department of Homeland Security.[158] Other tests tracked flowers from Kenya, oranges from California, and pineapples from Columbia to the Port of Rotterdam.[159] In January of 2018, IBM and Maersk announced plans to create a joint venture to move their blockchain solution to market.[160]

Wal-Mart. IBM also worked with Wal-Mart to track Chinese pork and Mexican mangos.[161] In December of 2017, IBM, Wal-Mart, JD.com and China's Tsinghua University National Engineering Laboratory, established the Food Safety Alliance. According the press release, '*The Alliance will work with food supply chain providers and regulators to develop the standards, solutions and partnerships to enable a broad-based food safety ecosystem in China.'*[162] IBM will provide the blockchain expertise and Tsinghua University will provide expertize on China's food safety ecosystem. IBM and Tsinghua will collaborate with Wal-Mart and JD '*to develop, optimize and roll out the technology to suppliers and retailers that join the alliance.'*[163]

The next case examines a startup in the supply chain space.

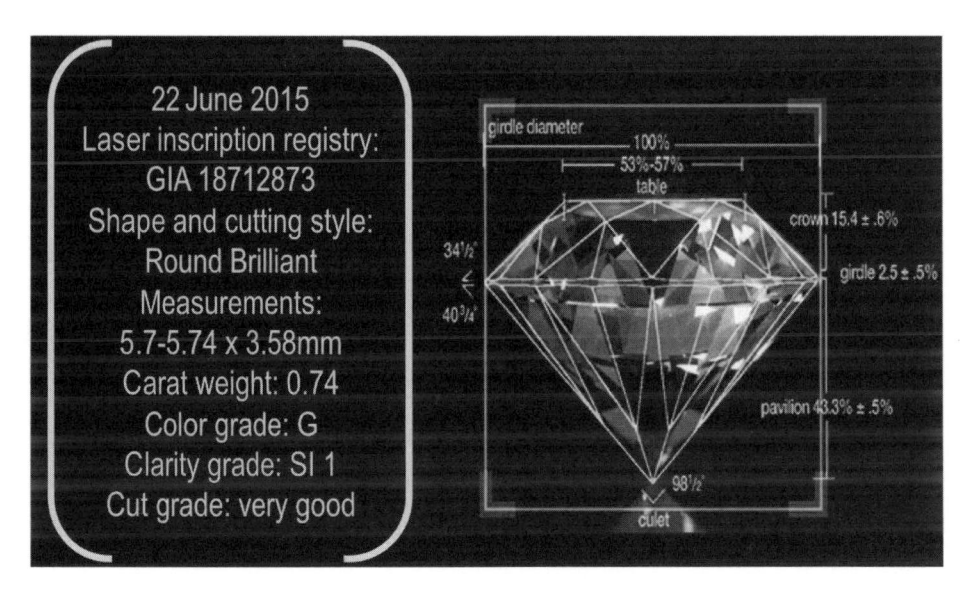

Figure 3:15: Everledger's digital identifier for a fair trade diamond

Source: https://www.youtube.com/watch?v=GAdjL-nultI

3.4.2. Provenance's tuna tracking

Provenance, a UK based startup, built a blockchain application to track and trace sustainably caught tuna from sea to store (see Figure 3.16). It conducted a six-month long pilot using smart tags and a mobile app interface to track tuna fish caught in Indonesia. Provenance worked with a non-government organization (NGO) to register and train local fishermen. For the first mile, fishermen used the mobile app to register their catch. At that point, the blockchain application assigned a unique ID to the catch. The local NGO updated the blockchain when it confirmed the fisherman's registration was compliant with fair trade using data sources such as global positioning system (GPS) data to verify the location of the catch. Fishermen used the mobile app to transfer the catch to the participating supplier. When the supplier sold the catch to the fish factory, the fish factory used the unique ID to print and adhere the label to each item. Provenance then worked with a UK supermarket to workshop the last mile of the supply chain.[164] Provenance foresees that supermarkets, restaurants, and end customers will use the mobile app to hover over the label to see the fish's entire journey from sea to table. Provenance also has projects to track coffee, cotton, fashion, organic produce,[165] and chicken.[166]

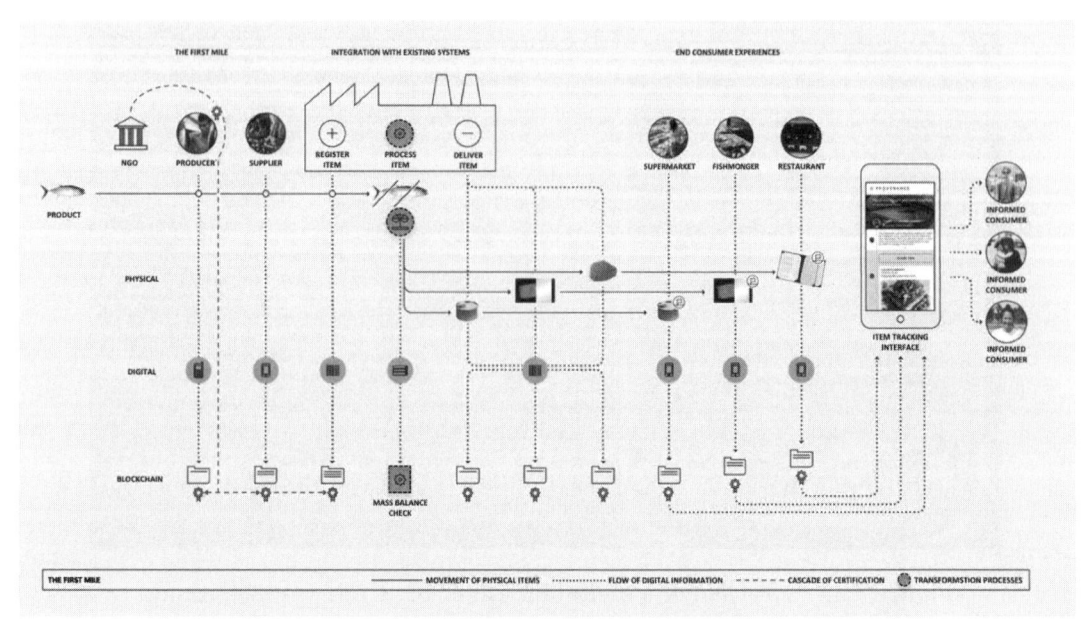

**Figure 3.16: Provenance's blockchain application for tracking
and tracing tuna from sea to table**

Source: https://www.provenance.org/tracking-tuna-on-the-blockchain

3.4.3. Moog, Inc.

"Moog made a deliberate business decision to be part of the disruption caused by 3D printing and Blockchain versus being disrupted by them. We realized the greatest impact our business was going to be how these technologies upended the business models and supply chains employed by manufacturers today."

George Small, Principle Engineer, Moog Inc.[167]

Source: https://www.provenance.org/tracking-tuna-on-the-blockchain "Coasian economics says firms exist because you have trust inside the company. Blockchain has allowed us to take trust outside of the four walls of the firm and distribute it, so we have distributed trust."

**James Allen Regenor, Business Unit Director, Transformative Technologies
Moog Inc.**[168]

Moog Inc. is a $2.5 billion US precision manufacturer and provider of integrated control systems. The company operates four divisions: Aircraft Controls, Space and Defense, Components, and Industrial Systems. Its biggest markets are defense (34 percent of 2016 revenues), commercial aircraft (24 percent), industrial (21 percent), followed by energy, medical, and space with seven percent each.[169] Our blockchain story begins in Aircraft Controls and features Colonel James Allen Regenor.

When Colonel Regenor retired after 31 years of military service in the US Air Force, he joined Moog in 2013 as Director of Business Development and Strategy. He was hired partly for his scenario-based planning skills to help Moog envision future business directions. One such scenario went as follows:

> *'Imagine a scenario where lives depend upon a mission being flown off the deck of an aircraft carrier far out at sea. The only available aircraft has just been grounded with a failed critical part. There is no part inventory on the carrier. But we do have a 3-D printer and a stock of powder aboard. A technical data package is available for the part, and a replacement is quickly printed. You are the responsible person who needs to get this part quickly fitted to the aircraft and to sign the plane off as safe and ready to fly. How would you know if the newly printed additive manufacturing part you are holding in your hand is good for use?'* [170]

Essentially, Moog imagined a completely decentralized manufacturing process in which military and commercial customers could print parts where they need them, when they need them. The potential business value was enormous, such as significantly less downtime, lower inventory costs, lower customs fees, and lower shipping and transportation costs.[171] The challenges to realize such a decentralized manufacturing process – particularly in such a highly regulated context – were equally as enormous. What if the 3-D printing instructions had been tampered with by a cyber-terrorist? Or what if the instructions were counterfeit? Moog would need a way to guarantee that the part that came off the printer was authentic and that the part was ready for use. Furthermore, the newly printed part would need to be tracked over its entire lifetime, so it would need an embedded unique ID when it came off the printer. Moog would need a decentralized network with the highest security. Technically, Regenor and his team quickly realized that blockchain technologies might be the ideal technical solution: a distributed blockchain application for distributed additive manufacturing.[172]

Moog is now building a platform-based business model for the entire lifecycle of 3-D printed parts – from design to decommissioning – called VeriPart (see Figure 3.17). The platform will integrate 3-D printing, blockchain, and artificial intelligence technologies. The long-term vision is that a joint venture with at least five equal partners (with Moog being one) will manage the platform and a separate consortium will govern each industry vertical. Moog is initially building the VeriPart platform for the aerospace industry, but it is actively exploring automotive, medical and other industries that use 3-D printed parts. Regenor is leading the effort.

Regenor became Moog's Business Unit Director of Additive Manufacturing & Innovation in April of 2016 and then Director of Transformative Technologies in 2017 to bring the vision to fruition. Regenor and his team are simultaneously building and testing the technical solution; seeking IP protection on new inventions; working with consortia; competitors and trading partners to define standards; working with government legislators and regulators to define regulations for military acquisition of 3-D parts; conducting POCs with key customers and partners; and defining a new viable business model to generate revenues and a marketing strategy to attract adoption. Here again, we have an example of why it takes longer than expected for enterprises to get blockchain applications out of innovation labs and into live production. The technical hurdles are jumpable… the ecosystem obstacles are more like a steeplechase. Let's examine what Moog is doing on each front.

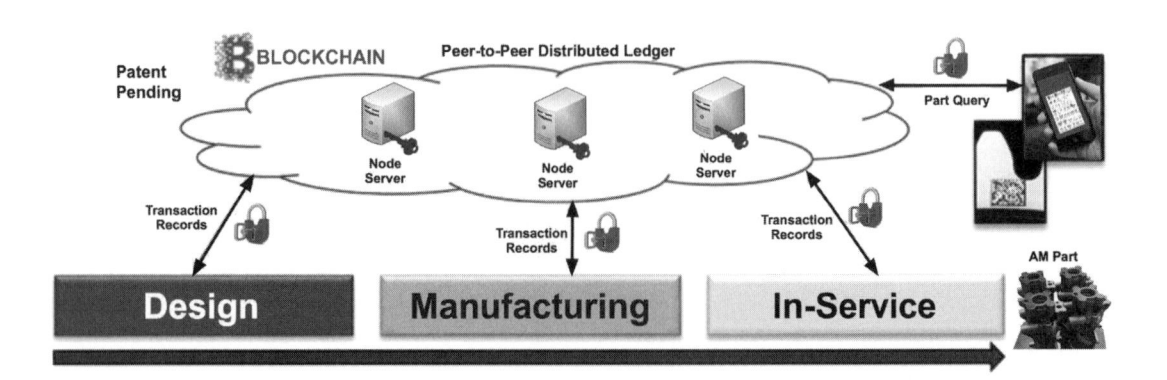

Figure 3.17: Moog Aircraft's blockchain application for verifying 3-D printed parts

Source: Moog Aircraft, http://www.moog.com/news/
blog-new/IntroducingVeripart_Issue3.html

Unique, embedded IDs on 3-D printed parts. Moog sought to offset the classic Blockchain 'Byzantine double spend' attack by creating a two-layer authentication protocol to insure the integrity of the parts in the supply chain. First, each part is printed with a unique hash that can be validated via a smart phone app. If in the hash verification process a part is identified as already existing in the supply chain… a counterfeit exists. Moog can then quickly determine which part is counterfeit by checking for a watermark, which Moog inserts in the build of each part. Additionally, the blockchain application could also store the part's every movement, every process, and every transfer of ownership, thus enabling track and trace through the supply chain.[173]

Blockchain platform. Moog is working with a number of blockchain partners because no single blockchain standard has emerged yet. Regenor related the current state of blockchain standards in 2018 to the state of railroad standards in the early 1800s. Initially, each railroad had its own gauge and could only operate on its own tracks until the UK government mandated the standard gauge of 4 feet 8 ½ inches in 1846. Given that we do not know which blockchain will become the defacto standard, Moog decided to partner with Nuco, a Toronto-based blockchain startup, that is building an interoperable blockchain network called 'Aion'.[174] Nuco's Aion white paper describes Aion as a 'third-generation' blockchain.[175]

Nuco describes Bitcoin as the 'first-generation' blockchain since it was built for one specific application; Ethereum is described as a 'second-generation' blockchain since it allows application-specific logic to be built on top of the Ethereum blockchain; Aion is described as a 'third-generation' blockchain because '*in the future, blockchains will federate data and value in a hub and spoke model similar to the internet. The future of mainstream blockchain adoption will be achieved by the development of a networked, federated blockchain to integrate these separate spokes. That integrated blockchain network is Aion.*'[176]

Aion will serve as the hub to VeriPart. Regenor said:

> *"Aion will allow us to move data between the multiple blockchains that could be present in our supply chain. We think this is a very important step, and we're glad to be participating in it."*[177]

Moog has also worked with a major ERP supplier because the VeriPart platform needs to connect not only with other blockchains, but also to legacy systems, particularly for Moog's enterprise customers. Moog is also working with Microsoft on adding plug-ins into the platform as well as on a major proof-of-concept (POC).

Proof-of-concepts. Moog has a number of POCs in partnership with industrial customers and technology providers. On February 7th 2018, Moog and Singapore Technology Aerospace (STA) announced the completion of a demonstration of the first digital end-to-end manufacturing of a 3-D printed part in the aerospace vertical on a blockchain. In the demonstration, STA bought a digital part from Moog using Microsoft's Azure blockchain application and printed the part on premises at their facility. When STA downloaded the file, the settlement happened instantaneously; the payment used a symbolic token that moved value from Moog's address to STA's address.

In another POC, Moog, Nuco (AION), and one of Moog's largest aerospace customers are testing the use of the blockchain for parts provenance using traditionally manufactured parts (rather than 3D printed parts). Moog wanted to involve its major aerospace clients early in the development of VeriPart rather than wait for the certification agencies to finalize regulations on 3D printed parts.

Finally, the US Department of Defense (DoD) is funding a POC with Moog, other government agencies, and an undisclosed blockchain company, to test the blockchain for parts provenance of several 3-D printed parts made out of plastic and metals. During phase I of the POC, the defense agencies will request the part designs, print the parts, and inspect the parts to test the efficacy of counterfeit part prevention and cybersecurity resiliency. During phase II, the Defense Logistics Agency will buy digital parts from a digital catalogue using smart contracts.

Working on standards and digital data. Moog is working with a nonprofit organization that conducts research and manages several US national laboratories, and other partners on an industry consortium for additive manufacturing in the aerospace industry. Regenor said:

> *"When they started with standards for aircrafts, the standards were based on wood, glue and fabric. Since then, they've helped develop standards for forgings and castings of metals, plastics, composites and everything else."*[178]

The consortium is building a digital library for general properties of 3-D printed materials. This step is needed so that manufacturers can pivot from 'point approvals' to 'design allowables'.

Regenor explained:

> *"Currently, when you make a part, you have to take it to the military or the FAA (Federal Aviation Authority) and seek approval for a particular part made from a particular pattern on a particular machine [i.e. a 'point approval']. It's extremely narrow. With additive manufacturing, we need to get approval for a family of parts from a family of patterns on a family of machines [i.e. a 'design allowable'] . In order to get there, you have to create the data, so that is what we have been doing."*[179]

Regenor foresees that the data will become part of an open digital catalogue available to VeriPart users. While some of Moog's competitors are building proprietary data catalogues that will have to be built on proprietary machines, Regenor believes that real customer value is generated from open architectures.

Moog is also working with the American Standards Association (ASA) on standards for 3-D printed parts, called, 'America Makes & ANSI Additive Manufacturing Standardization Collaborative (AMSC)'.[180] The AMSC published a roadmap for additive manufacturing in February of 2017.[181] A first draft of standards is expected in early 2018.

Working with legislators and regulators. If VeriPart was to become a reality, Moog needed the US government to create 3-D printing regulations for DoD acquisitions. Regenor described how he first approached getting regulations updated:

> *"In the Federal Acquisition Regulations for electronic parts, it says that there has to be providence. So I sat down with my pen and everywhere it said 'electronic', I put in the words 'additive manufacturing'. I went back to our lobbyist and said, 'Hey, let's put this in front of committee. Let's get this added to the Federal Acquisition Regulations.' So we decided to use federal regulation to help create market space."*[182]

Moog informed the US House Armed Services Committee about the threat of counterfeiting for additive manufactured parts. Regenor explained:

> *"With 3-D printing, you have to worry about complex parts being counterfeit. Anybody can print something that looks like the part they are holding in their hand. It won't have the same material properties or the same characteristics, but the guy pulling it off the shelf will not know the difference."*[183]

117

Legislators understood the concern; the National Defense Authorization Act of 2018 includes funds for additive manufacturing technology development and requires briefings on blockchain technologies from agencies.[184]

Working to protect IP. Moog has several internal and external lawyers working on protecting its intellectual property. So far, VeriPart's first extension for a registered trademark was granted on January 15, 2018.[185] Moog has also filed several patent applications. The patent for 'secure and traceable manufactured parts'[186] describes 3-D parts provenance, from initial requirements through the entire product life cycle using blockchain. The patent describes three integrities: data integrity, process integrity, and performance integrity. In December 2017, Moog extended the patent into the space domain. Regenor explained:

> *"If you are on a space station, space factory, space ship, or space colony, you'll need 3-D printed parts."*[187]

Moog also applied for a patent pertaining to the neural network part of the platform.

Working on the business model. Moog has a very simple strategy: How do you create value for customers in an ecosystem enabled by blockchain? To attract customers to the platform, Regenor foresees following Apple's strategy when it launched iTunes. Apple initially offered a seed catalogue of music to attract customers, then updated the catalogue each week to keep customers coming back. Similarly, Moog is seeding the digital catalogue for general properties of 3-D printed materials. This catalogue allows customers to move from 'point approvals' to 'design allowables'. Customers will initially go to the VertPart platform to access the digital catalogue, but as the ecosystem grows, other parties will be able to offer more services on top of the platform.

Conclusion. Moog has made a lot of progress on realizing the vision of building a blockchain-enabled platform that enables part providence for additive manufacturing. It aims to have its joint venture established, a shared governance model defined, and a consortium of 30 members by first quarter 2019. While that deadline may seem aggressive, Regenor said

> *"People say the Internet took 10 years, so blockchain will take ten years. But blockchain is built on the Internet, so we'll leverage the Internet protocols and fold those into blockchain so we can have an exponential acceleration rather than a linear acceleration."*

3.4.4. Center for Supply Chain Studies

"If the government had one iota how much fraud and abuse they could stop especially in pharmaceuticals, how they can purge the opioid thing, they would mandate blockchains tomorrow. It would be a mandated, you must participate on this within two years."

Head of Innovation for a US healthcare company[188]

"We are trying to figure out how can we use the blockchain as a technology to meet the DSCSA regulation, and just overall, how do we track and trace the product to secure the supply chain."

Enterprise Architect for a US healthcare company[189]

The Center for Supply Chain Studies is a non-profit, vendor neutral company started by Bob Celeste in 2015. The Center hosts group-funded studies to identify ways to improve the efficiency and compliance across the pharmacutical supply chain. One set of studies is examining ways the pharmaceutical industry can comply with the US Drug Supply Chain Security Act (DSCSA)[190], which was passed in November 2013. DSCSA aims to better trace pharmaceuticals throughout the entire supply chain. The law requires that all parties in the supply chain must participate, including pharmaceutical manufacturers, repackagers, wholesale distributors, and dispensers like hospital and retail pharmacies. The law is implemented in stages. Pharmaceutical manufacturers and repackagers needed to affix a unique product identifier on each package by November 2017. By 2023, the product's entire history must be traced as ownership passes through supply chain partners. The law requires that each party in the supply chain:

- Participates in electronic package-level traceability system
- Trades only with authorized partners
- Provides transaction information to trading partners in electronic format
- Responds to verification requests from trading partners
- Quarantines and investigates suspect products
- Identifies and remove illegitimate/counterfeit products and notifies the FDA
- Matches original transactions with returns
- Facilitates the gathering of previous transaction information[191]

Additionally, the package level tracing would need to be maintained for six years, and an additional six years if an investigation occurs on it. Thus, the regulation requires full data provenance and record immutability for over a decade. The context seems ideally suited for a blockchain-based application. In February 2017, the Center launched its first study called 'DSCSA and Blockchain' with 50 representatives from across the supply chain. Competitors like Cardinal Health, Amerisourcebergen, Becton Dickinson, Johnson & Johnson, and McKesson came together to consider the best ways to comply with the new regulation using a blockchain application.

While some consortia seek a consensus on a single standard, the DSCSA and Blockchain Study built nine reference models. The models varied from full-transparency to a very minimal set of encrypted data to be stored on the blockchain. Bob Celeste noted:

> *"The exploratory models helped us envision possibilities and to work around regulatory, operational and technology constraints. In the end, there was great interest in the 'state' model which could provide the most efficiencies and flexibility to expand beyond regulatory compliance."*

The study participants explored various rules for participation, shared governance models, services (such as maintaining master data and licensing), and the data that would actually be stored on the blockchain application or on another 'data persistent' database. The Center built and ran various simulations so the study members could see how the data would flow through an application and be permanently stored on a blockchain application.

Participants tackled tough questions about shared governance, industrial espionage, counterfeiters, shared intellectual property and investment. Questions such as: Who decides who sees which data under what circumstances? Will competitors learn too much about my volumes and trading partners? Will our design keep counterfeit drugs out of the supply chain? How do we protect the intellectual property we've built as a team? How will we finance the blockchain application development and ongoing operations? The output of the first study was a white paper that can be viewed from the Center's website.[192]

Even if the 50 members agree on the design and build the blockchain application, they will also face the daunting task of trying to become the defacto industry solution. There are over

85,000 participants in the US pharmaceutical supply chain. A second study called 'DSCSA & Blockchain Phase 2' and a third study called 'Blockchain for Cold Chain' were launched in January of 2018 to keep making progress.[193]

3.5. Conclusion

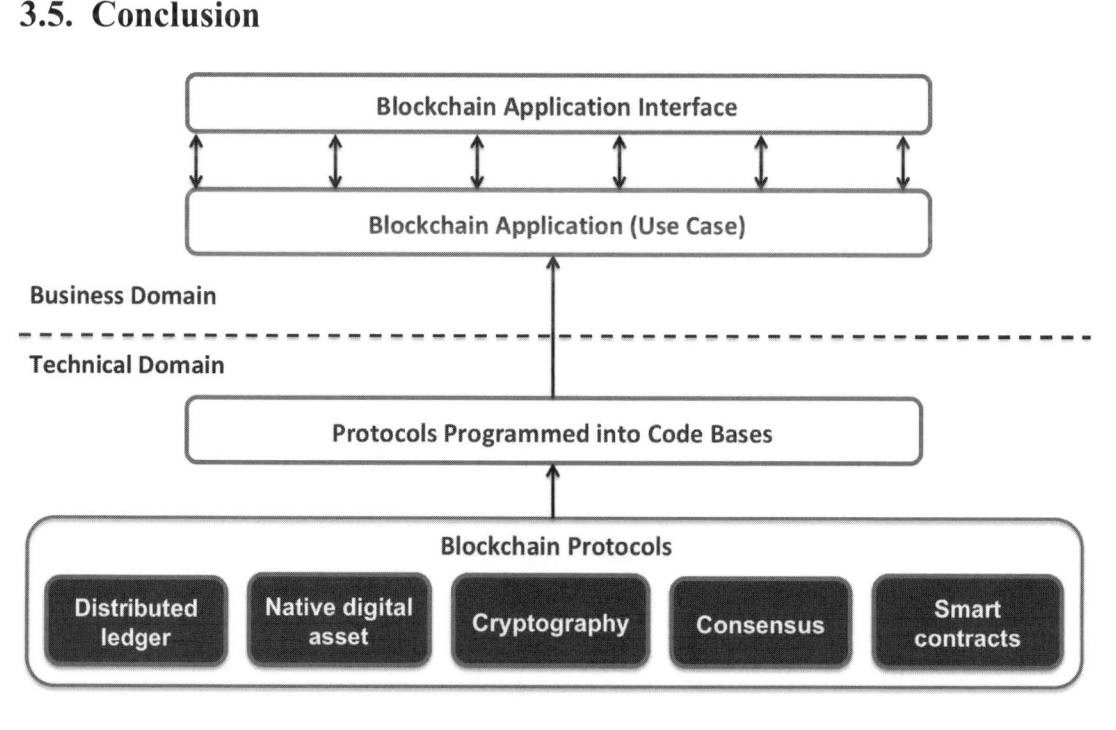

Figure 3.18: Business and technical domains of a blockchain application

The blockchain applications in this chapter aimed to capture a wide-range of blockchain application use cases. But even with 12 examples, we are still missing important use cases across other industries, such as governments, the sharing economy, insurance, healthcare, education, retail, and media. In particular, governments have huge opportunities to better manage identities, elections, registrations, and titles. Counties such as Estonia and Canada have explored blockchain applications.

While the sharing economy has been lauded for providing a market for peers, the pre-blockchain platforms themselves are third-party intermediaries that wield a lot of power and grab a disproportionate share of the value created by the individuals. Blockchains promise to change that. Essentially, it's the idea that buyers and sellers will find each other without the need for intermediaries like Uber, Lyft, Airbnb and others to serve as central market makers. How will these ideas come to life?

Technical and business maturity is needed to move more POCs from innovation labs to market. In general, technical challenges are the domain of protocols and code bases, in our blockchain application framework, and business challenges are in the domain of use cases (see Figure 3.18). In the next chapter, we'll explore the technical challenges and emerging solutions. In the final chapter, we'll address the business domain by specifying mindshifts, strategies and action principles to deploy live applications.

Citations

1. MacKenna, J. (January 10th 2018), *Hyperledger's Brian Behlendorf and How Blockchains Will Change the Enterprise World*, Nasdaq http://www.nasdaq.com/article/hyperledgers-brian-behlendorf-and-how-blockchains-will-change-the-enterprise-world-cm903367

2. Personal interview in 2017 with Mary Lacity

3. Personal interview in 2017 with Mary Lacity

4. CBInsights (2017), The FinTech 250, https://www.cbinsights.com/research-fintech250

5. The World Bank, *Financial Inclusion*, http://www.worldbank.org/en/topic/financialinclusion/overview

6. McKinsey (2016), *Global Payments 2016: Strong Fundamentals Despite Uncertain Times*, https://www.mckinsey.com/~/media/McKinsey/Industries/Financial Services/Our Insights/A mixed 2015 for the global payments industry/Global-Payments-2016.ashx

7. Again, the actual process depends on which services are used. Many banks use SWIFT (Society for the Worldwide Interbank Financial Telecommunication), an international payment network; members of the European Union might use SEPA (Single Euro Payments Area) to manage bank transfers of money. SEPA *"enables customers to make cashless euro payments to anyone located anywhere in the area, using a single bank account and a single set of payment instruments; SEPA guarantees that euro payments are received within a guaranteed time, and banks are not allowed to make any deductions of the amount transferred."* SEPA is also used by Iceland, Liechtenstein, Norway, Switzerland, Monaco and San Marino. https://en.wikipedia.org/wiki/Single_Euro_Payments_Area

8. http://paymentsviews.com/2014/05/15/there-is-no-such-thing-as-an-international-wire/

9. *Navigating the world of cross-border payments*, http://www.iqpc.com/media/1003982/57107.pdf

10. McKinsey (2015), *Global Payments 2015: A Healthy Industry Confront Disruption*, http://www.mckinsey.com/~/media/mckinsey/dotcom/client_service/financial services/latest thinking/payments/global_payments_2015_a_healthy_industry_confronts_disruption.ashx

11. American Bankers Association (2016), *Fees and Pricing of Banking Products*, http://www. texasbankers.com/docs/FeesandPricingofBankingProducts.pdf

12. McKinsey (2016), *Digital Finance for All*, http://www.mckinsey.com/~/media/McKinsey/Global Themes/Employment and Growth/How digital finance could boost growth in emerging economies/ MG-Digital-Finance-For-All-Full-report-September-2016.ashx

13. Peric, K. (April 18th 2017), *Fighting Poverty with Digital Payments*, presented at MIT Blockchain for Business Conference. http://events.technologyreview.com/video/watch/kosta-peric-bill-and-melinda-gates-foundation-fighting-poverty/

14. Most of the 150 person-to-person, mobile payment platforms in Africa and Asia can operate on a $5 phone and only need a basic 2G calls and SMS. Source: Peric, K. (April 18th 2017), *Fighting Poverty with Digital Payments*, presented at MIT Blockchain for Business Conference. http://events.technologyreview.com/video/watch/kosta-peric-bill-and-melinda-gates-foundation-fighting-poverty/

15. Peric, K. (April 18th 2017), *Fighting Poverty with Digital Payments*, presented at MIT Blockchain for Business Conference. http://events.technologyreview.com/video/watch/kosta-peric-bill-and-melinda-gates-foundation-fighting-poverty/

16. bKash, a mobile payment platform launched in 2011 in Bangladesh, had over 17 million users by 2015. Source: Young, Y. (January 20th 2016), *Bill Gates Invests in Mobile Payment Network bKash; Used by 10% of Bangladeshis*, https://btcmanager.com/bill-gates-invests-in-mobile-payment-network-bkash-used-by-10-of-bangladeshis/

17. Vodofone launched M-Pesa in 2007 is a mobile payment platform that operates in Kenya, Tanzania, Afghanistan, South Africa, Indian and Eastern Europe, https://www.mpesa.in/portal/

18. Dragos, A. (June 27th 2017), *Blockchain technology promises to drastically reduce the costs to offer a checking account*, https://medium.com/mit-media-lab-digital-currency-initiative/ blockchains-and-financial-inclusion-f767a2347e3d

19. *Blockchain and Financial Inclusion for Citizens in Poverty*, July 11th 2016, https://letstalkpayments. com/blockchain-and-financial-inclusion-for-citizens-in-poverty/

20. Arshadi, N. (2017), *Application of Blockchain to the Payment System: A Less Costly and More Secure Alternative to ACH*, working paper

21. https://ripple.com/network/financial-institutions/

22. Branson, R. (2015), *Ripple: The Ultimate Guide to Understanding Ripple Currency*, Elliot Branson Publications

23. https://ripple.com/

24. https://en.wikipedia.org/wiki/Ripple_(company)

25. https://ripple.com/

26. https://ripple.com/xrp/

27. https://ripple.com/use-cases/

28. https://ripple.com/use-cases/corporates/

29. https://ripple.com/network/financial-institutions/

30. Ripple case study: SBI remit https://ripple.com/files/case_study_sbi.pdf

31. Reuters (November 16th 2017), *American Express Is Getting Into Blockchain-Based Payments With Ripple*, http://fortune.com/2017/11/16/amex-payments-ripple-blockchain/

32. Branson, R. (2014), *Ripple: The Ultimate Beginner's Guide to Understanding Ripple Currency and What You Need To Know,* CreateSpace Independent Publishing Platform, UK

33. https://ripple.com/build/gateway-guide/

34. Schwartz, D., Youngs, N., and Britto, A. (2014), *The Ripple Protocol Consensus Algorithm*, https://ripple.com/files/ripple_consensus_whitepaper.pdf

35. https://ripple.com/build/ledger-format/

36. Branson, R. (2014), *Ripple: The Ultimate Beginner's Guide to Understanding Ripple Currency and What You Need To Know,* CreateSpace Independent Publishing Platform, UK

37. Branson, R. (2014), *Ripple: The Ultimate Beginner's Guide to Understanding Ripple Currency and What You Need To Know,* CreateSpace Independent Publishing Platform, UK

38. *Technical FAQ: Ripple Consensus Ledger*, https://ripple.com/technical-faq-ripple-consensus-ledger/

39. *Ripple Review*, http://www.toptenreviews.com/money/investing/best-cryptocurrencies/ripple-review/

40. Bob Way at Ripple.com, as reported in Seibold, S., and Samman, G. (2016), *Consensus: Immutable Agreement for the Internet of Value*, KPMG White paper.

41. Bauerle, N. (2017), *What is the Difference Between Public and Permissioned Blockchains?* https://www.coindesk.com/information/what-is-the-difference-between-open-and-permissioned-blockchains/

42. *Technical FAQ: Ripple Consensus Ledger*, https://ripple.com/technical-faq-ripple-consensus-ledger/

43. *Technical FAQ: Ripple Consensus Ledger*, https://ripple.com/technical-faq-ripple-consensus-ledger/

44. Barry, N. (May 19th 2015), *What is the main difference between Stellar and Ripple protocols?*, https://www.quora.com/What-is-the-main-difference-between-Stellar-and-Ripple-protocols

45. Maxim, J. (June 24th 2015), *Ripple Discontinues Smart Contract Platform Codius, Citing Small Market*, https://bitcoinmagazine.com/articles/ripple-discontinues-smart-contract-platform-codius-citing-small-market-1435182153/

46. Agarwal, H. (December 31st 2017), *Ripple (XRP) Wallet – Best Wallets For Ripple*, https://coinsutra.com/best-ripple-xrp-wallets/

47. https://ripple.com/build/gateway-guide/

48. Branson, R. (2014), *Ripple: The Ultimate Beginner's Guide to Understanding Ripple Currency and What You Need To Know,* CreateSpace Independent Publishing Platform, UK

49. Branson, R. (2014), *Ripple: The Ultimate Beginner's Guide to Understanding Ripple Currency and What You Need To Know,* CreateSpace Independent Publishing Platform, UK

50. Levy, A. (May 26th 2017), *Bitcoin rival Ripple is suddenly sitting on billions of dollars worth of cryptocurrency*, CNBC News, http://www.cnbc.com/2017/05/26/bitcoin-rival-ripple-is-sitting-on-many-billions-of-dollars-of-xrp.html

51. Maziières, D. (2016), *The Stellar Consensus Protocol: A Federated Model for Internet-level Consensus*, White Paper, https://www.stellar.org/papers/stellar-consensus-protocol.pdf

52. *Selecting Validators*, https://wiki.ripple.com/Consensus

53. According to this site, Ripple had 55 participants as of July 2017: https://www.coindesk.com/ripples-distributed-ledger-network-passes-50-validator-milestone/

54. According to this site, Ripple had 198 nodes on July 24th 2017; for an update, see https://xrpcharts.ripple.com/#/topology

55. *Stellar and Ripple Hacked: Justcoin to the Rescue*, October 14th 2014, https://cointelegraph.com/news/stellar-and-ripple-hacked-justcoin-to-the-rescue

56. https://www.stellar.org/how-it-works/stellar-basics/

57. Personal interview with Mary Lacity in 2017

58. https://www.stellar.org/about/mandate/

59. Maziières, D. (2016), *The Stellar Consensus Protocol: A Federated Model for Internet-level Consensus*, White Paper, https://www.stellar.org/papers/stellar-consensus-protocol.pdf

60. https://en.wikipedia.org/wiki/Stellar_(payment_network)

61. Stellar Funding, https://www.crunchbase.com/organization/stellar

62. *Business Solutions Powered by Stellar*, https://www.stellar.org/how-it-works/powered-by-stellar

63. Asatryan, D. (May 3rd 2016), *Deloitte Taps Blockchain Startups to Build New Core Banking System*, http://bankinnovation.net/2016/05/deloitte-taps-blockchain-startups-to-build-new-core-banking-system/

64. *Business Solutions Powered by Stellar*, https://www.stellar.org/how-it-works/powered-by-stellar

65. https://coins.ph/blog/conveniently-send-money-from-europe-to-the-philippines-with-tempo/

66. Personal interview with Mary Lacity in 2017

67. ShapShak, T. (2016), Instant Money Transfer Service Stellar Launches for Nigeria's Rural Women, *Forbes Magazine*, https://www.forbes.com/sites/tobyshapshak/2016/02/02/stellar-launches-mobile-money-service-for-nigerias-rural-woman/ - 5240e9c97183

68. Personal interview with Mary Lacity in 2017.

69. https://www.flutterwave.com/about/

70. Center for Financial Inclusion (August 8th 2017), *ICICI Bank and Stellar: Using Blockchain to Reach the Base of the Pyramid in India*, https://cfi-blog.org/2017/08/08/icici-bank-and-stellar-using-blockchain-to-reach-the-base-of-the-pyramid-in-india/

71. Roberts, J. (October 16th 2017) http://fortune.com/2017/10/16/ibm-blockchain-stellar/ and Suberg, W. (Oct 16, 2016) https://cointelegraph.com/news/ibm-blockchain-payments-to-use-stellar-in-major-partnership-deal

72. Personal interview with Mary Lacity in 2017

73. https://www.stellar.org/how-it-works/stellar-basics/

74. Personal interview with Mary Lacity in 2017

75. Bello, K. (May 2016), *Ripple vs Stellar Lumens*, https://www.youtube.com/watch?v=aeONeHlF9y4

76. https://www.stellar.org/how-it-works/stellar-basics/

77. *Difference between Ripple and Stellar*, https://galactictalk.org/d/242-difference-between-ripple-and-stellar

78. https://www.stellar.org/lumens/

79. https://www.stellar.org/about/mandate/

80. https://www.stellar.org/lumens/

81. Personal interview with Mary Lacity in 2017

82. https://www.stellar.org/lumens/

83. Mazières, D. (2016), *The Stellar Consensus Protocol: A Federated Model for Internet-level Consensus*, White Paper, https://www.stellar.org/papers/stellar-consensus-protocol.pdf

84. https://medium.com/a-stellar-journey/on-worldwide-consensus-359e9eb3e949

85. Personal interview with Mary Lacity in 2017

86. Blogpost on Reddit, *IBM just added 8 new validators from 8 different countries, on to the Stellar network!*, https://www.reddit.com/r/Stellar/comments/7gxc62/wow_ibm_just_added_8_new_validators_from_8/

87. To view live nodes, see https://dashboard.stellar.org/

88. Benoliel, M. (December 4th 2017), *Why Stellar could be the next big ICO platform*, https://hackernoon.com/why-stellar-could-be-the-next-big-ico-platform-f48fc3cb9a6c

89. https://www.stellar.org/lumens/

90. McCaleb, J. (May 11th 2017), *Introducing Lightyear.io*, https://www.stellar.org/blog/lightyear-announcement/

91. Personal interview in 2017 with Mary Lacity and Kate Moloney

92. Personal interview in 2017 with Mary Lacity and Kate Moloney

93. *History: two centuries of banking*, BNP Paribas, https://group.bnpparibas/en/group/history-centuries-banking

94. JahanZaib Mehmood, *The world's 100 largest banks,* S&P Global Market Intelligence, April

11th 2017, http://www.snl.com/web/client?auth=inherit#news/article?id=40223698&cdid =A-40223698-11568

95. *BNP Paribas worldwide*, BNP Paribas, https://group.bnpparibas/en/group/bnp-paribas-worldwide

96. *Our strategy and corporate culture*, BNP Paribas, https://group.bnpparibas/en/group/strategy-corporate-culture

97. Ibid., p. 51

98. Ibid., p. 58

99. *Digital Asset Closes Funding Round Exceeding $50 Million From Thirteen Global Financial Leaders*, Digital Asset press release, January 21st 2016, on the Digital Holdings website, http://hub.digitalasset.com/press-release/digital-asset-closes-funding-round-exceeding-50-million-from-thirteen-global-financial-leaders

100. Edward Robinson and Matthew Leising, *Blythe Masters Tells Banks the Blockchain Changes Everything*, Bloomberg, August 31st 2015, https://www.bloomberg.com/news/features/2015-09-01/blythe-masters-tells-banks-the-blockchain-changes-everything

101. *BNP Paribas joins the R3 Blockchain initiative*, BNP Paribas newsroom, November 23rd 2015, https://group.bnpparibas/en/news/bnp-paribas-joins-r3-blockchain-initiative.

102. *Building the New Operating System for Financial Markets*, R3, http://www.r3cev.com/about/

103. *BNP Paribas takes keen interest in Blockchain*, BNP Paribas newsroom, February 16th 2016, https://group.bnpparibas/en/news/bnp-paribas-takes-keen-interest-blockchain.

104. *Our model*, Caisse des Dépôts Group website, http://www.caissedesdepots.fr/en/our-model.

105. SEPA established a single set of tools and standards that enabled European customers to make and receive cashless euro transactions under the same basic conditions. SEPA covered all of the EU, and payments in Euros in Iceland, Liechtenstein, Norway, Monaco, San Marino, and Switzerland. 'Single euro payments area (SEPA)', the European Commission website, https://ec.europa.eu/info/business-economy-euro/banking-and-finance/consumer-finance-and-payments/payment-services/single-euro-payments-area-sepa_en

106. *Innovation, Fragmentation in Cross-border and Real-time Payments*, Payments Views, October 22nd 2017, http://paymentsviews.com/2014/05/15/there-is-no-such-thing-as-an-international-wire/

107. In 2017, Nxt was an open source cryptocurrency and payment network that built on the functionality of the first wave of cryptocurrencies such as Bitcoin. Nxt and Bitcoin had different protocols: NxT used a 'proof-of-stake' process called 'forging' to validate transactions and to add blocks to the blockchain, while Bitcoin used a 'proof-of-work' process called 'mining'. Nxt used a secret passphrase to protect private keys stored in users' wallets; Bitcoin placed responsibility on users to protect these keys. Nxt was written in Java; Bitcoin was written mostly in C++. *What is Nxt?*, Nxt Platform, https://nxtplatform.org/what-is-nxt/; *Frequently Asked Questions*, Bitcoin.org, https://bitcoin.org/en/faq#what-is-bitcoin

108. Barnett, T. (December 9th 2017), *Australian Securities Exchange Plans to Implement Blockchain Technology*, https://interestingengineering.com/australian-securities-exchange-plans-to-implement-blockchain-technology

109. ASX website: *ASX is replacing CHESS with distributed ledger technology (DLT) developed by Digital Asset*, http://www.asx.com.au/services/chess-replacement.htm

110. Pash, C. (September 19th 2016), *Australia's share market had a technical meltdown and stocks were left with no official closing prices*, https://www.businessinsider.com.au/the-asx-is-down-again-2016-9 - lBvWTTLkXBxdpGVt.99

111. ASX website: *ASX is replacing CHESS with distributed ledger technology (DLT) developed by Digital Asset*, http://www.asx.com.au/services/chess-replacement.htm

112. Barnett, T. (December 9th 2017), *Australian Securities Exchange Plans to Implement Blockchain Technology*, https://interestingengineering.com/australian-securities-exchange-plans-to-implement-blockchain-technology

113. ASX website: *ASX is replacing CHESS with distributed ledger technology (DLT) developed by Digital Asset*, http://www.asx.com.au/services/chess-replacement.htm

114. ASX Consultation Report (September 2016), *ASX's Replacement of CHESS for Equity Post-Trade Services: Business Requirements*, http://www.asx.com.au/documents/public-consultations/ASX-Consultation-Paper-CHESS-Replacement-19-September-2016.pdf

115. Stark, A. (2015), *American energy use up slightly, carbon emissions almost unchanged*, https://www.llnl.gov/news/american-energy-use-slightly-carbon-emissions-almost-unchanged-0

116. Conversion waste happens when converting natural gas, coal, nuclear, hydro, geothermal and wind to electricity. Transportation waste occurs when pushing electricity over long distances. About 5% of electric energy is lost in transit. Consumption waste occurs when consumer appliances lose electric energy to heat, for example. Source: Lempriere, M (April 11 2017), *The Brooklyn microgrid: blockchain-enabled community power*, http://www.power-technology.com/features/featurethe-brooklyn-microgrid-blockchain-enabled-community-power-5783564/

117. Ferris, R. (February 15th 2017), *US solar installations nearly doubled in 2016, and broke some records*, CNBC, https://www.cnbc.com/2017/02/14/us-solar-installations-nearly-doubled-in-2016-and-broke-some-records.html

118. Harrington, R. (October 13th 2015), *The US is about to hit a big solar energy milestone*, Business Insider, http://www.businessinsider.com/solar-panels-one-million-houses-2015-10

119. Energysage (2017), *Why go solar – Top 10 benefits of solar energy*, https://www.energysage.com/solar/why-go-solar/

120. Lempriere, M. (April 11th 2017), *The Brooklyn microgrid: blockchain-enabled community power*, http://www.power-technology.com/features/featurethe-brooklyn-microgrid-blockchain-enabled-community-power-5783564/

121. Orsini, L. (April 18th 2017), *Industry Impact: Peer-to-Peer Energy Transactions*, presentation Principal and Founder, LO3 Energy at the Business of Blockchain conference http://events.technologyreview.com/video/watch/lawrence-orsini-lo3-industry-impact/

122. https://vimeo.com/195896508

123. http://www.peci.org/

124. https://www.clearesult.com/

125. Spurlock, C. (December 6th 2017), *Hurricane Sandy New York City Power Outage Map: Thousands Without Electricity In Metro Area*, Huffington Post, https://www.huffingtonpost.com/2012/10/31/hurricane-sandy-new-york-city-power-outage-map_n_2050380.html

126. Lempriere, M. (April 11th 2017), *The Brooklyn microgrid: blockchain-enabled community power*, http://www.power-technology.com/features/featurethe-brooklyn-microgrid-blockchain-enabled-community-power-5783564/

127. http://brooklynmicrogrid.com/

128. Personal interview with Mary Lacity in 2017

129. *Can LO3 Energy Cut Through the Hype on Blockchain?*, Greentechmedia, https://www.greentechmedia.com/articles/read/can-lo3-cut-through-the-hype-on-blockchain - gs.ffx=I8Y

130. Orsini, L. (April 18th 2017), *Industry Impact: Peer-to-Peer Energy Transactions*, presentation Principal and Founder, LO3 Energy at the Business of Blockchain conference http://events.technologyreview.com/video/watch/lawrence-orsini-lo3-industry-impact/

131. Personal interview with Mary Lacity in 2017

132. http://microgridmedia.com/its-like-the-early-days-of-the-internet-blockchain-based-brooklyn-microgrid-tests-p2p-energy-trading/

133. Personal interview with Mary Lacity in 2017

134. http://microgridmedia.com/its-like-the-early-days-of-the-internet-blockchain-based-brooklyn-microgrid-tests-p2p-energy-trading/

135. Personal interview with Mary Lacity in 2017

136. Lempriere, M. (April 11th 2017), *The Brooklyn microgrid: blockchain-enabled community power*, http://www.power-technology.com/features/featurethe-brooklyn-microgrid-blockchain-enabled-community-power-5783564/

137. Googlemaps https://www.google.com/maps/@40.6844854,-73.98659,13z

138. Personal Interview with Lawrence Orsini, December 21st 2017

139. Orsini, L. (April 18th 2017), *Industry Impact: Peer-to-Peer Energy Transactions*, presentation Principal and Founder, LO3 Energy at the Business of Blockchain conference http://events.technologyreview.com/video/watch/lawrence-orsini-lo3-industry-impact/

140. https://www.sacramento.energy/

141. Financial Review (October 2017), LO3 to trial peer-to-peer energy sharing in South Australia, http://www.afr.com/business/energy/lo3-energy-to-trial-peertopeer-energy-sharing-in-south-australia-20171010-gyxw3s#ixzz53VrCB6MY

142. LO3 Energy Press Release (November 17th 2017), US start-up LO3 Energy begins two German projects, https://lo3energy.com/us-start-lo3-energy-begins-two-german-projects/

143. De, N. (December 13th 2017), Blockchain Startup LO3 Partners With Power Exchange, Coindesk, https://www.coindesk.com/blockchain-startup-lo3-partners-power-exchange/

144. Personal interview with Mary Lacity in 2017

145. Press Release: *LO3 Launches Exergy Token Sale Open for Accredited Investors*, https://lo3energy.com/lo3-launches-exergy/

146. Exergy Business White Paper (December 2017), https://exergy.energy/wpcontent/uploads/2017/12/Exergy-BIZWhitepaper-v5.pdf

147. Exergy Business White Paper (December 2017), https://exergy.energy/wpcontent/uploads/2017/12/Exergy-BIZWhitepaper-v5.pdf

148. Video from Innogy, https://youtu.be/uJx79G2Zmyo

149. https://innovationhub.innogy.com/

150. https://shareandcharge.com/en/

151. *Share&Charge Smart Contracts: the Technical Angle*, https://shareandcharge.com/sharecharge-smart-contracts-technical-angle/

152. *Share&Charge Smart Contracts: the Technical Angle*, https://shareandcharge.com/sharecharge-smart-contracts-technical-angle/

153. https://blockgeeks.com/guides/what-is-blockchain-technology/

154. Personal interview in 2017 with Mary Lacity

155. Presentation by Marie Wieck, General Manager of IBM's Blockchain business, at IBM Innerconnect in 2017, https://ibmgo.com/interconnect2017/search/?q=blockchain&tags=all&categoryType=video

156. https://en.wikipedia.org/wiki/Kimberley_Process_Certification_Scheme

157. Presentation by Everledger's CEO at IBM Interconnect: https://ibmgo.com/interconnect2017/?cm_mc_uid=19734726856314943335282&cm_mc_sid_50200000=1494367094&cm_mc_sid_52640000=1494367094 (About an hour and 15 minutes into the video)

158. Del Castillo, M. (March 5th 2017), *The World's Largest Shipping Firm Now Tracks Cargo on Blockchain*, Coindesk, https://www.coindesk.com/worlds-largest-shipping-company-tracking-cargo-blockchain/

159. IBM Press Release, *Maersk and IBM Unveil First Industry-Wide Cross-Border Supply Chain Solution on Blockchain*, https://www.prnewswire.com/news-releases/maersk-and-ibm-unveil-first-industry-wide-cross-border-supply-chain-solution-on-blockchain-300418039.html

160. IBM Press Release (January 16th 2018), *Maersk and IBM to Form Joint Venture Applying Blockchain to Improve Global Trade and Digitize Supply Chains*, https://www-03.ibm.com/press/us/en/pressrelease/53602.wss

161. Hackett, R. (August 22nd 2017), Wal-Mart and 9 Food Giants Team Up on IBM Blockchain Plans, *Fortune Magazine,* http://fortune.com/2017/08/22/walmart-blockchain-ibm-food-nestle-unilever-tyson-dole/

162. IBM Press Release (December 14th 2017), *Wal-Mart, JD.com, IBM and Tsinghua University Launch a Blockchain Food Safety Alliance in China*, https://www-03.ibm.com/press/us/en/pressrelease/53487.wss

163. IBM Press Release (December 14th 2017), *Wal-Mart, JD.com, IBM and Tsinghua University Launch a Blockchain Food Safety Alliance in China*, https://www-03.ibm.com/press/us/en/pressrelease/53487.wss

164. https://www.provenance.org/tracking-tuna-on-the-blockchain

165. https://www.provenance.org/case-studies

166. Nation, J. (August 2nd 2017), *Provenance Helps Arkansas Farmers Track Food With Ethereum*, https://www.ethnews.com/provenance-helps-arkansas-farmers-track-food-with-ethereum

167. Small, G., *Additive Manufacturing Reshaping Logistics*, http://www.moog.com/news/blog-new/IntroducingVeripart_Issue3.html

168. Regenor, J. (April 18th 2017), *Industry Impact: Aerospace Supply Chain*, presentation at the Blockchain for Business Conference at MIT, Cambridge Massachusetts

169. Moog 2016 Annual Report. http://www.moog.com/content/dam/moog/literature/Corporate/Investors/Annual_Report/2016/2016-Annual-Report.pdf

170. Small, G., *Additive Manufacturing Reshaping Logistics*, http://www.moog.com/news/blog-new/IntroducingVeripart_Issue3.html

171. Small, G., *Additive Manufacturing Reshaping Logistics*, http://www.moog.com/news/blog-new/IntroducingVeripart_Issue3.html

172. Regenor, J. (April 18th 2017), *Industry Impact: Aerospace Supply Chain*, presentation at the Blockchain for Business Conference at MIT, Cambridge Massachusetts

173. Regenor, J. (April 18th 2017), *Industry Impact: Aerospace Supply Chain*, presentation at the Blockchain for Business Conference at MIT, Cambridge Massachusetts

174. Nuco Global (October 5th 2017), *Moog Announces Partnership with Aion*, https://blog.aion.network/moogaionpartnership-6d37ce15b2fd

175. Nuco's Aion white paper: https://aion.network/downloads/aion.network_technical-introduction_en.pdf

176. Nuco's Aion white paper: https://aion.network/downloads/aion.network_technical-introduction_en.pdf

177. Galang, J. (October 10th 2017), *Nuco raises $27 million to build interoperable blockchain network*, https://betakit.com/nuco-raises-27-million-to-build-interoperable-blockchain-network/

178. Personal interview with Mary Lacity in 2018

179. Personal interview with Mary Lacity in 2018

180. America Makes & ANSI Additive Manufacturing Standardization Collaborative (AMSC), https://www.ansi.org/standards_activities/standards_boards_panels/amsc/

181. Standardization Roadmap for Additive Manufacturing https://share.ansi.org/Shared Documents/Standards Activities/AMSC/AMSC_Roadmap_February_2017.pdf

182. Regenor, J. (April 18th 2017), *Industry Impact: Aerospace Supply Chain*, presentation at the

Blockchain for Business Conference at MIT, Cambridge Massachusetts

183. Personal interview with Mary Lacity in 2018

184. National Defense Authorization Act for Fiscal Year 2018,
https://www.congress.gov/bill/115th-congress/house-bill/2810/text - toc-HBA0AA81CFC4F410E9 5EF87129909DC2A

185. https://www.battelle.org/homepage

186. Parent Application Abstract: 20180012311, *"A method for the verification and authentication of additive manufactured product, comprising the steps of receiving, from a customer, at least one customer requirement for a product, deriving at least one manufacturing requirement and generating a product geometry file for the product, recording, by a first computing device, to a distributed transaction register, a first transaction reflecting certification of the product geometry file, obtaining a first output reflecting the first transaction, printing the product with a 3D printer, recording, by a second computing device, to the distributed transaction register, a second transaction reflecting the printing of the product and the first output, obtaining a second output reflecting the second transaction, embedding within the product a unique code reflecting the second output, whereby the product geometry file and the printing of said product may be verified with the unique code such that the product may be authenticated."*
http://appft.uspto.gov/netacgi/nph-Parser?Sect1=PTO1&Sect2=HITOFF&d=PG01&p=1&u=%2Fn etahtml%2FPTO%2Fsrchnum.html&r=1&f=G&l=50&s1="20180012311".PGNR.&OS=DN/20180 012311&RS=DN/20180012311

187. Personal interview with Mary Lacity in 2018.

188. Personal interview in 2017 with Mary Lacity

189. Personal interview in 2017 with Mary Lacity and Kate Moloney

190. https://www.fda.gov/Drugs/DrugSafety/DrugIntegrityandSupplyChainSecurity/ DrugSupplyChainSecurityAct/

191. his website gives a timeline for each party's compliance requirements: http://www.pewtrusts.org/ en/multimedia/data-visualizations/2014/timeline-for-the-drug-supply-chain-and-security-act

192. DSCSA & Blockchain Study White Paper: https://www.c4scs.org/dscsa-blockchain-study-1-follow

193. https://www.c4scs.org/join-a-study

Chapter 4

Technical Challenges and Emerging Solutions

"There still remain those tech challenges, but those will probably be some of the more quickly resolved challenges, whereas a lot of the other ones such as regulatory challenges, challenges in collaboration, those are the ones that are probably going to take a lot longer for adoption."

John Burnett, Head of Blockchain Development for State Street[1]

"I am less worried about the technology. Although the technology is not mature, it is less of a problem than standards and regulations."

Nilesh Vaidya, SVP Head of Banking & Capital Market Solutions at Capgemini[2]

"I think that there is effective forward motion in the resolution and the ability to address some of the technical challenges that exist."

Eamonn Maguire, Global Lead, Digital Ledger Services, KPMG[3]

4.1. Introduction

Blockchain code is still considered nascent, with perhaps the exception of Bitcoin, which has been deployed since 2009. There are significant technical challenges around young source code, including security, scalability, interoperability, and massive resource consumption for certain protocols. Enterprises need to ensure the technologies are enterprise ready in that the software is secure enough and ready to handle the volume and speed requirements for enterprise applications. Fortunately, people from all around the world are collaborating to address these technical challenges for both permissionless and permissioned blockchains. As the quotes above attest, nearly all the blockchain experts we spoke to view the technical challenges as surmountable; the open source communities as well as private enterprises just need more time to identify, debate, and develop technical solutions. Managers in traditional enterprises certainly need to be aware of the technical challenges and should monitor the emerging solutions, which vary significantly between permissionless and permissioned blockchains. Technical issues also point to the skills enterprises need to start building today.

4.2. Security challenges

"Centralized security doesn't work. We need secure, decentralized messaging so devices cannot be hacked."

Andre de Castro, CEO and Founder, Blockchain of Things[5]

"For enterprise clients, we're usually dealing with things like Hyperledger or chain.com or even enterprise-grade Ethereum, which, in that case, you're rolling your own permissioned version of Ethereum. There are downsides to permissioned blockchains because you have fewer nodes verifying transactions. But if you deploy them correctly, what you can lose in security, you can make up in consortium security. What that means is, you might not have network security such as the Bitcoin or public Ethereum blockchain has in terms of all of the nodes that are verifying it, but you get a security in a different sense, which is all the nodes that are on the network can be trusted to a higher degree."

Dev Bharel, Blockchain Solutions Architect with Nussbaumer Projects[6]

"Blockchain presents a paradoxical situation when it comes to privacy and security. Blockchains are inherently secure with immutable transactions and hashing-based data-integrity. But most enterprises that I talk to have questions and concerns about confidentiality regarding who sees what. The hacking scandals, volatility of cryptocurrencies, and technological advancements such as quantum computing add to the perceived risk. The media hype and fake news, negative activity from threatened legacy stakeholders, also impedes adoption. For real enterprise adoption

of blockchain, we need to think about holistic security where it is not just a technical issue but a business challenge. In a lot of ways, it resembles the private versus public versus hybrid cloud debate."

Saurabh Gupta, Chief Strategy Officer, HfS Research[7]

One of blockchain's greatest selling points is heightened security over centralized systems that have single points of failure. In Chapter 2, we learned that blockchain applications still function properly even if a high percentage of nodes are faulty – or even malicious – promising unbeatable resiliency and 100 percent availability. In theory, the only way to break a blockchain application is to commandeer more than 50 percent of the nodes. If blockchains are so secure, why do we hear about so many heists? Examining some of the major heists will help managers understand the vulnerability points of today's blockchain technologies. People are also concerned that collusion among miners in permissionless blockchains (or powerful organizations within permissioned blockchains) could indeed result in a party or parties commandeering over 50 percent of nodes in a blockchain application. We'll also cover security threats of future technologies, most notably quantum computing.

4.2.1. Digital wallet security threats

"Traditional companies will not want to use cryptocurrencies just to utilize blockchain's other features. Can you imagine trusting your IT department with a blockchain wallet full of private keys?"

Andre de Castro, CEO and Founder, Blockchain of Things[8]

Most heists on blockchains happen at the vulnerable access points of digital wallets where private keys are stored. As noted in Chapter 2, once a hacker steals a private key, he or she controls the asset and can easily transfer funds to another address. Also noted in Chapter 2, while users may store their digital wallets on their own devices, most users rely on centralized exchanges. Exchanges are a lucrative target for hackers because some exchanges control millions of private keys. One of the largest heists occurred in August of 2014 when 850,000 bitcoins worth $450 million was stolen from the wallets managed by Mt. Gox, the largest Bitcoin exchange at the time. Mt. Gox's CEO, Mark Karpeles, was arrested in Japan for the crime. As of 2017, his trial was ongoing.[9]

Another famous heist was Dogecoin, initially released as a joke in 2014 by Jackson Palmer. Surprisingly, the coin took off. A person calling himself Alex Green using the handle 'Moolah' took over the exchange, shut it down, and disappeared with $4 million in funds.[10] A more recent heist of $70 million worth of bitcoin was stolen from NiceHash's digital wallet in December 2017.[11] In yet another attack, hackers stole $30 million worth of the digit currency tether in the fall of 2017.[12] Tether is interesting because the heist barely moved the price. Why? The reason is that Tether Limited, the company that issued the digital coins, backs each tether with one US dollar held in reserve, guaranteeing that one tether will equal one US dollar. Indeed, tether's price has hovered around $1.00 since its launch in March of 2015. Tether Limited works closely with Hong Kong-based Bitfinex, one of the largest bitcoin exchanges, which has also been hacked at least twice. In May 2015, 1500 bitcoins were stolen; $72 million worth of bitcoins were stolen in 2016.[13]

Managers will naturally worry about the risk implications of these incidents, but risks can be mitigated:

- *LESSON FOR MANAGERS: Enterprises will need build or acquire new IT, cybersecurity, and cryptography skills to protect digital assets, particularly if the private keys are stored in digital wallets.*

The specific technical skills include a deep understanding of asymmetric key algorithms like RSA and DSA, hashing algorithms like SHA-256, elliptic curve cryptography, and directed acyclic graphs (DAG) (see the Glossary for overview of terms).

4.2.2. Smart contact security threats

As defined in Chapter 2, a decentralized autonomous organization (DAO) is an organization or company that is run entirely by rules encoded as computer programs in smart contracts that execute on a blockchain. Our interest here is about a particular DAO, confusingly named 'The' DAO (as opposed to 'a' DAO). The DAO is perhaps blockchain's most ominous heist because its perpetrator(s) didn't steal private keys from a digital wallet stored off a blockchain. Rather, the perpetrator(s) exploited a weakness in a smart contract launched on the Ethereum blockchain. Here is the story…

Stephan Tual, Christoph Jentzsch and Simon Jentzsch proposed to launch a smart contract called 'The' DAO on Ethereum. They designed the DAO as an investment mechanism to fund Ethereum-related startups. Whoever invested in the DAO, by sending ether to it during the fundraising round, could vote on investment ideas pitched to the DAO after launch. The DAO was deployed in May of 2016. Despite the concerns some people voiced –like Professor Emin Gün Sirer of Cornell University – about the weaknesses in the code, money poured in.[14] Because the votes on future projects were weighted by the size of the investment, people who wanted a powerful vote invested heavily.[15] The DAO raised $150 million worth of Ethereum's native digital asset (ether), during its 28-day funding window, exceeding anyone's expectations as this represented 15 percent of the ether money supply. In June of 2016, a hacker (or hackers) exploited a weakness in the smart contract's code. He, she or they began draining the DAO's funds. The Ethereum community was powerless to stop it, as smart contracts run autonomously. The hacker syphoned $50 million in ether into another account. Vitalik Buterin, the co-founder of Etherum, called for a complete stop in trading until the problem could be addressed. The price of ether fell immediately from $20 to $13.[16]

What should be done? Opposing views swarmed in: Vitalik Buterin wanted to 'freeze the account', which would require new code that had to be run by at least 50 percent of the nodes. Stephan Tual argued that the blocks should be unwound and that all the stolen ether should be returned to the investors' accounts.[17] Some members of the open source community insisted that nothing should be done. The blockchain was not breeched; the coders of the smart contract did a poor job, so they should suffer the loss. Chat rooms were ablaze with analogies to the US federal government bailing out the banks during the Global Financial Crisis of 2008 and accused the Etherum Foundation of acting like a government. The decision was made to let miners vote, weighing their votes by their hashing power. The miners voted for a hard fork – a permanent divergence in the Ethereum blockchain. The blocks were rolled back and the stolen ether was returned. Those miners who refused to follow the fork proceeded mining with the original code, leaving us with Ethereum (fork followers) and Ethereum Classic (non-fork followers), where the thief can still cash out.

- ***LESSON FOR MANAGERS: Enterprises will need to build or acquire new legal to assess risks and to establish the legality of agreements and new coding skills to build and aggressively test smart contracts before live deployment.***

4.2.3. Code base security threats

Although much less frequent than the heists of private keys from digital wallets, all the major blockchains have had heists resulting from software weaknesses in the code base. These typically happen within the first year of launch when the code base is still very new. The Bitcoin blockchain was hacked in August 2010 when someone exploited a software vulnerability to create 184 billion bitcoins, a highly suspicious act given the maximum money supply is only 21 million bitcoins.[18] Thus far, this has been the only major attack on the Bitcoin blockchain itself. A hacker of Ripple was able to transfer 1000 bitcoins from an address that had only .0001 bitcoins in 2014.[19] Although the source code was fixed quickly, these episodes offer an important warning.

- *LESSON FOR MANAGERS: Enterprises will need software developers who understand how to build and test distributed applications.*

Since blockchain applications are distributed systems, enterprise will need to develop or attract talent capable of developing and testing decentralized applications ('DApps'). DApps offer benefits such as flexibility, transparency, and resiliency, but they are harder to test compared to traditional, centralized software. In particular, it's harder to identify computer programming logic errors (called 'bugs') in DApps. The enterprise will need software developers who can discover strange-sounding errors like mandelbugs, schrödinbugs, and heisenbugs (see Glossary).

4.2.4 Concentration of power security threats

As noted several times, the only way to break a blockchain application is to commandeer more than 50 percent of the nodes. How likely is this? And where are the biggest threats? For permissionless blockchains, the threat comes from the concentration of power by validators, i.e. the miners. We'll specifically look at the threats of concentration of power from the proof-of-work mining algorithms used in Bitcoin and Ethereum. For permissioned blockchains, the threat comes from giving the gatekeeper, or an organizational participant, too much control over the blockchain network.

4.2.4.1. Concentration of power security threats in Bitcoin and Ethereum

"Mining pools are groups of cooperating miners who agree to share block rewards in proportion to their contributed mining hash power. While mining pools are desirable

to the average miner, as they smooth out rewards and make them more predictable, they unfortunately concentrate power to the mining pool's owner."

Jordan Tuwiner, Founder of Buy Bitcoin Worldwide[20]

"I'm not overly concerned about the Chinese miners acting in unison as a cartel. It's a big mistake to lump all of them under the same umbrella because they're all Chinese. Over the course of the last year, especially the last couple of months, we've seen all of those mining pools and solo miners act quite independently from each other. They do not seem to be operating under the control of one person. We don't see that at all."

Professor Emin Gün Sirer of Cornell University, 2017[21]

Focusing on Bitcoin, the first miners back in 2009 could successfully compete for a block reward using their desktop computers. As Bitcoin's price skyrocketed, miners shifted to specialized hardware and shared computational power through mining pools. The main threat of concentration of power comes from China-based mining pools, which controlled over 80 percent of the mining power over Bitcoin in 2017 (see Figure 4.1). Antpool, Bixin, BTC, F2pool, ViaBTC and BW Pool are among the largest China-based mining pools. In theory, the miners could possibly collude, or the Chinese government could seize control.[22] Concerning the latter threat, complete takeover by the Chinese government would crash the price, so a more likely threat is if the government quietly seized control of a few mining pools.[23]

Ethereum also tracks its top miners on https://www.etherchain.org/charts/miner. In December of 2017, the top mining pools were Ethermine/Ethpool, f2pool2, nanopool, dwarfpool, miningpoolhub1, and ethfans.org2. At times, Ethermine/Ethpool controlled over 25 percent of the Ethereum network.[24]

The China-based company, Bitmain, poses another interesting threat to decentralization. Bitmain is both the world's largest bitcoin mining hardware manufacturer with 70 percent market share and owner of Antpool, one of the largest mining pools. Antpool mined around 20 percent of all blocks as of this writing (see Figure 4.1). Being the largest provider and consumer of bitcoin mining hardware poses a serious conflict of interest. In April 2017, it was discovered that Bitmain built-in a 'backdoor' program within its Antminer hardware so that the company could easily seize control and shut down other miners competing with its mining pool. Here's how this could occur:

'The firmware checks-in with a central service randomly every one to 11 minutes. Each check-in transmits the Antminer serial number, MAC address and IP address. Bitmain can use this check-in data to cross check against customer sales and delivery records making it personally identifiable. The remote service can then return 'false' which will stop the miner from mining.'[25]

Dubbed 'Antscape', Bitmain apologized and posted updates to the firmware.[26]

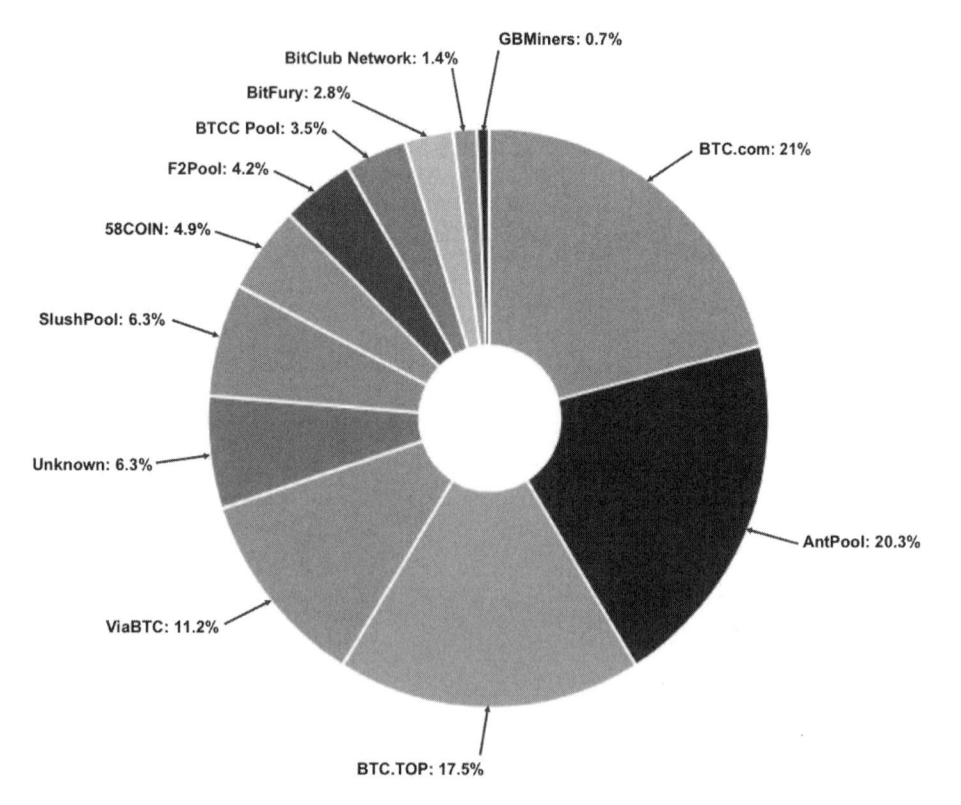

Figure 4.1: Bitcoin's largest winning mining pools on December 28th 2017

Source: https://blockchain.info/pools

Given that blockchains are supposed to be completely distributed applications, the dominance of a few key mining pools does pose a risk. The 2017 quote, above, from Professor Emin Gün Sirer, asserts that that the collusion concern is misguided because there is no evidence of collusion among Chinese mining pools. However, a 2018 study by Professor Sirer and his colleagues found that: *'Both Bitcoin and Ethereum mining are very centralized, with the top four miners in Bitcoin and the top three miners in Ethereum controlling more than 50% of the hash rate... The entire blockchain for both systems is determined by fewer than 20 mining entities.'*[27] The authors argued something that will ease many enterprises:

With just 20 nodes, the consensus mechanism used by many permissioned blockchains – namely, Byzantine consensus algorithms – can achieve more decentralization compared to proof-of-work algorithms used by many permissionless blockchains.

However, permissioned blockchains also have concentration of power threats.

4.2.4.2. Concentration of power security threats in permissioned blockchains

"The operators of a private blockchain may choose to unilaterally deploy changes with which some users disagree. To ensure both the security and the utility of a private blockchain system, operators must consider the recourse available to users who disagree with changes to the system's rules or are slow to adopt the new rules."

Allison Berke, Stanford Cyber Initiative[28]

Since most enterprises will use permissioned blockchains, it is important to understand the potential threat of a single organization having too much power in the network. If any one party operates 50 or more percent of the nodes, then they have the power to overtake the network and change the ledger, smart contracts, and source code. Let's consider a scenario where the gatekeeper also operates nodes in the blockchain network (see Figure 4.2). Provided that the gatekeeper operates a small percentage of nodes, it would not pose a risk. However, if it operates 50 or more percent of the nodes, then we revert back to the world of centralized systems where the gatekeeper in this scenario becomes a defacto trusted third party.

There may be legitimate use cases for an organization to control many – even all – of the nodes; for example, a global company might use a blockchain to facilitate transactions between its divisions as we saw in the case of BNP Paribas in Chapter 3. However, the majority of enterprises will likely be participating in inter-organizational blockchain applications, and thus should heed this lesson:

- *LESSON FOR MANAGERS: When participating in permissioned blockchains, be sure to understand which organizations are operating validator nodes. If your enterprise has an option to choose validator nodes, pick a variety of institutions across industries that would have a very low likelihood of colluding, such as a university, a non-profit, a manufacturer, and a financial services firm.*

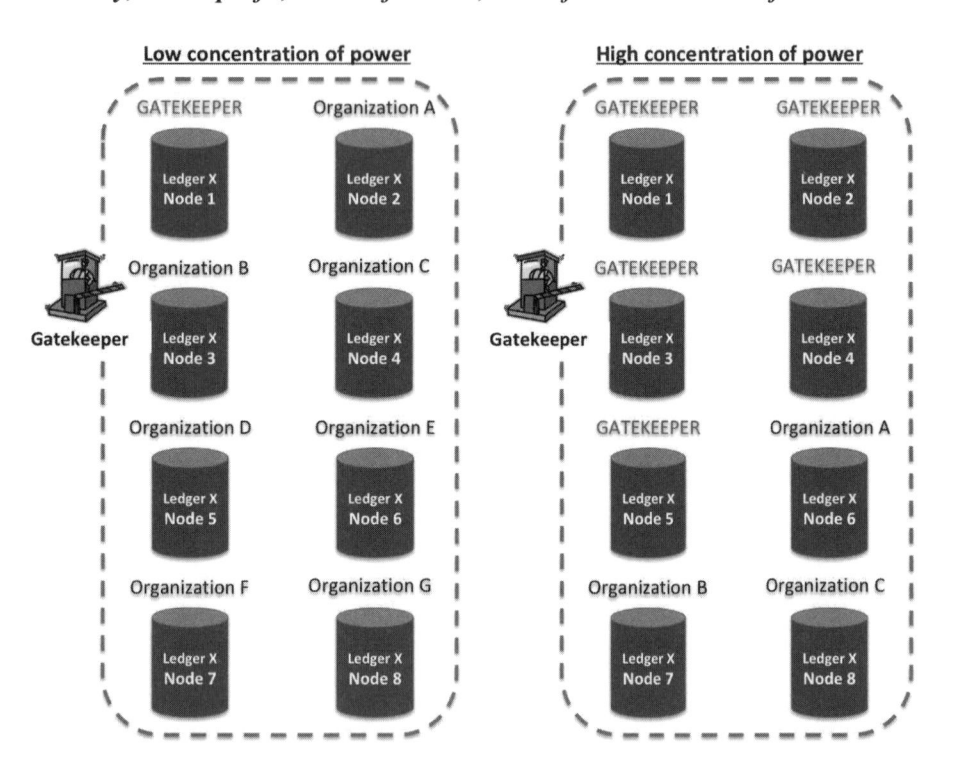

Figure 4.2: Concentration of power in a permissioned blockchain

On the left side, the gatekeeper operates just one node in the blockchain network, so concentration of power is low. On the right side, the gatekeeper operates more than 50 percent of the nodes, so the concentration of power is high.

4.2.5. Quantum computing security threats

Blockchain's cryptography is deemed secure because today's digital computers don't have enough computational power to make brute force guessing, say of a private key based on knowing only the public key, feasible. According to one source, today's digital computer would take billions of years to randomly guess a private key that matches a public key, even when assuming the computer was performing a trillion guesses per second.[29] Looking far ahead, some people are concerned that the cryptography we deem to be secure today may become vulnerable in the future. Keeping in mind that blockchain records are immutable, there is indeed a risk that future technologies could break the cryptography that protects the blockchains of today. Quantum computing is one such risk.

Quantum computing will speed computers in such a way that brute force searches that are impractical today could be practical in the future.[30] How? Today's digital computers are based on binary digits, called 'bits', which represent the state of a computation with a '0' or a '1'. Today, we make digital computers faster by processing more bits per second, but each bit can still only represent one computation. Quantum computers will change this; they will be based on quantum bits, called 'qubits', which can simultaneously represent multiple states and therefore do multiple calculations at the same time. A 30-qubit computer could do one billion calculations simultaneously.[31] Of course, blockchain technologies will also advance, so this particular risk might well be mitigated in the future.

- *LESSON FOR MANAGERS: Your enterprise will more likely be concerned with the immutability and permanence of records for reasons other than the future threat of quantum computing.*

Many organizations have data retirement or 'right to be forgotten' policies that will need to be re-examined for blockchain applications. (See next Chapter for more.)

4.3. Performance and scalability challenges

"Everyone calculating everything does not scale. Not at all... Ethereum is many magnitudes slower than today's databases."

Henning Diedrich, author of Ethereum: Blockchains, Digital Assets, Smart Contracts, DAOs[32]

"Certainly there has been developments, and, in most cases, blockchains can address the requirements for scalability."

Eamonn Maguire, Global Lead, Digital Ledger Services, KPMG[33]

Although performance and scalability affect each other, they are conceptually distinctive. Coindesk explains the difference as follows:

> *"Performance refers to how long it takes a system to process a request, while scalability relates to a system's ability to handle an increase in workload, such as when new users are added to a system."*[35]

Because performance and scalability issues are significantly greater for permissionless blockchains than for permissioned blockchains, we'll examine them separately.

4.3.1. Performance and scalability challenges of permissionless blockchains

Public, permissionless blockchains have significantly greater performance and scalability challenges than permissioned blockchains. Because the *a priori* trust among trading partners is nil in a permissionless blockchain, the computer networks need a lot of computational power to validate transactions and to constantly monitor the integrity of records. All this computation slows down performance (and consumes a lot of resources, which will also be addressed in this chapter). As we saw in the huge adoption surges of 2017, Bitcoin and Ethereum struggled to meet demand.

Performance: transaction processing and settlement times. Andre de Castro, CEO and Founder, Blockchain of Things, made an important distinction between transaction processing and settlement speeds in public blockchains like Bitcoin. He said:

> *"Most people do not understand the difference between the speed of settlement and the speed of transactions. Bitcoin settles in ten minutes, but transaction speed is in milliseconds. If you own both the endpoints, you have no counter party risk and can execute immediately in the case of IoT. Now, what gets stored on the blockchain for an auditor to see, that doesn't need to happen right away. Auditors ask what happened six months ago."*[36]

His company developed Catenis, an enterprise application that sits on top of Bitcoin and allows nearly instantaneous transactions between an organization's IoT devices. The key is trust in the sending and receiving devices.

For most uses, enterprises will not accept transactions as valid until they are settled, so performance is measured by settlement times. Bitcoin is designed to settle transactions every ten minutes and was indeed settling close to that time as of September 2017; Ethereum is designed to settle transactions in seven seconds, and the average was 15 seconds in December of 2017.[37] Even when public blockchains are performing optimally, the settlement times for some transaction types are still considered too slow. Public blockchains like Bitcoin and Ethereum settle some transactions like cross-border remittances much faster than the current global financial system, but they are not fast enough for transactions requiring nearly instantaneous reaction times, such as IoT devices that monitor the status of critical systems (Catenis was designed to solve this), or for retail applications where a customer will certainly not wait around for a transaction to settle.

Scalability: ability to take on increased transaction volumes. Permissionless blockchains like Bitcoin and Ethereum are considered too small in scale to handle the volumes that will be required for many enterprise applications. As of 2017, Bitcoin was handling about three or four transactions per second and Ethereum was averaging 20 transactions per second. In contrast, PayPal was handling 193 transactions per second, SWIFT – the global provider of secure financial messaging services – was processing about 329 messages per second,[38] and Visa was handling 1,667 transactions per second (and claimed it could accommodate up to 56,000 transactions per second).[39]

Ethereum's scalability issue was really highlighted when one smart contract for the game CryptoKitties started using 10 percent of Ethereum's network capacity in November of 2017; Cryptokitties created a backlog of tens of thousands of transactions.[40]

One consequence of permissionless blockchains' lack of scalability is higher transaction costs. For most of Bitcoin's history, transaction fees were indeed very small, averaging about 11 cents (in $US) per transaction in June 2014 and 28 cents in December of 2016.[41] For a specific example, we found a transaction on March 12th 2017, where a person offered just 45 cents worth of bitcoins to transfer over $8200 worth of bitcoins.[42] As Bitcoin gains in popularity, the network gets congested and fees have skyrocketed to as high as $55 in December 2017.[43] So what's going on?

To explain, we need to revisit the original Satoshi Nakamoto white paper...

In Nakamoto (2008), miners were incentivized to validate transactions and to create new blocks by the newly minted coins the miner would receive for doing so. Initially, miners were rewarded with 50 newly minted bitcoins for every block created, but the reward is halved every 210,000 blocks. (As of 2018, the mining reward is 12.5 bitcoins per block.) Eventually, the full stock of 21 million bitcoins would be released, so Nakamoto needed another method to incentivize miners. Nakamoto's idea was that senders would offer miners transaction fees to include their transactions in the next block. When the network is not congested, very small fees are enough to incentivize miners. However, when the network is congested, all the newly released transactions cannot be squeezed into the next block, which has a maximum block size of one megabyte. When miners cannot include all the newly validated transactions in the next block, the miners' algorithms select the transactions offering the highest fees. During peak times in 2017, senders offering smaller fees sometimes waited days to be added to the blockchain, or worse, their orphaned transaction eventually dropped out and needed to be resent.[44] Bitcoin's scalability problems are being hotly debated among the members of its open source community. At the time of this writing, Bitcoin had just forked again to accommodate a larger block size.

4.3.2. Performance and scaling solutions for permissionless blockchains

Open source communities and private enterprises are working on a number of solutions to scale blockchains to increase throughput. Public blockchains are examining solutions such as *sharding*, which involves segmenting the validation process so that not every node validates every transaction. *Segregated Witness*, called SegWit[45], is a proposal to move digital signatures from each address within a transaction to a single digital signature at the transaction level. Reducing the size of transactions means more transactions can be squeezed into a block. In the Bitcoin network, one consequence of the proposed adoption the SegWit[46] is that it also enables the use of *Lightning Network*. The Lighting Network tracks intermediate transfers of funds off-chain and only posts the value of the initial credit and the final account balance transfers to the blockchain. The solution helps unclutter the blockchain with intermediate transactions. Functionally, it's like opening up a bar tab. A person secures a bar tab with a credit card, orders several drinks (or sends a few drinks back), and then settles the final bill with one payment.

The *Raiden Network* is another protocol that builds another layer on top of a blockchain. Heiko Hees, CEO and founder of Brainbot in Germany, launched the Raiden Network as a high-speed network for micropayments on Ethereum.[47] Described as similar to the Lightning Network, the basic idea is to switch from a model where all transactions hit the shared ledger on the blockchain (which is the bottleneck) to a model where users can privately exchange messages which sign the transfer of value. Raiden nodes connect to Ethereum nodes using an API. The processing of a million, confidential transactions per second is possible, because they are not added to the blockchain. Furthermore, transaction fees are reported to be 'tiny'.[48]

4.3.3. Performance and scalability of permissioned blockchains

- *LESSON FOR MANAGERS: Permissioned blockchains solve the performance and scaling challenges by limiting the number of nodes needed to validate transactions and by allowing private messaging and channels among trading partners.*

Many permissioned blockchains create divisions of labor, so some nodes might be validating transactions while other nodes might be sequencing their outputs, and still others may be adding sequenced blocks to the ledger. Subsequently, permissioned blockchains like Corda, Quorum and Hyperledger Fabric can settle transactions within seconds. As of 2018, the exact scalability of permissioned blockchains is an unknown, as none have been adopted to scale. However, most permissioned blockchains claim they are highly scalable. For example, some people claim that Hyperledger Fabric can scale to more than 1,000 transactions per second.[49] The Hyperledger Project launched the Performance and Scalability Working Group in June 2017 to benchmark the actual performance of different blockchains.[50]

4.4. Anonymity challenges

Within a permissionless blockchain, every transaction is completely transparent to anyone with access to the Internet, but the identity of the owners of those transactions is anonymous. For example, Bitcoin's blockchain enables two parties to exchange value in anonymity, which is why Silk Road chose Bitcoin as it payment application (see Glossary for the story of Silk Road). Figure 4.3 illustrates the state of being public yet anonymous. Figure 4.3 is an example of an actual Bitcoin transaction that took place on Feb 25, 2016 at 10:24:44 am. The sending and receiving addresses have no means to identity the trading partners, yet the world can observe the transaction.[51]

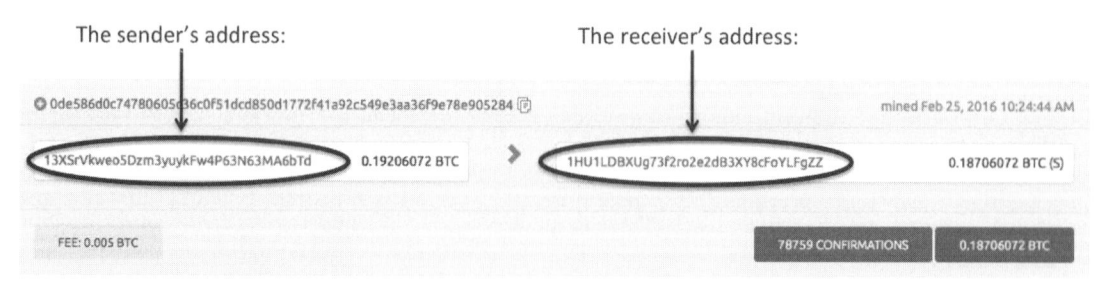

Figure 4.3: A Bitcoin transaction that occurred in Block 400000 on February 25ᵗʰ 2016

4.4.1. Threats to anonymity

Although public blockchains are anonymous in that no personal identities are revealed on the ledger, meta patterns can emerge where identities could be revealed. Many transactions are funded with multiple addresses, so patterns can emerge where one party can track another party's transactions.

Figure 4.4 illustrates how this can occur. If Party A sends value to an address owned by Party B on one date, Party A can later determine additional addresses owned by Party B when Party B spends the coins. This was something Satoshi Nakamoto acknowledged in his white paper. Nakamoto recommended that new addresses should be generated for new transactions:

> *"As an additional firewall, a new key pair should be used for each transaction to keep them from being linked to a common owner. Some linking is still unavoidable with multi-input transactions, which necessarily reveal that the same owner owned their inputs. The risk is that if the owner of a key is revealed, linking could reveal other transactions that belonged to the same owner."*[52]

4.4.2. Anonymity solutions

Open source communities are working to address these issues. We examine two such solutions: zero knowledge proofs and CryptoNotes.

Zero knowledge proofs are a method for one party to verify possession of a piece of information to other parties without revealing the information. Let's use an analogy to understand how it works:

Suppose Party A wants to prove to Party B that she knows the exact number of jellybeans that fills a large barrel without telling Party B the exact number. Party A instructs Party B to take any number of jellybeans out of the barrel after Party A leaves the room. Party A departs. Party B makes his choice. Party A reenters the room and Party B exits the room. Party A recounts the beans and compares the current count with the previous count to calculate exactly how many jellybeans (if any) Party B removed. When Party B returns, Party A tells Party B exactly how many jellybeans he took. If Party B thinks Party A made a lucky guess, rounds of the same choice could be made over and over again. Eventually, Party B will be convinced that Party A possesses the knowledge of the exact number of jellybeans without ever revealing the number.

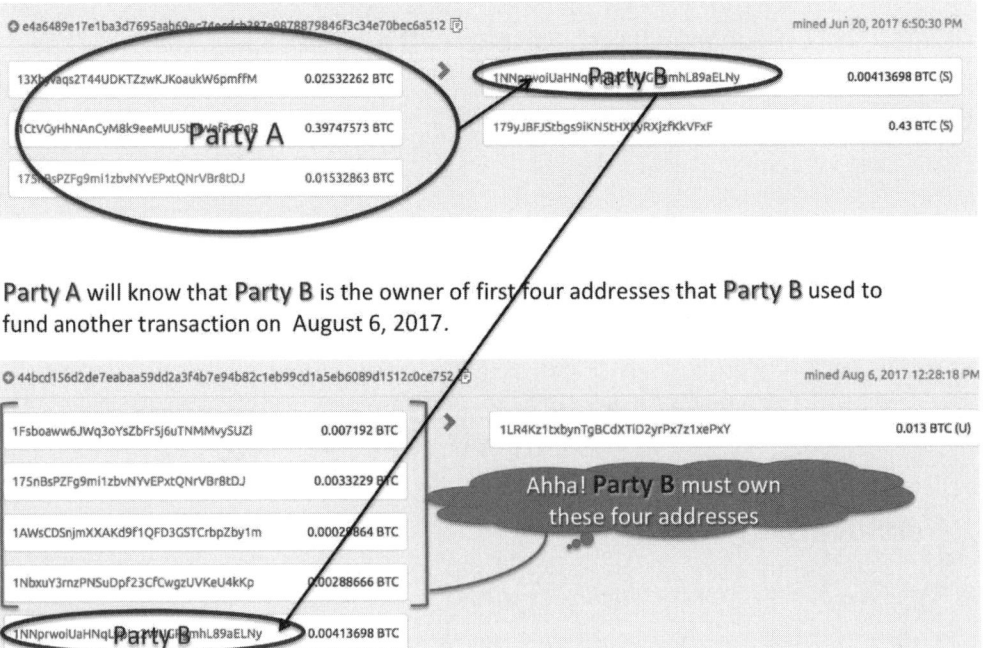

Figure 4.4: Meta patterns that can arise from a blockchain's transparency

Moving from an analogy to an actual algorithm, Zcash used a cryptographic zero-knowledge proof called 'zk-SNARK',[53] which stands for 'Zero-Knowledge Succinct Non-Interactive Argument of Knowledge.'[54] As a matter of practicality, this proof is verified within seconds and does not require rounds of communication like previous zero-knowledge proofs.[55] Quorum added this zero knowledge proof in May 2017.[56]

CryptoNotes is another protocol used in blockchains that offer more privacy than those used in Bitcoin and Ethereum. CryptoNote's transactions cannot be followed through the blockchain in a way that reveals who sent or received coins,[57] like we saw with Bitcoin. Instead, just an approximate amount of a transaction and a key image of the account are posted. As an example, compare what Monero posts on the public blockchain using the CryptoNote protocol in Figure 4.5 to Bitcoin's public blockchain in Figure 4.3 above.

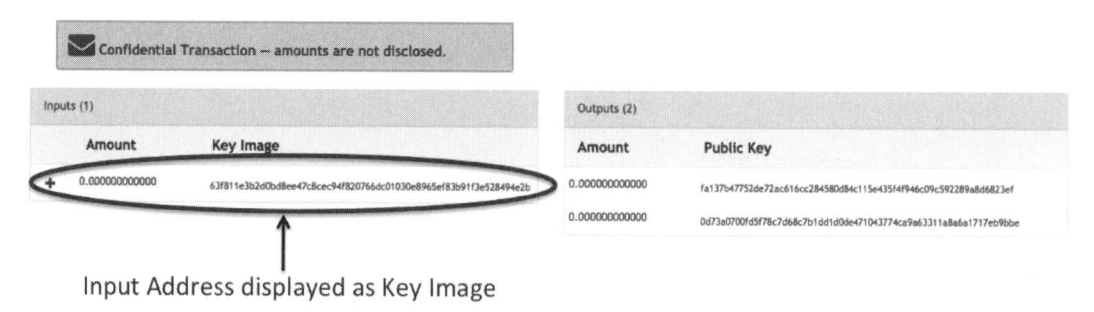

Figure 4.5: Monero transaction displayed with amount masked and with input address displayed as a key image[58]

4.5. Confidentiality challenges

"The issue is that some companies are afraid that information that's being collected for the blockchain will be used for other purposes. So let's say I'm a pharmacy. If I verified all the products I have on hand, I'm announcing my inventory. Companies are concerned that this added intelligence could be used for other purposes such as contract negotiations, etc."

Bob Celeste, CEO and Founder of the Center for Supply Chain Studies[59]

Moving from public, permissionless blockchains to permissioned blockchains, we obviously cannot allow anonymity among trading partners. Regulations require that enterprises know the identity of their customers, employees, suppliers, and third parties. However, enterprises are concerned about confidentiality. With one shared ledger, how do we allow some folks to view transactions while preventing other folks from viewing transactions when we are all sharing a blockchain application? The solutions discussed in Chapter 2 are rather straightforward. With permissioned blockchains, particular nodes play different roles, such as observe, transact, validate, and add transactions to the ledger.

Using Quorum as an example, participants can execute private and public smart contracts so that the ledger is segmented into a private state database and a public state database (see Figure 4.6).[60] Within a single ledger, all nodes can view Quorum's public states, but only those nodes party to private contracts can view private states.

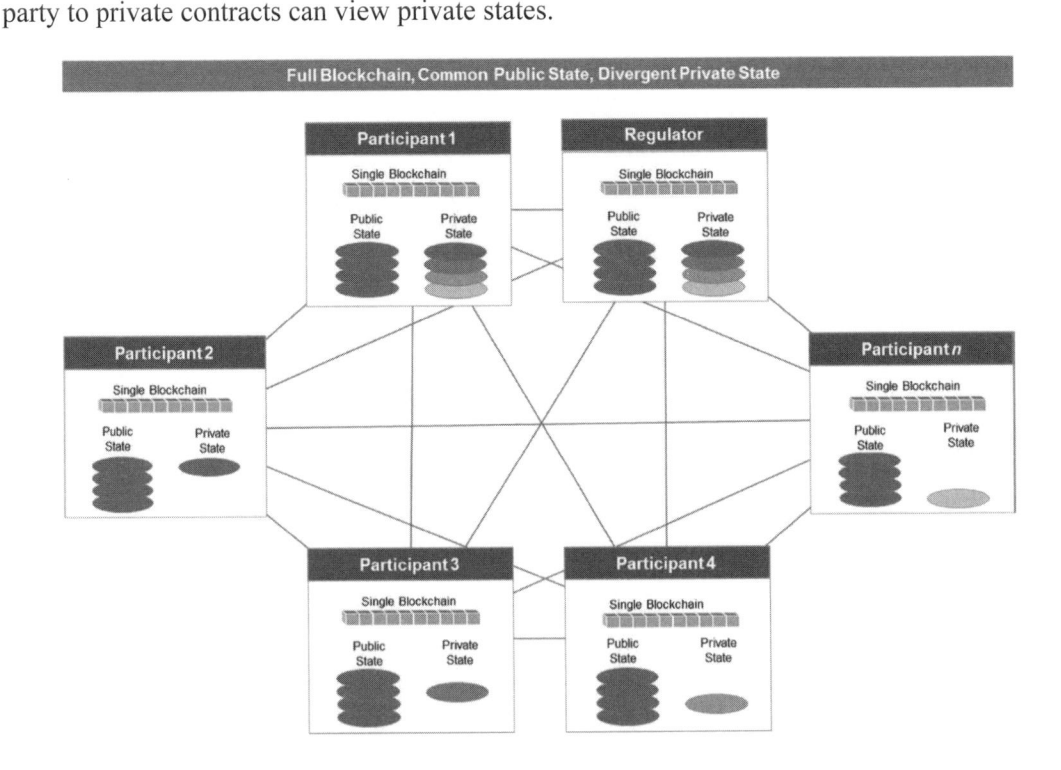

Figure 4.6: Quorum's architecture for separating public and private transactions

Source: Quorum White Paper[61]

151

Hyperledger Fabric uses the concept of channels, where channels help provide a data-partitioning capability, with only those needing to know the data able to see the number of transactions and the data itself.[62] Smart contracts (called Chaincode in Fabric) specify a channel's parties and the rules by which assets can be created and modified on the channel's ledger (see Figure 4.7).

Hyperledger Fabric is similar to Quorum in that non-confidential transactions are open to all participants, but the contents of confidential transactions are encrypted with secret keys known only to their originators, validators, and authorized auditors.[63]

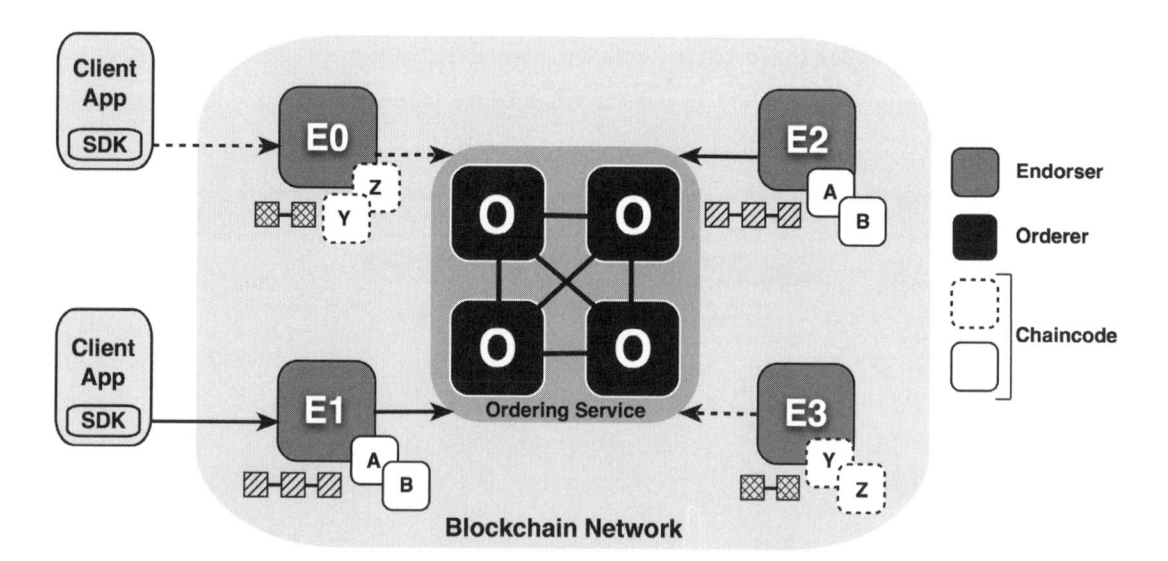

- PEERS **E0** AND **E3** CONNECT TO THE ▨ CHANNEL FOR CHAINCODES **Y** AND **Z**
- PEERS **E1** AND **E2** CONNECT TO THE ▨ CHANNEL FOR CHAINCODES **A** AND **B**

Figure 4.7: Channels in Hyperledger Fabric

Fabric allows parties to use a software development toolkit (SDK) to code smart contracts (called chaincodes) to create separate ledgers for different agreements

Source: *https://www.altoros.com/blog/hyperledger-fabric-v1-0-multi-ledgers-multi-channels-and-node-js-sdk/*

4.6. Interoperability challenges

"To connect across blockchains, you have to go on and off chain."

Dustin Byington, President Wanchain[64]

"When talking to the CIO at State of Illinois, he said, 'Sure, great. You come up with five, seven, eight different blockchain uses cases, but how does it make a difference if I can't connect the blockchains I'm using to my Oracle back-end?'"

Dev Bharel, Blockchain Solutions Architect with Nussbaumer Projects[65]

"Blockchains need to be integrated with different ERP systems. It really doesn't matter if you have great blockchain use cases if it doesn't add real value or if you can't make business decisions."

Rahul Shah, Strategy Manager, Axiom Technology Group[66]

For enterprises to adopt blockchain technologies, there will need to be interoperability – the ability for one system to use another system.[67] There is clearly a need for blockchain interoperability to eliminate reliance on intermediaries, to improve performance and scalability, and to bridge private and public blockchains.[68] For the foreseeable future, blockchains will not likely replace enterprise systems, but rather enterprises will bolt blockchains on top of their existing legacy systems. From our research, this issue is largely resolved by connecting to permissioned blockchains via Application Programming Interfaces (APIs). However, there remains a bigger issue: enterprises will need to make sure that records are locked in one system as they are processed in another system, lest we end up resurrecting the double spend problem blockchains aimed to solve in the first place.

Wanchain, Cosmos, Icon[69], Aion[70], Comit,[71] and other startups in the blockchain market are developing solutions to make blockchains interoperable. For example, Wanchain, founded in Beijing and Austin Texas, is a protocol that aims to connect blockchains. It proposes to accomplish this by locking an asset on one blockchain, minting a new proxy token for that asset as it enters the Wanchain, and connecting it to other blockchains. Wanchain itself is a blockchain that will record cross-chain and intra-chain transactions. (See Figure 4.8).[72]

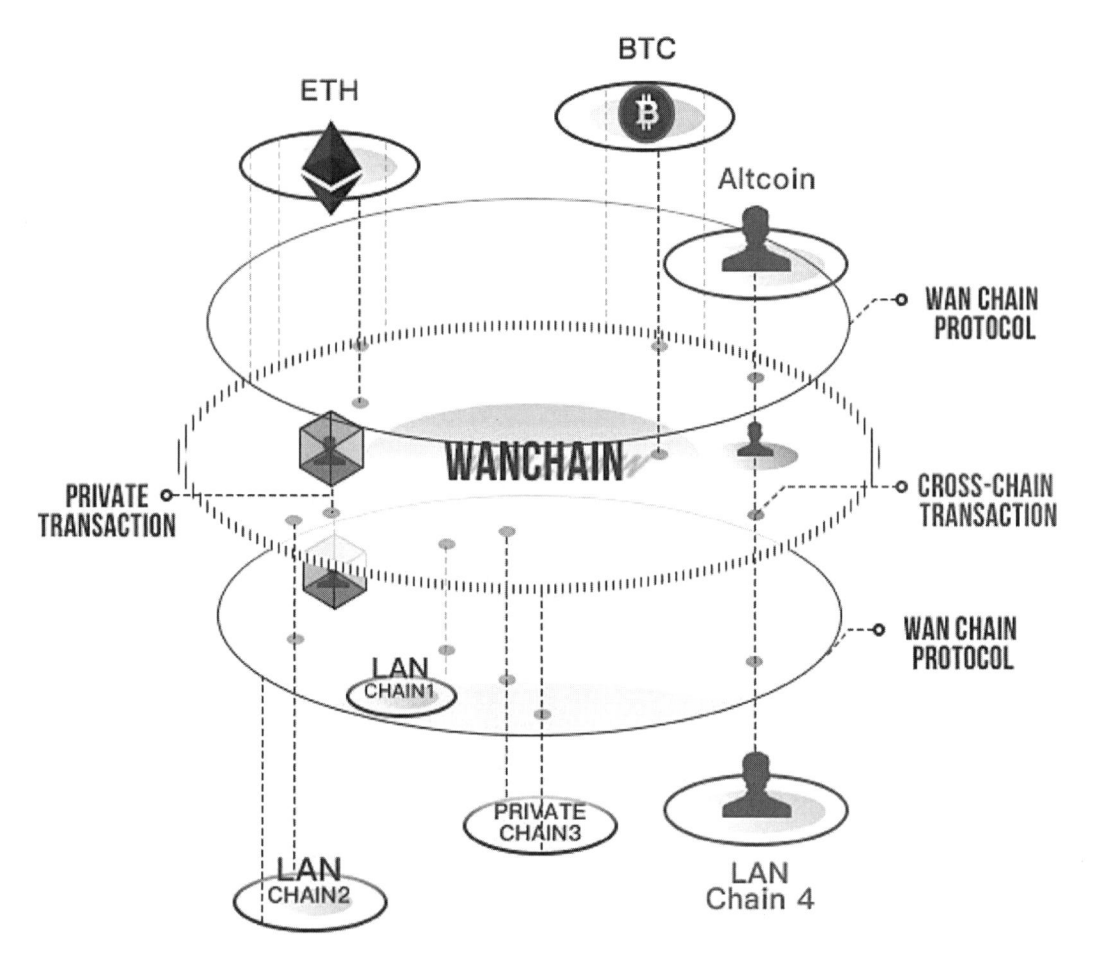

Figure 4.8: Wanchain's proposed solution for blockchain interoperability

Source: https://wanchain.org/

Cosmos is another proposed solution. Cosmos is a permissionless blockchain project that proposes to connect different blockchains through its hub (see Figure 4.9). The idea is that Cosmos will create the hub as the first blockchain and it will connect to other sovereign blockchains called zones, which can be either public or private.[73] Cosmos Hub can then be used as a secure pathway for inter-blockchain transfers of tokens without needing a liquid exchange between the two involved blockchains.[74] Cosmos raised $17 million in the first 8 minutes of its ICO in 2017.[75]

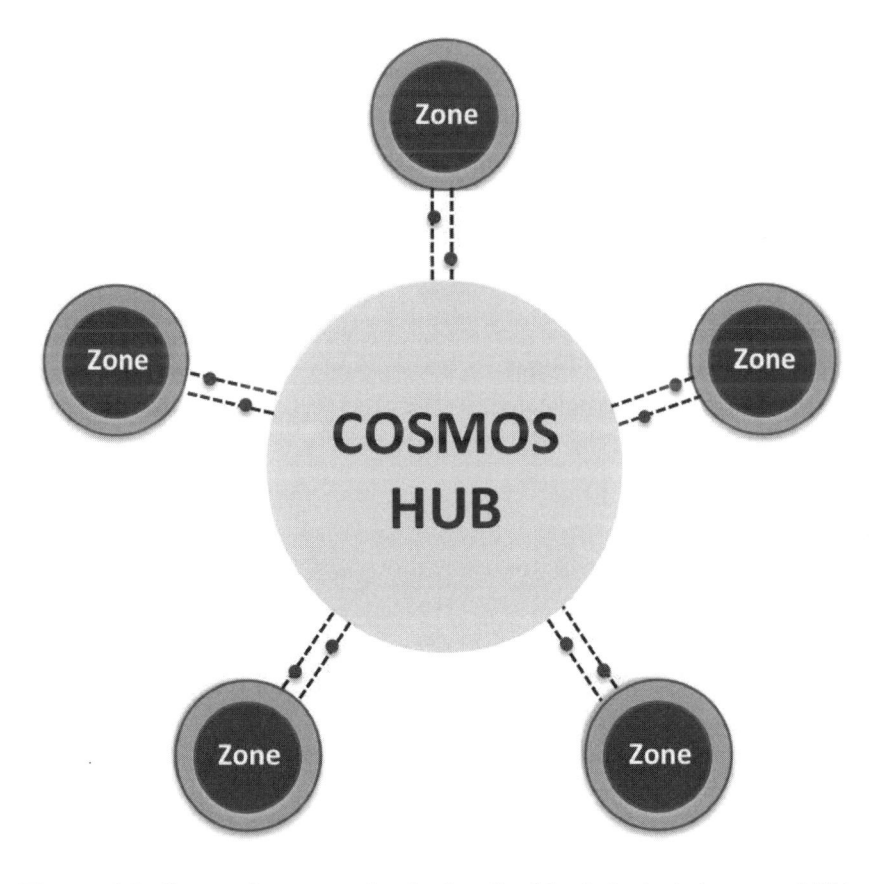

Figure 4.9: Cosmos' proposed solution for blockchain interoperability
Source: http://news.sys-con.com/node/4201542

Leaders from Wanchain, Icon[76], and Aion[77] decided it was in the best interests of all parties to share information. They formed the Blockchain Interoperability Alliance in 2017 to establish a common standard for inter-chain communications.[78]

- *LESSON FOR MANAGERS: Enterprises will need to build or acquire technical architecture skills that can understand how to connect blockchains and enterprise systems.*

Blockchain architects can earn salaries in the $200K to $400K range, so be prepared to pay.

4.7. Resource consumption challenges

"It's worth the price; a single security breech costs an average of $3.8 million"

Don and Alex Tapscott, authors of Blockchain Revolution[79]

Computers that run blockchain nodes consume resources in the form of electricity. While it makes sense that the more network nodes, the higher the electricity consumption, the computational intensity of a given blockchain's consensus protocol is the main driver of resource consumption. Recalling from Chapter 2, Bitcoin and Ethereum use the safest, yet computationally most resource-demanding protocol called a proof-of-work, which requires specialized hardware to increase chances of winning the mining reward. Bitcoin requires an Application-Specific Integrated Circuit (ASIC) and Ethereum requires a Graphics Processing Unit (GPU).

Proof-of-work is admittedly a resource hog. As of 2015, the process of mining and protecting the Bitcoin blockchain cost over $100 million in electricity each year.[80] According to one calculation, a bitcoin transaction required over 5,000 times more energy than a Visa transaction in 2015.[81] By the end of 2017, the electricity consumed exploded as the price of bitcoin rose, prompting more miners to add computer capacity to increase their chances of winning the mining reward. In order to compete, large mining centers have been established (see Figure 4.10 for an example). Digiconomist, a site that tracks blockchain energy consumption, calculated that by 2017, each bitcoin transaction required 268 kilowatts of electricity; Ethereum used 30 kilowatts of electricity per transaction. On an annual basis, those figures equate to the energy required to power 3.5 million US households for Bitcoin and 914,000 US households for Ethereum.[82]

Mining pools are incentivized to erect data centers near a low cost source of electricity. For this reason, large mining pools have sprung up in China, which controls over 80 percent of the mining power over Bitcoin in 2017. Iceland, Czech Republic, and Georgia (the country) are other popular mining sites.[83] Within the US, the price of electricity varies greatly across the 50 states. Louisiana has the lowest average cost of electricity for mining one Bitcoin, at $3,224 per bitcoin in the last week of 2017. Hawaii and Alaska were the most expensive at $9,483 and $7,059 per bitcoin respectively.[84]

Figure 4.10: Bitcoin mining site in Bowden, Sweden

Source: https://coinscage.com/wp-content/uploads/2017/05/bitcoin-mining-farm-1.jpg

- ***LESSON FOR MANAGERS: Solutions already exist today**.*

Other blockchains rely on less computationally intensive consensus algorithms, like proof-of-stake; permissioned blockchains rely on some form of Byzantine Fault Tolerance, which requires very little energy consumption – about as much energy as it takes to run an email server (See Chapter 2 for an explanation of these consensus methods).

4.8. Conclusion

As covered in this chapter, many people are working to make blockchains more secure, more private, faster, scalable and interoperable. Managers need to be aware of the technical risks, but their focus of attention should be on the issues discussed in our final chapter on mindshifts, strategies, and action principles.

Citations

1. Castillo, M. (January 3rd 2017), *State Street's Blockchain Strategy: Big and Bold for 2017*, https://www.coindesk.com/state-streets-blockchain-strategy-big-and-bold-for-2017/

2. Personal interview with Mary Lacity in 2017

3. Personal interview with Mary Lacity in 2017

4. Empty

5. Personal interview with Mary Lacity and Kate Moloney in 2017

6. Personal interview with Mary Lacity and Kate Moloney in 2017

7. Email interview with Mary Lacity in 2018

8. Personal interview with Mary Lacity and Kate Moloney in 2017

9. *Mt. Gox CEO Mark Karpeles pleads not guilty to embezzlement*, July 11th 2015, http://www.aljazeera.com/news/2015/08/japan-arrests-mtgox-bitcoin-head-missing-387m-150801054245349.html

10. Rogers, K. (March 6th 2015), *The Guy Who Ruined DogeCoin*, https://motherboard.vice.com/en_us/article/78xqxb/the-guy-who-ruined-dogecoin

11. Russolillo, S. (December 7th 2017), *Hackers Steal More Than $70 Million in Bitcoin: Theft prompts shutdown of NiceHash, which markets itself as the largest crypto-mining marketplace*, https://www.wsj.com/articles/millions-may-be-missing-in-bitcoin-heist-1512625176

12. RT (November 21st 2017), *Another big cryptocurrency heist raises questions about digital money safety*, https://www.rt.com/business/410479-bitcoin-tether-theft-safety-cryptocurrency/

13. https://en.wikipedia.org/wiki/Bitfinex

14. Segal, D. (June 25th 2016), *Understanding the DAO attack*, http://www.coindesk.com/understanding-dao-hack-journalists/

15. Diedrich, H. (2016), *Ethereum: blockchains, digital assets, smart contracts, decentralized autonomous organizations*, Wildfire publishing.

16. Segal, D. (June 25th 2016), *Understanding the DAO attack*, http://www.coindesk.com/understanding-dao-hack-journalists/

17. Segal, D. (June 25th 2016), *Understanding the DAO attack*, http://www.coindesk.com/understanding-dao-hack-journalists/

18. KPTX (October 6th 2016), *Cryptocurrency hacks: the biggest heists in blockchain history*, https://www.deepdotweb.com/2016/10/06/cryptocurrency-hacks-biggest-heists-blockchain-history/

19. *Stellar and Ripple Hacked: Justcoin to the Rescue*, Oct 14th 2014, https://cointelegraph.com/news/stellar-and-ripple-hacked-justcoin-to-the-rescue

20. Tuwiner, J. (July 13th 2017), *Bitcoin Mining Pools*, https://www.buybitcoinworldwide.com/mining/pools/

21. Emin Gün Sirer's presentation, *What Could Go Wrong? When Blockchains Fail,* Business of Blockchain conference, April 18th 2017, https://www.technologyreview.com/s/604219/blockchains-weak-spots-pose-a-hidden-danger-to-users/

22. BitcoinChaser (September 21st 2017), *The Chinese Bitcoin Mining Takeover Conspiracy*, http://bitcoinchaser.com/chinese-bitcoin-mining-takeover-conspiracy/

23. BitcoinChaser (September 21st 2017), *The Chinese Bitcoin Mining Takeover Conspiracy*, http://bitcoinchaser.com/chinese-bitcoin-mining-takeover-conspiracy/

24. Buchko, S. (November 14th 2017), *The 3 Best Ethereum Mining Pool Options*, Coincentral.

25. Crypto Mining Blog (April 27th 2017), *BitMain Up for Another Scandal With Antbleed Backdoor*, http://cryptomining-blog.com/8634-bitmain-up-for-another-scandal-with-antbleed-backdoor/

26. Rowley, J. (April 27th 2017), *Tensions Persist As Traders Largely Shake Off The 'Antbleed' Bitcoin Backdoor Scandal*, https://news.crunchbase.com/news/tensions-persist-traders-largely-shake-off-antbleed-bitcoin-backdoor-scandal/

27. Gencer, A.E., Basu, S., Eyal, I., cen Renesse, R., and Sirer, E.G, (January 15th 2018), *Decentralization in Bitcoin and Ethereum*, https://arxiv.org/pdf/1801.03998.pdf

28. Berke, A. (March 7th 2017), *How Safe are Blockchains? It Depends*, Harvard Business Review online, https://hbr.org/2017/03/how-safe-are-blockchains-it-depends

29. Sharma, N. (November 5th 2017), *Is Quantum Computing an Existential Threat to Blockchain Technology?* https://singularityhub.com/2017/11/05/is-quantum-computing-an-existential-threat-to-blockchain-technology/ - sm.00009y4jmx95sdww11rov5gdjdlzo

30. Schneier, B. (2015), *NSA Plans for a Post-Quantum World*, https://www.schneier.com/blog/archives/2015/08/nsa_plans_for_a.html

31. Sharma, N. (November 5th 2017), *Is Quantum Computing an Existential Threat to Blockchain Technology?* https://singularityhub.com/2017/11/05/is-quantum-computing-an-existential-threat-to-blockchain-technology/ - sm.00009y4jmx95sdww11rov5gdjdlzo

32. Diedrich, H. (2016), *Ethereum: blockchains, digital assets, smart contracts, decentralized autonomous organizations*, Wildfire publishing.

33. Personal interview with Mary Lacity in 2017

34. Empty

35. Castor, A. (June 14th 2017), *Hyperledger Takes on Blockchain Scaling with New Working Group*, https://www.coindesk.com/hyperledger-takes-on-blockchain-scaling-with-new-working-group/

36. Personal interview with Mary Lacity and Kate Moloney in 2017

37. https://etherscan.io/chart/blocktime

38. SWIFT Fin Traffic & Figures, https://www.swift.com/about-us/swift-fin-traffic-figures

39. *Bitcoin and Ethereum vs Visa and PayPal – Transactions per second*, Altcoin Today, April 22nd 2017, http://www.altcointoday.com/bitcoin-ethereum-vs-visa-paypal-transactions-per-second/

40. BBC News (December 5th 2017), *CryptoKitties craze slows down transactions on Ethereum*, http://

www.bbc.com/news/technology-42237162

Wong (December 4th 2017), *The ethereum network is getting jammed up because people are rushing to buy cartoon cats on its blockchain*, https://qz.com/1145833/cryptokitties-is-causing-ethereum-network-congestion/?utm_source=MIT+Technology+Review&utm_campaign=d6185c2892-EMAIL_CAMPAIGN_2017_11_02&utm_medium=email&utm_term=0_997ed6f472-d6185c2892-156469793

41. This website tracks average bitcoin transaction fee: https://bitinfocharts.com/comparison/bitcoin-transactionfees.html - 3m

42. The second transaction on block 456958 shows a miner was paid by the sender .00036955 bitcoins to add this to the transaction to the block. On March 12, one bitcoin was worth $1232.99 , so miner received 45 cents that day to include this transaction https://blockexplorer.com/block/0000000000000000015c7bd17dc9a82f457a8aed35bc6606cca57cb5932deb7e

43. To track average bitcoin transaction fee, see: https://bitinfocharts.com/comparison/bitcoin-transactionfees.html - 3m

44. *Bitcoin's Transaction Backlog Hits All-Time High, Fees Skyrocket*, May 11th 2017, http://www.trustnodes.com/2017/05/11/bitcoins-transaction-backlog-hits-all-time-high-fees-skyrocket

45. For a technical explanation of segregated witness, see http://learnmeabitcoin.com/faq/segregated-witness

46. For a technical explanation of segregated witness, see http://learnmeabitcoin.com/faq/segregated-witness

47. Hertig, A. (May 31st 2016), *Will Ethereum Beat Bitcoin to Mainstream Microtransactions?*, https://www.coindesk.com/ethereum-bitcoin-mainstream-microtransactions/

48. *The Raiden Network: High Speed Asset Transfers for Ethereum*, http://raiden.network/

49. *What Is Hyperledger? How the Linux Foundation builds an open platform around the blockchain projects of Intel and IBM*, https://blockgeeks.com/guides/what-is-hyperledger/

50. Castor, A. (June 14th 2017), *Hyperledger Takes on Blockchain Scaling with New Working Group*, https://www.coindesk.com/hyperledger-takes-on-blockchain-scaling-with-new-working-group/

51. To further protect privacy, users are advised to generate new addresses every time they receive bitcoins to prevent previous trading partners from detecting usage patterns.

52. Nakamoto, S. (2008), *Bitcoin: A Peer-to-Peer Electronic Cash System*, p.6, https://bitcoin.org/bitcoin.pdf

53. *What are zk-SNARKs?*, https://z.cash/technology/zksnarks.html

54. *What are zk-SNARKs?*, https://z.cash/technology/zksnarks.html

55. Here is a simple explanation of zk-SNARKs: Lundkvist, C. (2017), *Introduction to zk-SNARKs with examples*, https://media.consensys.net/introduction-to-zksnarks-with-examples-3283b554fc3b

56. Allison, I. (May 22nd 2017), *Zero-knowledge proofs added to JP Morgan's Quorum*, http://www.ibtimes.co.uk/zero-knowledge-proofs-added-jp-morgans-quorum-blockchain-1622573

57. en.wikipedia.org

58. https://moneroblocks.info/tx/898764c111ed490300fa58623c905ae335737a98ab28c49af34c8d9045915f82

59. Personal interview with Mary Lacity in 2018

60. Quorum White Paper, available at https://github.com/jpmorganchase/quorum-docs/blob/master/Quorum Whitepaper v0.1.pdf

61. Quorum White Paper: https://github.com/jpmorganchase/quorum-docs/blob/master/Quorum Whitepaper v0.1.pdf

62. Cocco, S. and Singh, G. (March 20th 2017), *Top 6 technical advantages of Hyperledger Fabric for blockchain networks*, https://www.ibm.com/developerworks/cloud/library/cl-top-technical-advantages-of-hyperledger-fabric-for-blockchain-networks/index.html

63. https://medium.com/chain-cloud-company-blog/hyperledger-vs-corda-pt-1-3723c4fa5028

64. Presentation at Invest Conference, November 28th 2017 https://youtu.be/SPk1-PRrafU

65. Personal interview with Mary Lacity and Kate Moloney in 2017

66. Personal interview with Mary Lacity and Kate Moloney in 2017

67. Ross, C. (December 5th 2016), *Blockchain Brings Us Into The Future, But Only After It Drags Up The Past: Interoperability Becomes An Actual Issue Again*, http://www.horsesforsources.com/blog/christine-ferrusi-ross/the-interoperability-problems-blockchain-brings_120616

Ross, C. (April 18th 2017), *Simplify Blockchain by Refusing to Let Interoperability Issues Bog You Down*, posted on http://www.horsesforsources.com/Simplify-Blockchain-Refusing-Interoperability-Issues_041817

68. https://www.coindesk.com/events/invest-2017/live/ - streams

69. Icon Foundation, (2017), *icon: Hyperconnect the world*, white paper, https://docs.icon.foundation/ICON-Whitepaper-EN-Draft.pdf

70. Spoke, M. and Nuco Engineering Team, (July 31st 2017), Aion white paper, https://aion.network/downloads/aion.network_technical-introduction_en.pdf

71. Hosp. J., Hoenisch, T., and Kittiwongsunthorn, P., *Comit: Cryptographically-secure Off-chain Multi-asset Instant Transaction network*, white paper, http://www.comit.network/doc/COMIT white paper v1.0.2.pdf

72. Wanchain is a fork of Ethereum and uses Monero style-ring signatures (it's a tumbling mechanism that creates privacy) to help secure multi-party compute. https://wanchain.org/

73. https://cosmos.network/about/whitepaper

74. Cryptojudgement, (March 7th 2017), *Cosmos: Discovering interoperability of blockchains*, https://medium.com/@cryptojudgement/cosmos-discovering-interoperability-of-blockchains-5f284d7867b7

75. http://cryptoeconomy.info/2017/04/06/cosmos-ico-over-17-m-raised-in-just-8-minutes/

76. Icon Foundation, (2017), *icon: Hyperconnect the world*, white paper, https://docs.icon.foundation/ICON-Whitepaper-EN-Draft.pdf

77. Spoke, M. and Nuco Engineering Team, (July 31st 2017), Aion white paper, https://aion.network/downloads/aion.network_technical-introduction_en.pdf

78. Presentation at Invest Conference, November 28th 2017, https://youtu.be/SPk1-PRrafU

79. Tapscott, D. and Tapscott, A (2016), *Blockchain Revolution*, Penguin, New York City

80. Scheider, N. (2015), After the bitcoin Gold Rush, *The New Republic*, https://newrepublic.com/article/121089/how-small-bitcoin-miners-lose-crypto-currency-boom-bust-cycle

81. Malmo (2015), *Bitcoin is unsustainable*, June 29th 2015, http://motherboard.vice.com/read/bitcoin-is-unsustainable

82. https://digiconomist.net/bitcoin-energy-consumption

83. Tuwiner, J. (July 13th 2017), *Bitcoin Mining Pools*, https://www.buybitcoinworldwide.com/mining/pools/

84. Sedgwick, K. (December 21st 2017), *These Are The Five Cheapest US States for Bitcoin Mining*, https://news.bitcoin.com/these-are-the-five-cheapest-us-states-for-bitcoin-mining/

Chapter 5

Mindshifts, Strategies and Action Principles: Making Enterprise Blockchains Real

"I think the first important lesson is this: there is something real here."

Vice President for a global bank[1]

"In my opinion, it will take a village to realize the true promise of blockchain. No one player or even one set of players (be it large ISVs or start-ups) can be everything to everyone. We are already starting to see a healthy and collaborative blockchain ecosystem beginning to emerge comprising of platform/framework players, technology providers, service providers, start-ups, consortiums, academia, legal firms, regulators, and industry associations."

Saurabh Gupta, Chief Strategy Officer, HfS Research[2]

"If you look at today's enterprise grade applications, they provide a lot of capabilities like security (not to be mistaken for immutability) and the ability to recover from a disaster. Blockchain implementations nearing production are now increasingly paying more and more attention to all of these traditional, well-known practices that will also apply to blockchain applications."

Kiran Nagaraj, Managing Director, KPMG[3]

"Blockchain technology brings some amazing innovations in computing and in the kind of work organizations can do. But in many cases it's not a great replacement for technology we use today – it's not always more efficient or effective than current systems. If someone really wants to harness the power of blockchain, then she or he should stop asking 'what can I do better with blockchain?' and ask 'what can I do with blockchain that I couldn't do before?' Don't buy an airplane just to turn it into a faster car."

Christine Ferrusi Ross, Advisor and Strategist, Decision Changers, Inc.

5.1. Introduction

Thus far in our journey, we've examined the blockchain landscape, the promised benefits of enterprise blockchains, actual examples of enterprise blockchains across industries, and the major technical challenges and emerging technical solutions. Now we turn to business issues. In this chapter, we examine what it takes for traditional enterprises to actually gain value from enterprise blockchains. It's not easy; enterprises face a daunting 'technology-embeddedness' challenge. Endemic to all technologies, live blockchain applications must be assimilated within complex institutional, political, regulatory, legal, social, economic, and physical systems.[4] We developed a succinct yet comprehensive roadmap to help executives move blockchain applications out of innovation labs into the real world (see Figure 5.1).

Traditional enterprises will need to **shift their mindsets** when moving from command-and-control, centralized applications to distributed applications. They will need to build new capabilities in a market where such skills are scarce. They are going to have to ignore the general maxim that 'strategy drives technology adoption' for a while as they learn how blockchains work. We call this the *'cart before the horse' exploration phase*. Once enough learning has accumulated, enterprises can roll up their sleeves to build sustaining, disruptive, or consortium-led innovations, each of which has a different strategic intent. We call this the *'horse before the cart' strategic intent phase*. Embedding strategic innovations is going to require more change management than most executives are accustomed to handling; in addition to working with internal stakeholders and current customers, enterprises will have to work with trading partners, open source communities, consortia, and regulators. Once theses hurdles are overcome and the application is deployed, there remains the formidable task of trying to become the go-to, defacto application. We call this the *critical mass phase*. Although each enterprise's blockchain journey will be its own, we offer 16 action principles to help navigate the trip.

'Action principles' are practices identified by our research that produced desirable results in real world implementations. Action principles are therefore grounded in our data and are designed to assist other thoughtful agents as they embark on their own implementation journeys. Action principles are similar to best practices in that both seek to share knowledge from prior experiences. But whereas 'best practices' imply that mimicry is always recommended and will always produce similar results, action principles recognize that context matters. The

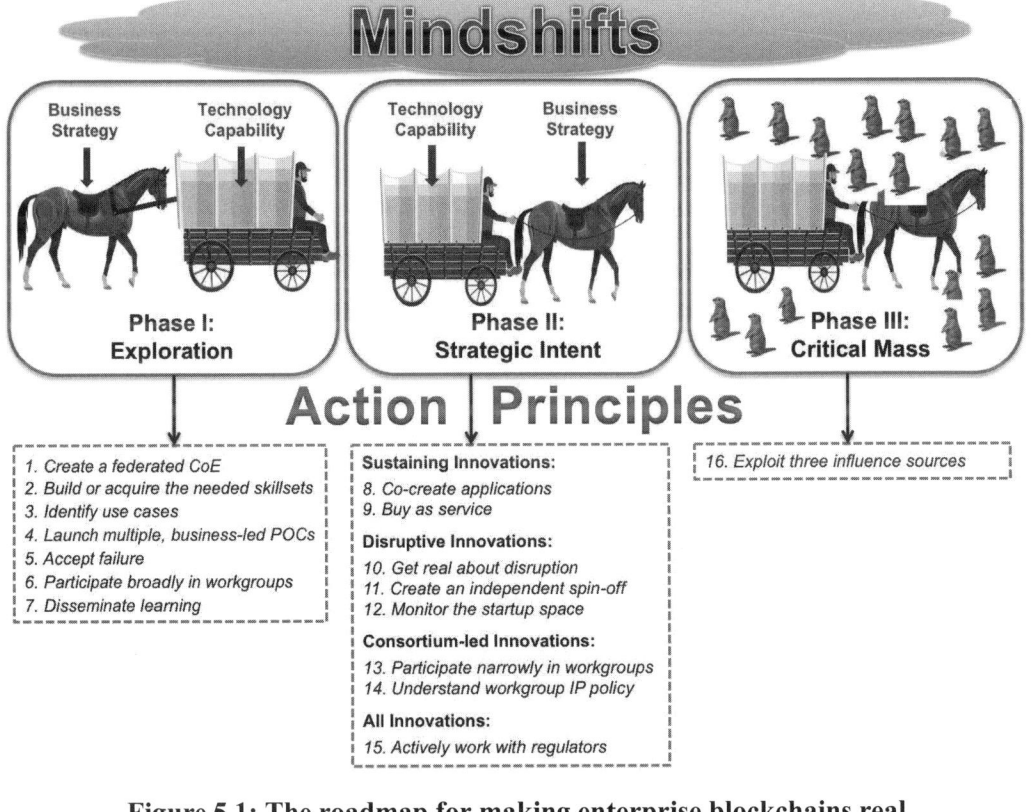

Figure 5.1: The roadmap for making enterprise blockchains real

Enterprises need to change their mindsets when moving from command-and-control, centralized applications to the shared governance models of distributed applications. Enterprises will pass through three phases: exploration to build technical capabilities, enactment of strategic intents, and gaining a critical mass of adopters. Action principles help enterprises navigate each phase.

usefulness of a practice depends on the objectives the organization is trying to achieve, whether the organization has the absorptive capacity to implement the practice effectively; and timing – there are better times than others to apply a specific practice. As social scientists, we view managers as thoughtful agents who scrutinize 'best practices' derived from other people's learnings to decide when and whether practices need to be modified, or perhaps discarded, within their organizations.[5]

5.2. Mindshifts: The blockchain mindset

"Business agreements are the hardest things. We need to have rules of entry and play that protect consumers and protect the overall ecosystem. Taking it live is the easy thing once you have a business agreement. Getting people to play ball, that's the real tough thing."

Innovation Director for a US healthcare company[6]

A blockchain application promises an abundance of business benefits, like transacting directly with trading partners; eliminating the need for reconciliations; instantly tracking and tracing assets; providing data provenance; settling transactions quickly and cheaply; and enabling a security model that is fault tolerant, resilient, and available. All this sounds great on the surface, until managers from traditional enterprises realize the implications like losing control over data, abiding by the wishes and decisions of shared governance bodies, and committing the enterprise's resources to validate and store other parties' data. Blockchain applications require six significant mindshifts from old to new ways of thinking (see Figure 5.2).

5.2.1. Mindshift: From command-and-control to shared governance models

Is your traditional enterprise ready for shared governance models? Both permissionless and permissioned blockchain applications rely upon shared governance models. No one entity can unilaterally make decisions about changing the rules, upgrading the code base, or altering the immutable records. (The only exception is under the circumstance in which an enterprise assumes the gatekeeping role and operates at least 50 percent of the nodes – we'll get to this circumstance later in the chapter.)

If an enterprise participates in a permissionless blockchain application, an open-source community likely governs the decisions about changing rules, upgrading the software, or altering the permanent records, say in the case of a hack. The enterprise must be willing to defer to the community's will and live with the consequences of its majority rule. Hard forks happen when agreements cannot be reached (see Glossary entry, Forks (Hard)). Hard forks at Ethereum and Bitcoin are two prominent examples. Ethereum split into Ethereum and Ethereum Classic in June 2016 when the Ethereum community could not agree on how to handle the DAO hack discussed in Chapter 4; Bitcoin split into Bitcoin and Bitcoin Cash in August 2017 when the

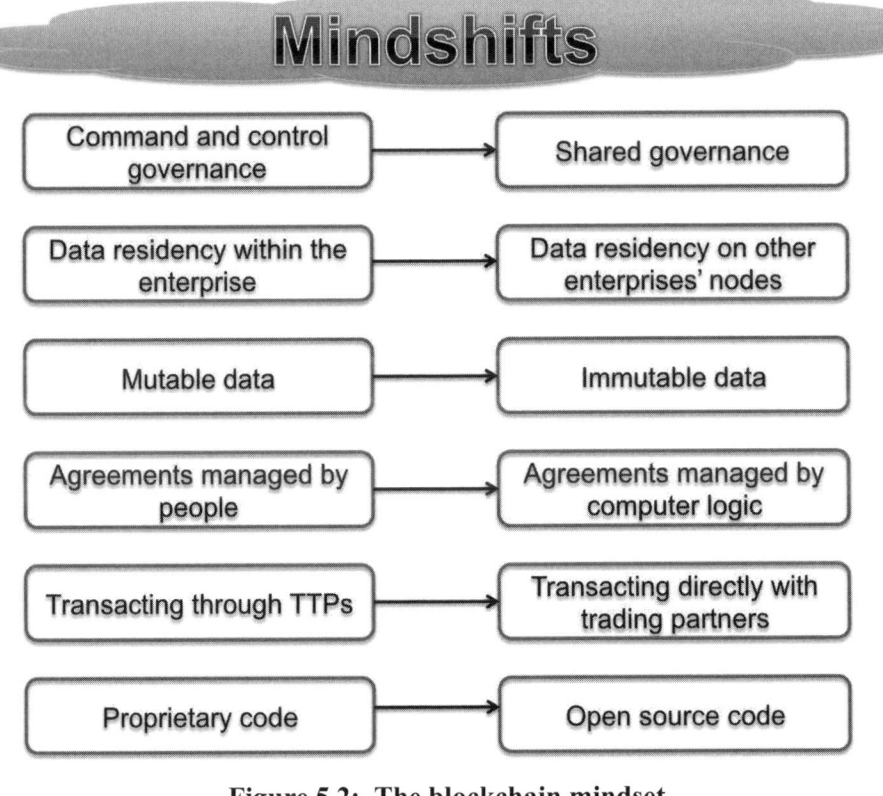

Figure 5.2: The blockchain mindset

community could not agree on the proposed increase in block size. Their stories are important reminders of the implications of shared governance.

If an enterprise participates in a permissioned blockchain application, again, a shared governance model will likely oversee the access rights and rules of the application. The parties will debate, deliberate and ultimately vote on proposed upgrades or fixes to address unexpected events like breeches or unintentional consequences from poorly crafted smart contracts. The enterprise may have a weighted vote in deliberations in proportion to their stake, but it will not be able to control them. However, at least with a permissioned blockchain application, there will be fewer voices in deliberations. The smallest viable permissioned blockchain application requires only four independent nodes, so coordinating changes will require less effort than in a permissionless blockchain.

5.2.2. Mindshift: From nodes in the enterprise's silos to immutable data residing on other parties' nodes

Is your enterprise ready to let its data reside on nodes operated by other parties? Granted, the data will be encrypted and smart contracts can create private states so only those privy to the smart contract can observe those records, but some of an enterprise's data will exist on trading partners' nodes. Additionally, an enterprise will also be using its computer resources to validate and store transactions for other parties, perhaps even when the enterprise is not a participant in those agreements.

5.2.3. Mindshift: From mutable data to immutable data

Is your enterprise ready for data permanency? Immutable records cannot be altered or erased, which assures parties that they are always relying on the same historical record of events. However, data permanency may violate some enterprise's data policies or some government's regulations. For example, some enterprises require that records be destroyed after a certain time period. Some regulations give individuals the 'right to be forgotten'. There's a lot to think about.

Practice Head for FS Analytics & Blockchain at a global technology and consulting organization explained that blockchain technologies could be designed to comply with data protection / retirement regulations. He said:

> *"We've developed a blockchain based application around GDPR – General Data Protection Regulation, a legal framework that sets guidelines for the collection and processing of personal information of individuals within the European Union (EU). We have built a very extensive application, which we are right now working on taking into production."[7]*

5.2.4. Mindshift: From agreements managed by people to agreements managed by computer logic

Is your enterprise ready for legal agreements that automatically execute? Most enterprises will use permissioned blockchains with smart contracting features, which is just programming logic to codify agreements that reside and execute on the blockchain. According to Deloitte:

"Careful and unambiguous wording is very hard to achieve, and remains so, whether contracts are written on paper or recorded on a blockchain. But if the scope of the smart contract is small enough, with limited complexity, foreseeing the consequences and testing for correctness are much easier."[8]

However, a key feature is that once deployed, smart contracts are supposed to be immutable – it would take a consensus among the shared governors to unwind them in the case of bad contract. While users are still getting accustomed to the idea of immutable data, they have not yet grown comfortable with immutable smart contracts. Vitalik Buterin, the creator of Ethereum, warned:

"It's hard for regular users to know that contracts they are interacting with do what they say they do, and do not have accidental or malicious bugs."[9]

Another question that often arises is this: Are smart contracts legal? Many people will state the maxim, 'code is not law', but smart contracts can be legal agreements. Thus, enterprises will need legal talent that understands how smart contracts work. An easy solution is to create a system that translates legal contract templates into smart contract code. Barclays Bank, for example, developed a user interface where people fill in variables on a legal contract template and the underlying smart contract code is automatically generated (see Figure 5.3). Barclays Bank envisioned that standard-making bodies ultimately would be in charge of the legal/smart contract 'templates' to ensure compliance and to facilitate standard agreements.[10]

5.2.5. Mindshift: From engaging trusted third parties to transacting directly

"There is a huge challenge to understand the way blockchain technology can really add value in traditional financial services. I think it really has the better proposition when we dispense with the trusted intermediaries."

Lead Digital Architect for a large global bank[11]

Is your enterprise ready to disengage from trusted third parties (TTP)? Blockchains promise to replace the functions of TTP intermediaries with computer algorithms. The entire risk profile shifts – a traditional enterprise will have to trust programs instead of other intuitions to mediate counter-party risks. Who does the enterprise sue if the computer algorithm malfunctions? Who reimburses the enterprise in cases of fraud or heists? Furthermore, even if an enterprise can get over these risk hurdles, they may not be able to disentangle from TTPs easily. Enterprises

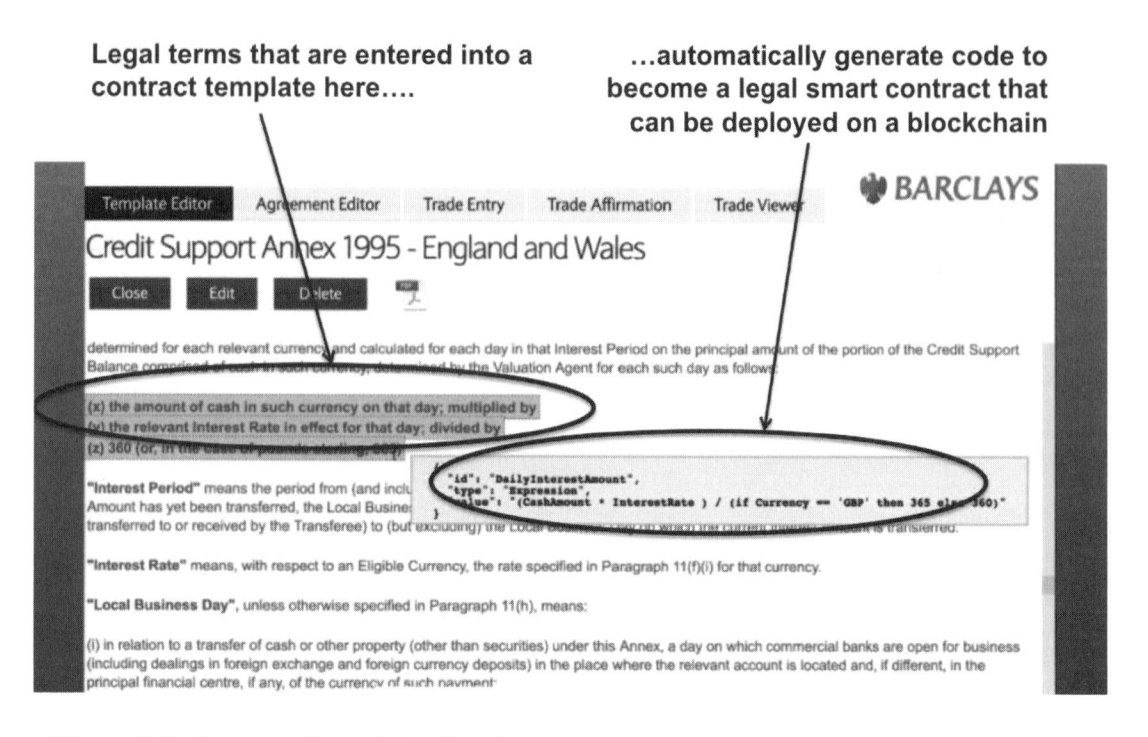

Figure 5.3: A screen shot of Barclays' prototype for a legal contract that automatically codes a smart contract for deployment on a blockchain

Source: adapted from Bitcoinwiki[13]

may have long-term contracts that cannot easily be broken, idiosyncratic investments in the relationship that cannot be recouped, or integrated services that are difficult to decouple. Certainly, disintermediation poses great threats to TTPs, and they therefore likely will strongly resist being replaced by blockchains and will seek to protect their business interests. Few people, for example, will be surprised to know that TTPs are among the top spenders lobbying the US Congress.[12] Even if an enterprise can eliminate part of its reliance on a TTP by moving to a blockchain application, the enterprise may rely on the TTP for other services for whose fees may escalate to compensate for the TTP's losses.

What if your enterprise is the trusted third party? The enterprise is advised to heed the action principles under the 'disruptive innovation' discussion later in this chapter.

5.2.6. Mindshift: From proprietary code to open source code

"Open source means we inherit the contributions of thousands of highly-qualified developers."

Amber Baldet, Program Lead for J.P. Morgan's Blockchain Center of Excellence[14]

"How do you get companies over the hurdle of going from a no to a yes to open innovation?"

General Manager for a large multinational conglomerate[15]

"Blockchains are not one man's story... you cannot build one prototype and produce an outcome. We have to work with all sorts of people, competitors, academics, startups, so it's a different mindset."

Head of Blockchain Innovation Lab for a multinational bank[16]

Is your enterprise ready to accept open-source code bases? There are pros and cons to open source software, and it's not easy for traditional enterprises to embrace them. On the positive side, when source code developed by an open community has had time to mature, it can be more secure, less expensive, with greater interoperability and auditability compared to proprietary software – provided there is a vibrant community of core developers, co-developers, bug reporters, and users.[17] Open source software also means that there are low barriers to entry – anyone can download the software and start experimenting. On the other hand, immature open source code means that vulnerabilities are public. Furthermore, an open source community does not always agree on the path a code base should follow.

Of course, many enterprises will convert open source code bases to propriety applications. This was indeed the route several enterprises in our study were considering:

"For healthcare, we are working with a private company developing proprietary source code because it's harder to hack than open source software. It can sit on top of open source, but will be shielded with proprietary code."

Innovation Director at a healthcare company[18]

"Open source through the Linux foundation allows a company to do plug-ins. So, if you had differentiation in, for example, a consent model, you could develop your own plug-in to support a differentiated business model."

Vice President for a global bank[19]

In summary, traditional enterprises will need to shift their mindsets about governance, data residency, data permanence, contract as code, contract permanency, open code bases, and mitigating counter-party risks when moving to distributed blockchain applications. The blockchain mindset helps the enterprise maneuver through the three phases of hard work, beginning with exploration.

5.3. Phase I: 'Cart before the horse' exploration

In the organizations we studied, an enterprise's initial interest in blockchains came from many places. Some senior executives read about blockchains in the business press; some operations managers learned about blockchains from an industry event; some innovation lab leaders downloaded open source software and played around with the code; some employees pursued it as a hobby. Yes, inspiration may come from anywhere! Moving from inspiration to action, many enterprises sought to more purposefully build technical blockchain capabilities, identify use cases, and build business-focused proof-of-concepts. A focus upon business uses of technical capabilities arose as a key theme. Here are the action principles research participants used:

1. ACTION PRINCIPLE: Create federated blockchain Center of Excellence (CoE)

"We think that because the solution comes from the study of pain points of clients, it needs to come from the business units."

Jacques Levet, Head of Transactional Banking, EMEA at BNP Paribas[20]

"You'll notice that our Center of Excellence is not massive in terms of the number of people. We are being very judicious about the skills we bring in. And the skills we want are more of the typical skills that you'd have in a technology firm."

Vice President for a global bank[21]

Given the technology-embeddedness challenge, traditional enterprises need to assemble a unit that focuses on coordinating the exploration of blockchain applications led by business operations. Several research participants erected a federated blockchain Center of Excellence (CoE) that reported high up in the organization but had deep ties to business operations. The CoE might have had other names, like the blockchain innovation 'hub' or 'lab', but in general, a federated CoE provided the technical expertise to support business units. The CoEs worked with stakeholders to identify use cases, led proof-of-concepts (POCs) that were owned by business sponsors, selected consortia with which to participate, and generally educated the enterprise about blockchains.

Within the large, traditional enterprises we studied, the number of dedicated people to a federated CoE was quite small, ranging from two to ten people. However, the number of part-time people from within and outside the enterprise could swell headcounts to three or four times those numbers, depending on the amount of POCs underway. Let's look at some specific examples of CoEs:

BNP Paribas. BNP Paribas bank believed that blockchain projects should be owned by the decentralized business units, but facilitated their activities with the centralized CoE for tool and knowledge sharing. Each blockchain project is linked via the centralized blockchain lab in Paris. The blockchain lab oversees the bank's blockchain toolkits and serves as a central repository and source of knowledge sharing across the divisions. The lab has only a few full-time employees as of 2017, as the bank's blockchain applications are developed and owned by the business units. The lab helps to mobilize needed resources, like coders, to support the decentralized blockchain teams. Another function of the lab is to encourage reuse of blockchain component parts.[22]

Capgemini. Capgemini, the Paris-based multinational IT consulting company, has nine Applied Innovation Exchange (AIE) centers around the world that coordinate technological innovations, including blockchains. Capgemini's client-facing blockchain services are embedded in the divisions because the most important blockchain capability, according to one executive, is its deep understanding of an industry's ecosystem. Its clients in financial services and in energy and utilities are the most interested in the potential effects of blockchains on their industries. Nilesh Vaidya, SVP Head of Banking & Capital Market Solutions at Capgemini explained:

"We have different parts in the company exploring their strategies on their own because various sectors feel the impact of Blockchain differently. So we have energy and utilities looking at it in one direction. Financial services are looking at it in another direction. Clients from other sectors will not be affected as quickly, so they will jump into it a little while later."[24]

World-wide, Capgemini filled 100 blockchain positions between 2016 and 2017.

The leaders of a federated CoE need to guard against redundancy and islands of innovation. One interviewee explained:

"Federalists allow business units to operate relatively independently. You get lots of benefit from that, but you also get some expected negative consequences and those are things like redundancy in the capabilities that are built independently across these businesses. We're at a point where we're trying to pull back from that and say, 'these should be enterprise platforms.'"

2. ACTION PRINCIPLE: Build or acquire the needed skillsets

"The underlying technology is very difficult to grasp; solving distributed problems is difficult. Companies need to find someone with experience to actually go and look at the underlying protocols and see which of these things will actually work, and then invest their time in those things."

Jed McCaleb, Cofounder and CTO of Stellar Development Foundation[25]

"The first thing we say is: Don't make a new blockchain. Developing a new blockchain requires quite a few masters degrees; quite a succinct understanding of mathematics and cryptography; and even after you have a whole team like that, then you need a marketing team to make people believe in you, to download and verify your platform."

Dev Bharel, Blockchain Solutions Architect with Nussbaumer Projects[26]

As with all innovations, human talent is a critical organizational resource for exploiting blockchain's capabilities. An enterprise needs subject matter experts (SMEs) and scarce technical skills like architects, decentralized application (DApp) specialists, blockchain coders and cryptographers. One of our interviewees estimated that there were only 5,000 people in the world with such technical skills. Enterprises likely will need to partner with consulting firms who snagged much of the global talent. Luckily beyond talent, proof-of-concepts among a few trading partners are not that expensive. Some POCs only cost $50,000 out of pocket (not accounting for staff time). Such small-scale experiments quickly build tomorrow's blockchain capabilities today.

Experience with open source software is another skill that is needed. Several companies in our study highlighted that for the first time ever in their organizations' long histories, they were serious about using and contributing to open source projects and recruited top managers specifically to help with the mindshift.

State Street Corporation. State Street hired Moiz Kohari to become Chief Technology Architect in September of 2016, in part because of his long history with open-source projects. He founded Mission Critical Linux in 1998, an open-source company, to build enhancements to the Linux operating system. He said:

> *"When State Street brought in my team, they understood they were signing up for open-sourced projects. If we were to leverage open source as core components and core technologies, the bank was going to have to participate in the open-source community. We have had senior management support around this from the beginning and I'm very grateful for that."* [27]

3. ACTION PRINCIPLE: Identify the process suitability of blockchains for potential use cases

> *"One of the biggest challenges is coming up with the right use case. Use cases range from provenance all the way to global payments, micropayments. We want to make sure that we can answer the question: How does this really add value to our clients?"*
>
> **Rahul Shah, Strategy Manager, Axiom Technology Group** [28]

> *"Blockchains are going to be valuable where there is friction and processes are actually broken. The current trend to try to apply blockchains for everything will change."*
>
> **Kiran Nagaraj, Managing Director, KPMG** [29]

"From a business perspective I'd always advise clients to ask themselves: 'Is there a need for decentralization?' Is there a need for removing multiple parties who are in the process just for the sake of infusing trust? Is there a need for data provenance to trace the transactions throughout the process? Those are the right use cases to look into."

Practice Head for FS Analytics & Blockchain at a global technology and consulting organization[30]

Identifying an impactful use case requires assessing both the technical and business suitability of a blockchain solution (see Figure 5.4).

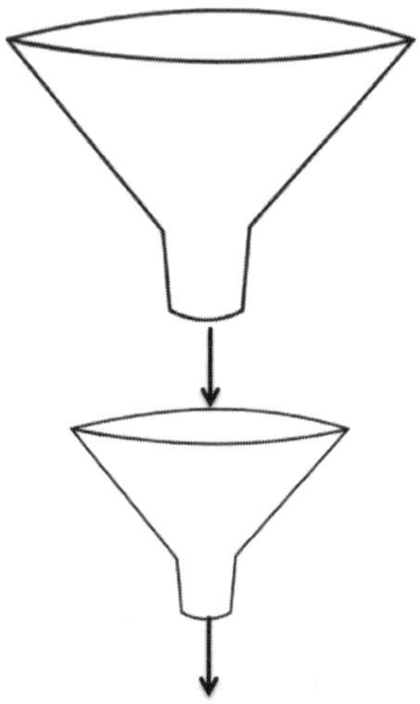

Generic Process Criteria:

- Inefficient intermediaries
- Lack of trust among trading partners
- Complex interdependencies
- Need for sharing data
- Need to improve the IT architecture

Business Specific Criteria:

- The sponsor comes from business operations
- The sponsor funds the POC
- The sponsor accepts the risks and knows many POCs will initially flounder

Use Cases for POCs

Figure 5.4: Criteria for identifying multiple uses cases for POCs

As a general set of criteria, blockchain applications are most suitable for processes with the following characteristics:

Inefficient intermediaries: The current business process relies on intermediaries that are too slow or too costly. Allowing trading partners to transact directly without relying on trusted third parties (TTP) is the main impetus for a blockchain application. Indeed, it was Satoshi Nakamoto's *raison d'être* for designing Bitcoin. A current business process where the TTPs add significant fees and slow transactions just to verify asset ownership and to prevent double spending, is the poster child use case for a blockchain application.

Some relevant questions to ask:

- For a given business process, would the enterprise benefit significantly from transacting directly with trading partners?
- Would the transaction cost savings more than compensate for the investment and change management costs of the blockchain?
- Would services be delivered at least an order of magnitude faster?

Lack of trust: Blockchains allow multiple parties who do not trust each other to share and update information safely. Some institutional organizations, particularly small-sized enterprises, do not trust their larger and more powerful trading partners.[31] A blockchain application levels the playing field by making all parties follow the same set of rules. Gideon Greenspan, CEO and Founder, Coin Sciences explained why the absence of trust is a use case criterion:

> *"Absence of trust: I mean that one user is not willing to let another modify database entries which it owns. Similarly, when it comes to reading the database's contents, one user will not accept as gospel the 'truth' as reported by another user, because each has different economic or political incentives."*[32]

Concerning Greenspan's last point, many business processes require an organization to verify signatures, identities, certifications, or documents provided by another organization or person. Because the receiving organization cannot trust the sending organization, time and resources are spent simply to verify information provided by other parties. For example, the US Council for Higher Education Accreditation estimated that more than 100,000 fake degrees are sold each year, costing, on average, just $1,000.[33] For this reason, HR Departments spend a lot of resources verifying information provided by job applicants. As another example, organizations use a lot of resources protecting themselves from duplicate or fake invoices. Antony Lewis, Founder of Bits on Blockchain, wrote:

> *"Even with a distributed ledger, does each party need to validate the results of someone else's calculations? Of course they do. It would be bonkers to rely entirely on someone else's calculations. The difference now is that the reconciliation comes*

before data is stored, rather than after. I wrote about distributed ledgers being 'confirm as you go' rather than 'confirm after the fact'. Switching the order makes a huge difference to operational risk."[34]

Some relevant questions to ask:

- Would the enterprise benefit from trusting computer algorithms instead of institutions or individuals?
- How would the risk profile for mitigating counter-party risks change?

Complex interdependencies: the business process requires multiple writers. Global supply chains provide a suitable example. As we learned in Chapter 3, today's global supply chains comprise a messy web of trading partners. Each party relies on others to synchronize the data about the flow of physical goods and services with the actual flow of goods and services. We learned that while manufacturers, exporters; couriers; freight forwarders; customs; inspectors; exporters; shippers; and importers are moving physical goods around the globe, they are also creating data about those movements with bills of lading; certifications; consignments; customs forms; inspections data; insurance forms; invoices; lines of credit; purchase orders; shipping manifestos; and receiving documents to name just a few. As a consequence of so many players with their own centralized systems and so much paperwork, assets get lost, shipping containers get delayed in ports because of missing paperwork, inconsistent records across trading partners trigger disputes, and counterfeit products slip through supply chains. A blockchain application promises to solve many of these problems, but requires a significant amount of cooperation and participation from other parties to define standards.

Some relevant questions to ask:

- How long and how much effort will be required to coordinate trading partners to define standards and to develop shared governance and funding models?
- How long and how much effort will be required to build, test, and deploy a shared blockchain solution?
- Could the enterprise join a working group, joint venture, or startup that already has made significant headway?

Need for sharing: The business process requires that the enterprise share its information with other parties.

Even when multiple writers are not involved in a transaction, some processes require enterprises to share information with 'observers', such as regulators. A blockchain application can store the minimal data needed for compliance and safely share it with authorized observers.

Need to improve the IT architecture: The centralized technology architecture poses significant security risks or is very inefficient.

> *"Our perimeter model of cybersecurity is broken. It's incredibly costly to maintain. And fundamentally is not going to be serviceable in the long-term as more and more economies come together. Right now, it's held together through sheer amount of brute force. But, we could do better. So, imagining how we can redesign our applications so that we have truly secure financial transactions could be very, very revolutionary."*
>
> **Amber Baldet, Program Lead for J.P. Morgan's Blockchain Center of Excellence[35]**

> *"No single point of failure exists because the entire distributed ledger is continuously replicated on all or at least a group of nodes in the network."*
>
> **McKinsey Report[36]**

Blockchain applications can de-risk critical infrastructure systems through distributed redundancy.[37] A blockchain application ignores faulty, malicious, or suspicious transactions and nodes. A blockchain application will continue to operate normally even if a high percentage of nodes are attacked. Redundancy also means 100 percent availability – a distributed data network cannot be shut down. If, for example, an enterprise's node goes offline, the other nodes in the network will continue to function properly and those other nodes will update the organization's node once it is back online.

Which critical infrastructure systems might be de-risked? Anthony Lewis, founder of Bits on Blocks, argued that a country's Real Time Gross Settlement (RTGS) is vulnerable to cyberterrorism and therefore suitable for a blockchain. If a country's RTGS system were hacked, Lewis noted that:

"A terrorist could halt commerce, hold the system for ransom, or steal billions of dollars. Moving an RTGS system to a blockchain application would mean the network could not be killed, it will always be running." [38]

Several large enterprises in our study planned to deploy internal blockchains to strengthen security and to simplify the architecture. The current IT architecture for these firms grew through mergers and acquisitions, resulting in a plethora of ledgers and systems across divisions. Blockchains were seen as a cost effective way to connect disparate systems. One participant from a Canadian bank explained:

"We've got internal use cases where we're looking at blockchains as simply a tool that can consolidate and bring efficiency to legacy systems."

The five criteria – inefficient intermediaries; lack of trust; complex interdependencies; the need to share data; and weak cybersecurity – focus attention on exploiting the technical benefits of blockchains. Enterprises will need to explore specific business use cases. Research participants uniformly agreed that business sponsors should conceive of use cases, with the CoE serving as expert advisors. An idea for a use case should only become a proof-of-concept if the business sponsor comes from operations, the business sponsor partly or wholly funds the POC, and the business sponsor understands the risks (see Figure 5.3).

4. ACTION PRINCIPLE: Launch multiple, business-led POCs

"You need a diverse mix of use cases and the kind of benefits you might expect from them, a diverse mix of the different business units that participate in the exercise, and diversity in the platforms such as Hyperledger, R3, Ethereum or Chain."

Head of a blockchain CoE for a global financial services firm [39]

Many enterprises chose to explore multiple business contexts simultaneously since POCs can be coded in as few as two weeks for mini-cases, and at very little cost. According to the executives we interviewed, out-of-pocket costs for a bootstrap, do-it-yourself blockchain POC ranged from $0 to $75,000. Of course these estimates did not consider indirect costs, such as time invested by stakeholders, or facilities costs, such as running servers and hosting meetings. In addition to low costs, many POCs did not require that much effort. Many enterprises in our research began by engaging some enthusiastic in-house technologists who downloaded an open source code base from somewhere like Github, and played with the code in the safety of a sandbox test environment. Next, enterprises brought together some business sponsors – as well as some eager-to-learn customers – to brainstorm thoughts, and then picked a few ideas for POCs. Let's look at how one enterprise identified business-focused use cases.

BNP Paribas. At BNP Paribas, the bank used two-day events called 'Bizhackathons' to bring both internal and external stakeholders together to identify how blockchains might impact their businesses. Internally, BNP invited stakeholders from across the enterprise, including people from business operations, IT, legal, and marketing. Externally, BNP invited key customers, as well as blockchain experts. On day one, BNP blockchain and outside blockchain experts explained blockchain technologies. On day two, the participants generated ideas about how blockchains might be used to disrupt the business. Experts were available for consultation, but the use cases were lead by business and customer stakeholders. BNP Paribas had done Bizhackathons for securities, big data distribution, trade finance, asset management, insurance, and real estate.[40]

5. *ACTION PRINCIPLE: Accept that high failure rates of POCs may be the fastest learning accelerator*

According to a study by TCS, between 70 and 80 percent of blockchain proof-of-concepts (POC) fail to meet their goals.[41] Blockchain advocates argue that failures are a natural part of the learning process. For example, Professor Emin Gün Sirer said:

> *"We're going to have to learn not to make a big deal out of failures… failures will happen… we should be comfortable with them."*[42]

Amber Baldet, Program Lead for J.P. Morgan's Blockchain Center of Excellence, echoed this:

> *"Failures shouldn't stop us from progressing... maybe four out of five pilots are going to fail. That should be okay as long as we're doing these in sandboxes or in ways that we're testing out the cybersecurity and operational implications."*[43]

While such failure rates may deter some managers from considering blockchain applications, we return to those arguments from Chapter 1 as to why many managers should proceed with their own exploration. Blockchain applications are coming, and every enterprise will need some in-house capabilities to assess whether they want to lead, be fast followers, or take a slower pace to adopting enterprise blockchains. Furthermore, while blockchain POC failure rates may be initially high, the learning gained will more than offset what often can be a minor expense.

6. ACTION PRINCIPLE: Participate broadly in blockchain workgroups

"The way we go about investing in blockchain is really multifaceted since nobody knows today which players will prevail… you cannot put all your eggs in one basket, so we have a very diversified approach with whom we work on the blockchain."

Jacques Levet, Head of Transaction Banking, EMEA at BNP Paribas[44]

"At this stage in the game, we're not informed enough to pick a winner. There are lots of people vying for this strategic high ground, so I think it's important for us to engage in places and keep our fingers on the pulse of all of them rather than try and pick a winner at a way too early stage."

Head of a blockchain CoE for a global financial services firm[45]

"So, from a strategy point of view, it's early days. We're probably in the situation that all the other big financial institutions are at the moment. Nobody's really backing one horse. We're all trying to get to know as much about it as possible and see where it takes us. All we know is that it's going to be extremely disruptive."

IT Consultant and Architect for an African-based bank[46]

In Chapter 1, we introduced the idea of working groups – organizations that are defining blockchain standards and developing code bases upon which to build blockchain applications. Large blockchain consortia may be the best bet for scalability in the long-run, but some are slow to agree upon standards or to develop actual applications. The value of smaller consortia is that players can move faster; the downside risks are lack of wider-spread adoption or eventual obsolesce if a new standard or platform emerges in the industry. As the quotes above exemplify, many global firms mitigate the risk of backing the wrong horse by participating in both large and small consortia.

BNP Paribas. For example, BNP Paribas participated in both large and small consortia and had invested in several FinTechs to influence, learn, and contribute to blockchain initiatives. A large consortium like R3 was very valuable because it brings many financial institutions into the conversation. Jacques Levet said:

> *"R3 is very useful because it's a way to organize discussions between the banks. Banks have historically not been very good at doing that on their own, so having a third party who organizes that is quite useful."*

BNP Paribas also joined two smaller consortia, with the goal that the banks will define standards and create a Request for Proposal (RFP) for FinTechs to develop the specified blockchain application.[47]

7. ACTION PRINCIPLE: Disseminate learning broadly across the enterprise

> *"Initially, it's important to evangelize new ideas internally. People miss that step."*
>
> **James Allen Regenor, Business Unit Director, Transformative Technologies Moog Inc.**[48]

> *"That's kind of our mandate. Education, awareness – making sure everyone knows what blockchains are and how they will affect them. More importantly let's not push this to the back burner, let's make sure that we're actively engaged in exercising the technology and exercising the business concepts as well as the business opportunities, through use cases and prototypes."*
>
> **Head of a blockchain CoE for a global financial services firm**[49]

Senior managers, colleagues, and employees may have formed opinions based solely on popular media coverage, particularly around cryptocurrencies. Therefore blockchain champions will need to disseminate broadly knowledge about the business value of blockchains. Champions may need to overcome the negative publicity caused by malicious acts like stolen cryptocurrencies, money laundering,[50] and illegal markets.[51] Equally of concern are the blockchain prophets who exaggerate the current maturity of blockchain applications and understate the challenges.

How can blockchain champions educate the entire enterprise about blockchains? Executives we interviewed used seminars, webinars, business hackathons, new digital tokens and cryptocurrency mining. Here are a few examples:

183

At State Street, the Emerging Technology Center hosted a blockchain seminar for 300 employees, with an additional 1200 employees attending remotely. Given that State Street only has 33,700 employees, this number of attendees is significant – representing five percent of the company with just a single event.[52]

Fidelity Investments made Bitcoin available for use in its company cafeteria, and allowed employees to donate Bitcoin assets to the company's Fidelity Charitable Donor program.[53]

Several organizations use their own cryptocurrencies to widely disseminate knowledge about blockchains, including Deloitte and Capgemini. Deloitte launched Dcoin to serve as an internal employee rewards program. Capgemini created SRTCoin (Satoshi Roundtable Coin) in 2015 to experiment, test and disseminate knowledge about cryptocurrencies. Rather than a proof-of-work mechanism to earn new coins, Capgemini used a 'proof of listening' mechanism. Once a week, there was a blockchain call where a 'magic word' would be revealed. Employees could retrieve coins by entering the magic word on a web-based application that stored the wallets.[54]

"It was a fun experiment. We used it to evangelize it [blockchain] internally."

Nilesh Vaidya, SVP Head of Banking & Capital Market Solutions at Capgemini[55]

Once enterprises have built up enough understanding about blockchain technologies, they are better able to decide which POCs to move to pilots and eventually into production.

5.4. Phase II: 'Horse before the cart' strategic intent

"I think that there are selective examples where a blockchain can be disruptive… like remittances, custody, and transfer agent work. Blockchain is not universally disruptive. It is certainly universally transformative and in strategic areas, it is selectively disruptive."

Eamonn Maguire, Global Lead, Digital Ledger Services, KPMG[56]

As noted in Chapter 2, enterprises have experimented with hundreds of blockchain uses cases across all industries.[57] From the perspective of a traditional enterprise, our research found traditional enterprises pursuing blockchain applications for three different strategic intents, of which the first two come from Clayton Christensen's Theory of Disruptive Innovation (see Table 5.1).[58] The three strategic intents are:

(1) as a **sustaining innovation** that strengthens the enterprise's current business model by improving the performance of its products and services for its high-end customers;[59]

(2) as a **disruptive innovation** that supplants the enterprise's current business model with a new business model to deliver a product or service that targets underserved customers or creates an entirely new market;[60]

(3) as a **consortium-led innovation** that is shared across trading partners to create benefits for all parties.

	Sustaining Innovations	Disruptive Innovations	Consortiun-led Innovations
Strategic Intent	Strengthen the prevailing business model by improving the performance of current products and servcies to better serve today's high-end customers	Build a new bisiness model to sell to under-served customers or to create a new market where none exists.	Coordinate transactions among trading partners to benefit all parties.
Locus of Control	The enterprise	The enterprise	Shared among trading partners
Motto	"We keep getting better"	"If we don't disrupt ourselves, someone will do it to us"	"Rising tides raise all ships"
Action Principles	8. Co-create applications with select customers 9. Buy as a service	10. Get real about disruption 11. Create an independent spin-off; else ... 12. Closely monitor the noisy yet well-funded startup space to possibly invest in, acquire or rapidly respond to viable threats	13. Narrow participation to a few, key working groups 14. Understand the workgroup's IP policy
	15. Actively work with regulators		
Examples	• Cross-border payments • Trade settlements • Securities lending	• Solar energy sharing • Additive manufacturing • Electric car charge sharing	• Track & trace pharmaceuticals

Table 5.1: Strategic intents of blockchain applications

Whereas an enterprise can control the first two innovation types within the boundaries of the firm, the last innovation type requires a neutral organization – like a non-profit consortium – to comply with anti-trust regulations. At first glance, the first two types seem counter to the spirit of a blockchain application – aren't we just back to a centralized system governed by a single enterprise? The answer depends on which organizations are actually operating nodes. In the circumstance where a single enterprise operates all of the nodes, yes we are back to a centralized governance model. For example, a large global enterprise might use a blockchain application for inter-divisional transactions. However, in the circumstance where a single entity operates less than fifty percent of the nodes, then power stays distributed. The case studies of Ripple and Stellar from Chapter 3 provide good examples. Ripple and Stellar are companies that built and operate their blockchain applications, but institutional customers also operate nodes. Let's closely examine each strategic type…

5.4.1. Sustaining innovations

"Blockchains bring the ability to significantly reduce costs to our clients. If our clients surrender the reduction of costs to their competition when using the blockchain, they will be at a significant disadvantage from both profitability and pricing points of view. I think that there are selective examples where a blockchain can be disruptive, but for the vast majority of our clients, blockchains are at the forefront of transformations that will reduce costs."

Eamonn Maguire, Global Lead, Digital Ledger Services, KPMG[61]

"In all the use cases, we have to define a strategy. Let's say we streamline the collateral process first – there's an element of cost elimination, and there's an element of additional revenues because you can onboard more customers when you streamline the process, make it less cumbersome and less workload heavy."

Head of Distributed Ledger Technologies for a global bank[62]

"I do think that you're going to see, certainly, internal applications of blockchain going forward in 2017 because it's a lot easier in a lot of ways when it's within your own walls."

John Burnett, Head of Blockchain Development for State Street[63]

Enterprises are rapidly exploring blockchains to improve the performance of their existing products and services to better serve today's high-end customers. These applications keep incumbents competitive within their existing markets by "sustaining" the enterprise's current business model.[64] As of 2018, we found that sustaining innovations were the most common type among traditional enterprises, as they fit well within an enterprise's existing business models.

With the motto, *'we keep getting better'*, sustaining innovations have the lowest organizational resistance to change among the three types. Sustaining blockchain applications are led by the enterprise and can run in parallel with existing systems for side-by-side comparison. BNP Paribas, Australian Securities Exchange and State Street, exemplify sustaining innovations.

BNP Paribas. BNP Paribas built a blockchain application to settle its customers' cross-border payments within hours instead of days and at a fraction of the cost compared to the legacy route of national payment systems and corresponding banking relationships. BNP Paribas expected that this and other blockchain applications would not change what the bank does, but rather how the bank does it. The bank was also exploring the use of blockchains to improve the existing IT architecture. Like most global banks, BNP has grown through mergers and acquisitions, resulting in a legacy of non-integrated and inefficient systems of record. In the future, the bank foresees that blockchain technologies will enhance or even replace legacy systems with a more efficient and cost effective infrastructure.[65]

The Australian Securities Exchange (ASX). The ASX planned to replace its existing post-trade settlement system[66] with a blockchain application in the later part of 2018.[67] The new blockchain application aims to benefit both investors and traders by giving them more control over their transactions and by enabling faster and less costly settlements.[68] Thus, ASX is improving the performance of its current services for its high-end customers.

State Street Corporation. State Street was also building blockchains to improve services. It had nearly a dozen proof-of-concepts for two types blockchains by mid-2017: internal blockchains with existing clients and for back offices (sustaining innovations) and blockchains with trading partners for business-to-business transactions or for multi-party transactions (consortium-led innovations).[69] State Street will first move internal blockchains from POC to deployment. Securities lending is an example.[70] State Street did not have an automated way to determine to which account collateral should be returned and thus required a lot of manual intervention. The bank also had to keep diligent records of securities lending transactions to comply with regulations. State Street built an internal blockchain application in 2016 that automated collateral management for securities lending while at the same time creating an auditable trail. The blockchain application transforms the investor's posted collateral into a digital token that can be used for other transactions. This creates a permanent record of how the collateral had been used and how to return the collateral to the borrower's account once the transaction was complete.[71]

8. ACTION PRINCIPLE: Co-create applications with select customers to make sure the sustaining application will be truly valued by customers

Because a sustaining innovation aims to add value for an enterprise's high-end customers, it follows that those customers should be included in the development process. ASX, BNP Paribas, and State Street all involved customers in the conception, development and testing of their blockchain applications. ASX completed its POC in 2016, but spent the next year and a half seeking customer input on required system features and on desired transition and implementation services.[72]

BNP Paribas. The bank will not launch an innovation project unless it has clients co-developing projects with it. Jacques Levet, Head of Transaction Banking for EMEA, said,:

> "We believe that if the idea is good, we should be able to convince at least one or two clients to do co-development."

Co-development does not mean that clients fund the blockchain projects – indeed they do not. Rather, clients work with the bank to identify pain points, brainstorm ideas, define requirements and participate in testing and feedback.[73] When Jacques Levet was asked to offer advice to other financial institutions, he answered:

> "The one [piece of] advice I would give [to other financial institutions] is to include your clients from day one, because you learn that most of the time they know exactly what they need and what they want. They have a vision that is very different from ours and it's extremely important to make sure that whatever we develop is actually an answer to a particular client need." [74]

Levet credits client participation for the rapid development and for the ultimate success of the bank's POCs.

9. ACTION PRINCIPLE: Buy sustaining innovations as service

Incumbent enterprises do not necessarily have to build sustaining innovations – they can buy them as a service. From Chapter 3, we learned that Ripple's customers are primarily institutional enterprises like banks, corporates, payment providers and exchanges. For banking customers, Ripple promises that banks will capture new revenue by booking new corporate and consumer clients, reduce their transaction costs, and provide one integration point and a consistent experience for rules, standards and governance.[75]

Microsoft, Hewlett-Packard Enterprise (HPE), and IBM provide 'Blockchain-as-a-Service' (BaaS). Microsoft was one of the first service providers to offer BaaS in 2015. Its Azure cloud platform supports many code bases such as Ethereum, Hyperledger Fabric, R3 Corda, Quorum, Chain Core and BlockApps. HPE's BaaS supports Corda;[76] IBM's BaaS supports Hyperledger Fabric.[77]

5.4.2. Disruptive innovations

"Large banks are obviously enamored by blockchain. They all have innovation labs that are digging into it, but I don't see the change coming from there. Going from proof-of-concept to actual production is a huge, long road. It's hard to basically cannibalize your own business. It's hard to give up centralized control. Large institutions are calcified, they benefit form the status quo. So that's why we don't focus that much on large banks. We spend most of our time on these smaller, innovative financial institutions because they're able to move much quicker."

Jed McCaleb, Cofounder and CTO of Stellar Development Foundation[78]

"How do you actually get folks who are so heavy driven by meeting a quarter and making the numbers to actually look at technologies that could completely disrupt their business? They're just too busy and they don't have time."

General Manager for a large multinational conglomerate[79]

Disruptive blockchain applications aim to dramatically reduce costs and thereby target undemanding customers who want low cost alternatives to existing products or services. Disruptive applications can also create entirely new markets.[80] Theory tells us that most disruptions come from nimble startups because it's very hard for incumbent enterprises to break their successful business models and cannibalize revenues from existing products and services. The quote above from Jed McCaleb certainly indicates this view. The theory also asserts that global enterprises rationally ignore disruptive innovations because they are initially too risky, the market is too small, the quality is too poor, and they target a different set of customers. Of course, many potentially disruptive technologies fail. The theory says that by the time a disruptive innovation moves from a potential threat to a serious threat, it is often too late for the incumbents to act.[81] What should incumbents do today? Incumbent enterprises should create an independent spin-off if they are serious about disrupting themselves; else closely monitor the noisy yet well-funded blockchain startup space to possibly invest in, acquire, or rapidly respond to viable threats.

Much of our empirical evidence aligned with theory. Most notably, Moog and Innogy – covered in Chapter 3 –were creating low-end market disruptions and new markets, and were doing so as predicted by Christensen – by creating an independent joint venture and spin-off, respectively. As predicted by theory, we have also seen corporations investing in blockchain startups and projects. Corporations have invested over $1.2 billion in blockchain companies between 2012 and 2017.[82] USAA; NYSE; CME Group; Wells Fargo; JP Morgan; Visa; MasterCard; Citi; Google; DTCC; SBI holdings; Google; Overstock.com; Goldman Sachs; and Nasdaq are just some examples[83] (see Chapter 1).

The following action principles may help enterprises maneuver through the challenges:

10. ACTION PRINCIPLE: Get real about disruption

We interviewed many executives from traditional enterprises who expressed some form of the motto, "If we don't disrupt ourselves, someone will do it to us."[84] No organization wanted to be the next Blockbuster. Representative quotes include:

> "You see some things, particularly in radiology, where a patient pays $800 for an MRI in a physician's office, and ours cost $2,400. Which do you think somebody's going to go to for an MRI? There's a point where you have to disrupt yourself."
>
> **Innovation Director for a healthcare company**[85]

> "If we don't change our business model and look where we can add value, where we will earn income, somebody else is going to come and do it for us."
>
> **IT Consultant for a large global bank**[86]

Upon closer inspection, however, many traditional enterprises in our study were actually building sustaining innovations, but calling them 'disruptive'. It's hard to truly embrace disruption when an enterprise is faced with potential losses of millions or billions of dollars. Consider the perspective of a healthcare payer.

Healthcare Company. Healthcare insurance companies have amassed some of the largest holds on cash compared to any other industry.[87] According to one interviewee, healthcare payers don't want to be disrupted – they make money by sitting on huge stores of cash. He said:

> *"Payers don't want claims to be streamlined with a blockchain. One of them told me he took it to their executives for review and was told, 'don't bring this back up... it is career limiting for you.' That's what we are fighting against. They can see losing money if claims are immediately adjudicated."*

He fears that the only thing that will prompt real change in healthcare is a complete financial collapse – or perhaps a completely new business model? Despite the obstacles, he is committed to disrupting his own company's business model and spends time evangelizing the message to senior management. He continued:

> *"We need to design a consumer-centric, transparent healthcare system. I want to use blockchains to disrupt the current system, because it will be insolvent in ten years if we don't."*

11. ACTION PRINCIPLE: Create a joint venture or independent spin-off

For large enterprises, joint ventures or spin-offs may be the easiest path to disruption. As covered in Chapter 3, RWE's Innogy, the German-based electric utility, spun-off a separate company called Share&Charge from its corporate innovation center to launch a blockchain-based application that creates a market for individuals to buy and sell capacity from electric car charging stations.[88] Moog was building a blockchain-enabled platform to verify 3-D printed parts. It planned to launch a joint venture by first quarter 2019. Maersk announced plans to create a joint venture with IBM to move their blockchain solution to market.[89] As noted above, these practices are consistent with Christensen's theory.

12. *ACTION PRINCIPLE: Monitor the blockchain startup space to possibly invest in, acquire, or rapidly respond to viable threats*

In Chapter 1, we noted that there are over 1500 blockchain startups. New start-ups will be the most common source of disruptive blockchain applications because they have no legacy barriers. In Chapter 3, we featured several startups. Ripple and Stellar had already deployed live blockchains. Provenance was about as far along as other supply chain giants, with successful pilots and headed towards a wider variety of applications.

LO3 Energy. LO3 Energy was running an operational blockchain application with 560 participants; it was just awaiting a license before switching the application from a shadow market to a live market. Concerning LO3, we asked Lawrence Orsini, the CEO, this question: How were incumbent utilities responding to LO3? Orsini made it clear that LO3's business model does not rely on cooperation from the incumbent utility provider, but he foresees that incumbent utilities could become adopters (or partners of adopters) of its transactive energy platform. He added:

> *"Nobody is suggesting that we're going to put utilities out of business. What we're suggesting is that it's time to evolve a business model that hasn't changed for a hundred years. So, we're talking with them about active participation in this future."*

Indeed Ameren, the electricity utility provider that services the US states of Missouri and Illinois, seems willing to look at its business model. It invested in Omegagrid, a startup that aims to build a blockchain-enabled energy grid in 2017.

5.4.3. Consortium-led innovations

> *"The benefit of the Center is that we adhere to Anti-Trust Laws and participants recognize that, even if they are competitors, we are working for the common good of the industry."*
>
> **Bob Celeste, CEO and Founder of the Center for Supply Chain Studies**[90]

> *"Blockchains will affect market structures. This is not a change internal to the organization. Unlike some technologies, which you want to automate, then, fine, you develop your own business classes, you use your own technology; you change your*

192

own organization. Blockchains are going to impact market structures: How will interactions between partners change? What will be the incentives? Who has the power in the market to make those changes?"

Nilesh Vaidya, SVP Head of Banking & Capital Market Solutions at Capgemini[91]

"Blockchains are a very ambitious technology platform. It's not like web services that can easily be adopted. It's more far-reaching than that and will take time to fully mature."

Vice President for a Global Bank[92]

Blockchains have the potential to help all trading partners in an existing market – think 'rising tides raise all ships'. Consortium-led innovations likely will require the most time among the three types to move to market. Indeed, deployed applications may be years away because many challenges first must be addressed. Success requires a high level of collaboration among traditional competitors to agree upon standards about which information to store on a blockchain, message types and formats, what access rights should be given to whom, whether permanency and immutability of records is desirable, and who should govern the blockchain, particularly if there are disputes. To comply with anti-trust regulations, traditional competitors need a neutral third-party like a consortium to coordinate activities.

The Center for Supply Chain Studies. In Chapter 3, the Center for Supply Chain Studies[93] in the pharmaceutical sector provides an example of a consortium-led innovation. The center is helping 50 companies – including pharmaceutical manufacturers, distributors, and retail pharmacies – to define requirements for a shared trading platform that will comply with new US government regulations that will require the entire US pharmaceutical supply chain to trace certain drug classes on one shared electronic system by 2023. Phase 1 of the study is complete. The group defined several different reference models for which data might be shared and stored on a blockchain, as well as the access rights and rules by which parties may transact. Phase 2, launched in January 2018, will develop a POC based on Phase 1's reference models.

While consortium-led blockchains have the power to transform entire industry structures[94], there are indeed challenges. Some executives felt they were paying industry consortia for the right to give away their intellectual property. Others worried that a blockchain might allow competitors to mine the blockchain to reveal secret information about sales volumes, returns, prices, and major customers. Even the very visible and successful consortia have faced significant challenges. R3 serves as one such example. It's been successful in deploying the Corda code base and building POCs with its members, but struggled to manage so many participants.

Nine banks initially joined a consortium called R3 in 2015: Barclays; Banco Bilbao Vizcaya Argentaria (BBVA); the Commonwealth Bank of Australia; Credit Suisse; Goldman Sachs; J.P. Morgan; Royal Bank of Scotland; State Street; and the Swiss bank, UBS.[95] Membership continued to expand, and by 2016, it had more than 80 members from across the globe. Its membership numbers fluctuate, and several early members subsequently left R3. Goldman Sachs, for example, left the consortium in 2016 because it had gotten too large. According to an article in Fortune Magazine:

> *"A person familiar with Goldman's internal thinking said that the bank did not expect R3 to mushroom to 70-plus members when it initially joined. The number of participants and competing interests made negotiations more difficult."*

Morgan Stanley, Santander Bank and JP Morgan also left the R3 consortium. Large membership fees prompted some departures."[96]

R3's membership evolution is typical. Early on, enterprises participate widely in many consortia (see Action Principle 6), but as they gain experience, they focus attention and investments.

13. *ACTION PRINCIPLE: Narrow participation to a few key working groups*

> *"Initially, State Street cast a reasonably wide net in our search for blockchain initiatives. We were really looking at pretty much every effort under the sun. However, last year, we began to devote more of a focus on specific projects supported by the Linux Foundation. Many of its initial contributors are from my team."*
>
> **Moiz Kohari, SVP and Chief Technology Architect, State Street Corporation**[97]

> *"Eventually a few chains will mature, and we'll be left with four or five key blockchains, perhaps by the end of 2018."*
>
> **Rahul Shah, Strategy Manager, Axiom Technology Group**[98]

During the exploration phase, enterprises typically 'hedged their bets' by engaging with many blockchain working groups. But as learning accumulated and clear strategies emerged, many enterprises decided to 'double down' on a few, or even a single group. For example, State Street initially investigated many types of blockchain technologies and had joined several groups.

State Street Corporation. State Street was a founding member of the R3 consortium in 2015, the Hyperledger Project in 2015, and the Ethereum Alliance in 2017. It also participated in proof-of-concepts with several groups such as the Post Trade Distributed Ledger Group in Europe and the Irish Funds Industry Association for regulation compliance. As recently as January 2017, State Street aimed to be 'blockchain agnostic'. By August 2017, State Street decided to focus participation on Hyperledger Fabric. According to Moiz Kohari, SVP and Chief Technology Architect for State Street:

> *"We decided to concentrate on Fabric because it's open-sourced and one of the more scalable solutions available. It was also significant to me that many of Fabric's strategic contributors are State Street employees."*[99]

State Street will continue to monitor all major blockchain projects, but deployments, at least for the near-term, will be developed using Fabric.

As part of a working group, the enterprise will have to work with members to define shared governance structures, shared funding models, and shared intellectual property (IP). Concerning this last item, the following action principle applies:

14. ACTION PRINCIPLE: Be sure to understand the working group's IP policy

As noted in Chapter 1, there are over 40 major global blockchain consortia and countless smaller ones. Some consortia like the Hyperledger Project have visible IP policies, while others like R3 do not. For example, Hyperledger's charter includes a clearly worded IP clause that in part reads:

> *'Members agree that all new inbound code contributions to HLP (Hyperledger Project) shall be made under the Apache License, Version 2.0. All contributions shall be accompanied by a Developer Certificate of Origin sign-off that is submitted through a Governing Board and LF-approved contribution process. Such contribution*

process will include steps to also bind non-Member Contributors and, if not self-employed, their employer, to the licenses expressly granted in the Apache License, Version 2.0 with respect to such contribution... Subject to available Project funds, HLP may engage The Linux Foundation to determine the availability of, and register, trademarks, service marks, and certification marks – which shall be owned by the LF.'[100]

R3's IP policies were not available to the public as of May 2017. An article by the Business Insider reported:

'Details about R3's share structure are not being disclosed, neither are details about the division of the intellectual property built atop the open-source Corda platform. However, Rutter (R3's CEO) did explain that while Corda itself is being open-sourced, the results of experiments conducted with partners within the R3 lab would be guarded more closely.' [101]

We interviewed leaders and members from consortia that required members to sign non-disclosure agreements, but they did not all have signed IP agreements. One interviewee from a large bank explained:

"Our industry is behind some other industries in our management of shared IP and our ability to collaborate and cooperate. We all jumped in to explore a use case and did some joint design thinking with two or three traditional competitors without thinking about who owns the intellectual capital that comes out the tail end of that workshop. Then, if you do highlight the need for some agreement there, getting to common ground on what that agreement needs to look like and who should own the IP, it's sometimes weeks or even months in lead time. We as an industry need to work faster on those kind of repeatable processes."

For one consortium, the group did not want to delay the project to wait for large members to maneuver through the onerous process of signing an IP agreement. To protect the group's IP in the absence of formal IP agreements, the head of one consortium recorded all meetings so that none of its members could subsequently file a patent.

For one small French consortium, our question about IP protection amused the interviewee:

"In the US, your motto 'In God We Trust' should be 'In IP We Trust'. In France, the motto is 'Liberty, Equality, Fraternity', so we share IP. That's a cultural difference between the US and Europe."

Regardless of whether an enterprise is pursuing sustaining, disruptive, or consortia-led innovations, all enterprises must comply with laws and regulations. Thus, the following action principle applies to all enterprises during Phase II:

15. ACTION PRINCIPLE: *Actively work with regulators*

"So far, the interactions with regulators have been really positive. We've met with central banks in various places like Luxembourg, Bahrain, and India. They understand that this technology can be very useful. Stellar doesn't change the regulatory story for the financial institutions that are using it, but it gives regulators a more transparent view."

Jed McCaleb, Cofounder and CTO of Stellar Development Foundation[102]

"We don't know how the regulators are going to respond. At the end of the day, I think the early indications suggests that they're as intrigued by the value proposition associated with Blockchain as anybody. No regulator has come out of the gates telling you what you can and cannot do yet. That's a big unknown in our world."

Head of a blockchain CoE for a global financial services firm[103]

"Regulators should embrace blockchains. Instead of trolling through emails and multiple systems to reconstruct history, a regulator can just look at the provenance through blockchain. Imagine if a brokerage could show the SEC the trades history through a blockchain. They could show, 'this is how the transaction started, this is how the front office processed it, this is how the middle office made changes, this is how the risk department assessed it, and then the settlement was done here.'"

Practice Head for FS Analytics & Blockchain at a global technology and consulting organization[104]

Chapter 1 spoke about the regulatory uncertainty in the context of blockchains. As of 2018, some regulators are supportive, some are not, and still others have yet to deliberate. Many participants in this research wanted to educate regulators about blockchains, but at the same time, did not want regulators participating too closely in consortia lest their compliance weaknesses be exposed. Among all the enterprises examined, LO3 Energy and Moog, Inc. had the most lessons to offer about regulations.

LO3 Energy. Lawrence Orsini has worked very closely with regulators and policy makers since he launched the company in 2012. He's met with regulators from the US at both the State and Federal levels, as well with regulators from Australia and Europe.[105] He views his job as explaining the technology to help them understand what his blockchain enables: a local, renewable, efficient 'microgrid' that operates separately, but alongside, the utility grid. He hired lawyers who understood regulatory requirements. Orsini said:

> *"We've spent a fair amount of time and a decent amount of investment making sure that we can work within existing regulations. Lots of other people talking about doing something similar to us have never even considered how that impacts regulation. It takes a real strong team of regulatory attorneys to understand, and be able to fit legally within the existing regulation."*[106]

Orsini was among a minority of research participants who praised regulators for being receptive. He said:

> *"We have a very good relationship with the regulators. The regulators in New York are pretty excited about and engaged in what we're doing, particularly for the transactive energy platform."*[107]

Moog, Inc. James Allen Regenor, Business Unit Director for Transformative Technologies Moog Inc., was also an early advocate of getting regulations for verifying parts created by additive manufacturing. As covered in Chapter 3, he needed the US government to create 3-D printing regulations for Department of Defense (DoD) acquisitions. Regenor took the current federal regulations for electronic parts and substituted the word 'electronic' for 'additive manufacturing' and brought it to legislators.[108] Moog also informed the US House Armed Services Committee about the threat of counterfeiting for additive manufactured parts. Legislators understood the concern; the National Defense Authorization Act of 2018 includes funds for additive manufacturing technology development and requires briefings on blockchain technologies from agencies.[109]

As a final note on Moog, we have focused on VeriPart as a disruptive innovation, but Regenor sees VeriPart as a **hybrid innovation** that will better serve high-end customers as well as target underserved customers. Most certainly, Moog's most demanding customers in aerospace will gain tremendous value from VeriPart and some of its largest customers are eager participants in its POCs. Regenor also sees how the platform will attract new customers. He said:

> *"A Mom & Pop 3-D print shop may not have a metallurgist expert on staff, but they could access the services of a metallurgist across the platform."*

5.5. Phase III: Critical mass

> *"Most of the organizations that we're speaking to are at an exploratory phase. Pretty much saying, 'we're trying to understand this'. Very few have really identified use cases that they're going to production scale and get a critical mass of partners on within the next six to ten months. But this is changing fast."*
>
> **Practice Head for FS Analytics & Blockchain at a global technology and consulting organization**[110]

As of 2018, few enterprises have reached this final phase of reaching a critical mass of adopters to truly transform trading. Traditional enterprises, startups, joint ventures, and consortia working on blockchain applications, will each aim to become their industry's defacto standard. Among all the challenges discussed in this guide, gaining a critical mass is the greatest one. Unfortunately, the enterprises we interviewed had not advanced enough to offer concrete action principles. For those enterprises ready to gain critical mass but do not know how, theory again informs the process.

The Theory of Institutional Isomorphism models the process of homogenization among organizations facing similar environmental conditions.[111] Essentially, the theory seeks to answer the question: Why do organizations within an industry eventually change to become more alike? Paul DiMaggio and Walter Powell (1991) posited that organizations eventually adopt similar structures, processes, philosophies, practices, and technologies through three mechanisms of influence (see Figure 5.5).[112]

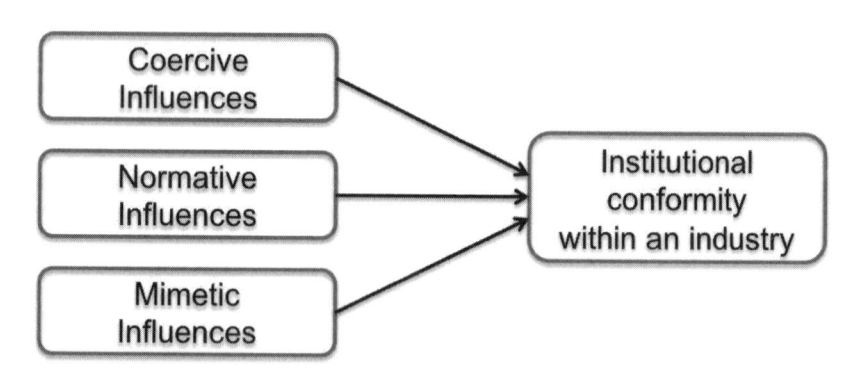

Figure 5.5: Three influences that pressure institutions to conform

Adapted from DiMaggio and Powell (1991)[113]

16. ACTION PRINCIPLE: *Exploit three influence sources to gain a critical mass of adopters*

"The only motivation for a shift to blockchains would be aggressive new regulation."

Gideon Greenspan, CEO and Founder, Coin Sciences[114]

"If people see positive ROIs and they see benefits or they see market shifts, they'll jump all over it."

Innovation Director for a US healthcare company[115]

1. Coercive influences come from political pressures exerted on an organization by other organizations upon which they are dependent. Government regulations, legal requirements, and powerful trading partners' mandates are examples of coercive influences. Within the context of blockchains, several interviewees thought government regulations would be the fastest route to mass adoption. For example, one interviewee thought new US government regulations would be the way to force the adoption of better healthcare processes that could be enabled with blockchains. He said:

"The government may need to step in at some point. All we have to do is have a couple of use cases, and then we go public about it and say, 'This is the kind of thing we could do. Why can't we do this with healthcare?' We let the government ask, 'Why aren't you doing this?' Then, there's going to be a bunch of payers who say, 'Oh, this

is going to be bad for the consumer.' What are they talking about? Consumers are getting screwed to the nth degree right now. There have never been higher insurance rates."

However, he was not confident the US government is competent enough to act.

2. Normative influences arise from duties, obligations, and norms of professionalism, including formal education and professional and trade associations that seek to legitimize their existence.[116] In the context of blockchains, we see that powerful advisory firms – those companies that have built considerable blockchain services – will influence their client's blockchain adoptions. While advisory firms seek to be technology neutral, they will have insights as to which applications are the most enterprise-ready and the most context-suitable, thereby moving a sector towards adopting a winning application.

3. Mimetic influences arise from the perception that peer organizations are more successful; by mimicking peer behavior, the organization aims to achieve similar results. Mimetic influences are particularly strong when environmental uncertainty is high, goals are ambiguous, and when technologies are poorly understood.[117] IBM's strategy to attract 'anchor tenants' like Maersk and Wal-Mart for its major blockchain applications can be considered a mimetic influence.[118] One interviewee thought this was an effective strategy:

> *"There's also a little bit of a herd mentality.*
> *People are afraid to be left out."*

DiMaggio and Powell stress that the three influences are analytically distinctive but may not be empirically indistinguishable. For example, some might view anchor tenants as a 'coercive influence in mimetic clothing' if they are powerful enough to require smaller partners to use a particular blockchain platform.

5.6. Conclusion

These final words are being written on Valentine's Day, February 14th 2018. Reflecting upon the 18-month research journey, we are convinced that blockchains for business are coming. Leaders will produce blockchain applications that deliver the abundance of business benefits so often repeated in this guide: transacting directly with trading partners; eliminating the need for reconciliations; instantly tracking and tracing assets; providing unbeatable data provenance; settling transactions quickly and cheaply; and enabling a security model that is fault tolerant, resilient, and available.

One of the final questions we asked participants during interviews was about the timing of live blockchain deployments. Interviewees in 2017/early 2018 offered many timelines, ranging from one to 20 years. We are going to let their voices close out *A Manager's Guide to Blockchain Applications for Business*:

> *"In the next one to two years, we're going to start to see a lot of real production implementations, but they will coexist and run in parallel with existing systems. Somewhere in the two to three year range, they'll start decommissioning those. And In the four to six year range, blockchains may become the primary choice of processing."*
>
> **Kiran Nagaraj, Managing Director, KPMG**[119]

> *"The evolution of blockchain is going to continue for a while. It's another three or five years for clients to really adopt it."*
>
> **Rahul Shah, Strategy Manager, Axiom Technology Group**[120]

> *"My conviction is to say that, we will have pilots and production activity before 2030, but mainly on niche products."*
>
> **Philippe Denis, Head of BNP Blockchain Lab**[121]

"In the near term, I think blockchain initiatives will drive significant business impact and create a frenzy of excitement as ambitious businesses jump on the potential of new technology developments like never before. I am optimistic that 2018 might be the year where we start to see some real impact. Several pilots are on track to go-live this year even if they will start on a smaller scale and in a parallel environment (where legacy solutions are not getting replaced). Overall, I expect a five to seven-year horizon for blockchains to displace intermediaries and create new business models."

Saurabh Gupta, Chief Strategy Officer, HfS Research[122]

"We're definitely several years away from large applications. A few applications will be in production maybe in three years. But mass production won't likely be here for five years."

Nilesh Vaidya, SVP Head of Banking & Capital Market Solutions at Capgemini[123]

"At some point, I'm sure someone will say, this is actually 10 or 20 years away. And that's true, but it's infinite years away if we're not actually working on the problem."

Amber Baldet, Program Lead for J.P. Morgan's Blockchain Center of Excellence[124]

Citations

1. Personal interview with Mary Lacity and Kate Moloney in 2017

2. Email interview with Mary Lacity in 2018

3. Personal interview with Mary Lacity in 2017

4. Lacity, M. and Willcocks, L. (2018), *Robotic Process and Cognitive Automation: The Next Phase*, SB Publishing, UK

5. Lacity, M. and Willcocks, L. (2018), *Robotic Process and Cognitive Automation: The Next Phase*, SB Publishing, UK

6. Personal interview with Mary Lacity in 2017

7. Personal interview with Mary Lacity in 2017

8. www2.deloitte.com

9. Buterin, V. (2017), *The most valid criticisms of Ethereum, Reddit*, https://www.reddit.com/r/ethtrader/comments/6lgf0l/vitalik_drops_the_mic_on_rbtc/djtxbyr/
   See also the commentary by De Silva, M. (July 6th 2017), *Seven Critiques of Ethereum According To The Creator*, https://www.ethnews.com/seven-critiques-of-ethereum-according-to-the-creator

10. Braine, L. (April 18th 2016), *Barclays' Smart Contract Templates*, presented at Barclays Accelerator London Demo Day, http://www.r3cev.com/projects

11. Personal interview in 2017 with Mary Lacity

12. Wilson, M (February 7th 2017), *Lobbying's top 50: Who's spending big*, http://thehill.com/business-a-lobbying/business-a-lobbying/318177-lobbyings-top-50-whos-spending-big

13. *How Barclays Used R3's Tech to Build a Smart Contracts Prototype*, http://bitcoinwiki.co/how-barclays-used-r3s-tech-to-build-a-smart-contracts-prototype/

14. Personal interview with Mary Lacity in 2017

15. Personal Interview with Jeanne Ross and Kate Moloney in 2017

16. Personal interview with Mary Lacity and Kate Moloney in 2017

17. Bahamdain, S. (2015), Open Source Software Quality Assurance: A Survey Paper, *Procedia Computer Science*, Vol. 56, 459-464
Spinellis, D, Gousios, G. Karakoidas, V.and Louridas, P. (2009), Evaluating the Quality of Open SourceSoftware, *Electronic Notes in Theoretical Computer Science*, Issue 233, 5–28
Spinellis, D., *Code Quality: The Open Source Perspective*, Addison-Wesley, Boston, MA, 2006

18. Personal interview with Mary Lacity in 2017

19. Personal interview with Mary Lacity and Kate Moloney in 2017

20. Personal interview with Mary Lacity and Kate Moloney in 2017

21. Personal interview with Mary Lacity and Kate Moloney in 2017

22. Lacity, M., Moloney, K., and Ross, J. (2018), *Blockchain at BNP Paribas: The Power of Co-Creation*, CISR Case Study

23. Capgemini 2015 Annual Report, https://more.capgemini.com/annual-report/2015/ - exp_innovation

24. Personal interview with Mary Lacity in 2017

25. Personal interview with Mary Lacity in 2017

26. Personal interview with Mary Lacity and Kate Moloney in 2017

27. Personal interview with Mary Lacity and Kate Moloney in 2017

28. Personal interview with Mary Lacity in 2017

29. Personal interview with Mary Lacity in 2017

30. Personal interview with Mary Lacity in 2017

31. Healy, J. (March 29th 2017). Give SMEs the banking system they deserve, *The Australian*, http://www.theaustralian.com.au/
Canning Corporate Communications, (March 29th 2017), *Why small businesses distrust big banks*, http://www.canningsstrategiccommunications.com.au/article/why-small-businesses-distrust-big-banks
Pymnts.com (May 12th 2015), SMEs Distrust Banks, But they Distrust Alt lenders too, https://www.pymnts.com/in-depth/2015/smes-distrust-banks-but-they-distrust-alt-lenders-too/

32. Greenspan, G. (November 15th 2015), *Avoiding the pointless blockchain project,* https://www.multichain.com/blog/2015/11/avoiding-pointless-blockchain-project/

33. Tutton, M. (January 12th 2010), Uncovering the multi-million dollar fake degree, industryhttp://www.cnn.com/2010/BUSINESS/01/11/fake.college.degrees/index.html

34. Lewis, A, (July 24th 2017), *Avoiding blockchain for blockchain's sake: Three real use case criteria*, https://bitsonblocks.net/2017/07/24/avoiding-blockchain-for-blockchains-sake-three-real-use-case-criteria/

35. Quote from Amber Baldet's presentation, *Building Tomorrow's Financial Markets Today,* MIT Blockchain for Business, April 18th 2017, https://events.technologyreview.com/video/watch/amber-baldet-jpmorgan-building-tomorrows-financial-markets/

36. Lorenz, J. et al. (July 2016), *Blockchain in insurance –opportunity or threat?*, McKinsey & Company, https://www.mckinsey.com/~/media/McKinsey/Industries/Financial Services/Our Insights/Blockchain in insurance opportunity or threat/Blockchain-in-insurance-opportunity-or-threat.ashx

37. Lorenz, J. et al. (July 2016), *Blockchain in insurance –opportunity or threat?*, McKinsey & Company, https://www.mckinsey.com/~/media/McKinsey/Industries/Financial Services/Our Insights/Blockchain in insurance opportunity or threat/Blockchain-in-insurance-opportunity-or-threat.ashx

38. Lewis, A, (July 24th 2017), *Avoiding blockchain for blockchain's sake: Three real use case criteria*, https://bitsonblocks.net/2017/07/24/avoiding-blockchain-for-blockchains-sake-three-real-use-case-criteria/

39. Personal interview with Mary Lacity and Kate Moloney in 2017

40. Lacity, M., Moloney, K., and Ross, J. (2018), *Blockchain at BNP Paribas: The Power of Co-Creation*, CISR Case Study

41. Efstathiou, A. (July 11th 2017), *Adventures in Blockchain: TCS Focuses on the Building Blocks of a Successful Blockchain Ecosystem*, https://research.nelson-hall.com/blogs-webcasts/nelsonhall-blog/?avpage-views=blog&type=post&post_id=694&utm_source=NelsonHall+-+Industry+Insight&utm_campaign=3abeba8088-NH_Industry_Insight_July18&utm_medium=email&utm_term=0_9d9720677e-3abeba8088-316614105

42. Emin Gün Sirer's presentation, *"What Could Go Wrong? When Blockchains Fail,"* at the Business of Blockchain conference, April 18th 2017, https://www.technologyreview.com/s/604219/blockchains-weak-spots-pose-a-hidden-danger-to-users/

43. Quote from Amber Baldet's presentation, *Building Tomorrow's Financial Markets Today*, MIT Blockchain for Business, April 18th 2017, https://events.technologyreview.com/video/watch/amber-baldet-jpmorgan-building-tomorrows-financial-markets/

44. Personal interview with Mary Lacity and Kate Moloney in 2017

45. Personal interview with Mary Lacity and Kate Moloney in 2017

46. Personal interview with Mary Lacity in 2017

47. Lacity, M., Moloney, K., and Ross, J. (2018), *Blockchain at BNP Paribas: The Power of Co-Creation*, CISR Case Study

48. Personal interview with Mary Lacity in 2017

49. Personal interview with Mary Lacity and Kate Moloney in 2017

50. The Guardian (January 20th 2016), *Ten arrested in Netherlands over bitcoin money-laundering allegations*, https://www.theguardian.com/technology/2016/jan/20/bitcoin-netherlands-arrests-cars-cash-ecstasy

51. Popper, N. (2015), *Digital Gold: Bitcoin and the Inside History of the Misfits and Millionaires Trying to Reinvent Money,* Harper, New York.

52. Castillo, M. (January 3rd 2017), *State Street's Blockchain Strategy: Big and Bold for 2017*, https://www.coindesk.com/state-streets-blockchain-strategy-big-and-bold-for-2017/

53. Keynote speech by Abby Johnson at Consensus 2017, https://www.bloomberg.com/news/articles/2017-05-23/fidelity-s-abby-johnson-urges-resolution-to-blockchain-barriers; https://www.fidelitylabs.com/2017/05/18/fidelity-chairman-ceo-at-consensus-2017/

54. Bart Cant (2015), *Introducing Capgemini's Own Digital Crypto-currency*, https://more.capgemini.com/beyond-the-buzz/cryptocurrency-blockchain/

55. Personal interview with Mary Lacity in 2017

56. Personal interview with Mary Lacity in 2017

57. Many sites track blockchain uses cases; for example, Ledra Capital compiled a list of top 84 uses cases, Redit posted a slide of 88 blockchain use cases by industry; Moody's posted a more manageable list of top 25 blockchain use cases

58. Clayton Christensen has developed the theory of disruptive innovation over two decades, beginning with this first book published in 1997, *The innovator's dilemma: when new technologies cause great firms to fail,* (Boston, Massachusetts, Harvard Business School Press). For a thoughtful and current synopsis of the theory, see Christensen, C., Raynor, M., and McDonald, R. (2015), Disruptive Innovations, Harvard Business Review, 93(12): 45-53

59. Christensen, C., Raynor, M., and McDonald, R. (2015), Disruptive Innovations, Harvard Business Review, 93(12): 45-53

60. Christensen, C., Raynor, M., and McDonald, R. (2015), Disruptive Innovations, Harvard Business Review, 93(12): 45-53

61. Personal interview with Mary Lacity in 2017

62. Personal interview with Mary Lacity and Kate Moloney in 2017

63. Castillo, M. (January 3rd 2017), *State Street's Blockchain Strategy: Big and Bold for 2017*, https://www.coindesk.com/state-streets-blockchain-strategy-big-and-bold-for-2017/

64. Christensen, C., Raynor, M., and McDonald, R. (2015), Disruptive Innovations, *Harvard Business Review,* 93(12): 45-53

65. Lacity, M., Moloney, K., and Ross, J. (2018), *Blockchain at BNP Paribas: The Power of Co-Creation*, CISR Case Study

66. The current system is called CHESS (Clearing House Electronic Subregister System)

67. ASX website: A*SX is replacing CHESS with distributed ledger technology (DLT) developed by Digital Asset*, http://www.asx.com.au/services/chess-replacement.htm

68. Barnett, T. (December 9th 2017), *Australian Securities Exchange Plans to Implement Blockchain Technology*, https://interestingengineering.com/australian-securities-exchange-plans-to-implement-blockchain-technology

69. Castillo, M. (January 3rd 2017), *State Street's Blockchain Strategy: Big and Bold for 2017*, https://

www.coindesk.com/state-streets-blockchain-strategy-big-and-bold-for-2017/

70. Securities lending is defined as 'the act of loaning a stock, derivative or other security to an investor or firm. Securities lending requires the borrower to put up collateral, whether cash, security or a letter of credit. When a security is loaned, the title and the ownership are also transferred to the borrower.' Source: https://www.investopedia.com/terms/s/securitieslending.asp

71. Irrera, A (December 21st 2016), *State Street tests blockchain system for securities lending, Reuters*, http://www.reuters.com/article/us-state-str-blockchain-idUSKBN14A23X

72. ASX website: *ASX is replacing CHESS with distributed ledger technology (DLT) developed by Digital Asset*, http://www.asx.com.au/services/chess-replacement.htm

73. Lacity, M., Moloney, K., and Ross, J. (2018), *Blockchain at BNP Paribas: The Power of Co-Creation,* CISR Case Study

74. Lacity, M., Moloney, K., and Ross, J. (2018), *Blockchain at BNP Paribas: The Power of Co-Creation*, CISR Case Study

75. https://ripple.com/use-cases/

76. Mearian, L. (November 2017), *Blockchain-as-a-service allows enterprises test distributed ledger technology, Computerworld,* https://www.computerworld.com/article/3237465/enterprise-applications/blockchain-as-a-service-allows-enterprises-test-distributed-ledger-technology.html

77. Miller, R. (March 19th 2017), *BM unveils Blockchain as a Service based on open source Hyperledger Fabric technology,* Techcrunch, https://techcrunch.com/2017/03/19/ibm-unveils-blockchain-as-a-service-based-on-open-source-hyperledger-fabric-technology/

78. Personal interview with Mary Lacity in 2017

79. Personal Interview with Jeanne Ross and Kate Moloney in 2017

80. Christensen, C., Raynor, M., and McDonald, R. (2015), Disruptive Innovations, *Harvard Business Review*, 93(12): 45-53

81. Christensen, C., Raynor, M., and McDonald, R. (2015), Disruptive Innovations, *Harvard Business Review*, 93(12): 45-53

82. Source: *Blockchain in Review: Investment Trends and Opportunities*, October 2017, CB Insights

83. Source: *Blockchain in Review: Investment Trends and Opportunities*, October 2017, CB Insights

84. Some authors contest that blockchains are disruptive and instead argue that they are foundational. See Iansiti, M. and Lakhani, K. (January / February 2017), The Truth About Blockchain, Harvard Business Review, 118-127

85. Personal interview with Mary Lacity in 2017

86. Personal interview with Mary Lacity and Kate Moloney in 2017

87. Larson, C. (July 25th 2017), *Humana has billions in cash on hand – did Obamacare really hurt that much?* https://www.bizjournals.com/louisville/news/2017/07/25/humana-has-billions-in-cash-on-hand-did-obamacare.html

88. See http://shareandcharge.com/en/; Lielacher, A. (May 5th 2017), *Innogy Charges Electric Car*

Fleet Using Ethereum Blockchain, https://www.nasdaq.com/article/innogy-charges-new-electric-car-fleet-using-ethereum-blockchain-cm785270

89. IBM Press Release (January 16th 2018), *Maersk and IBM to Form Joint Venture Applying Blockchain to Improve Global Trade and Digitize Supply Chains*, https://www-03.ibm.com/press/us/en/pressrelease/53602.wss

90. Personal interview with Mary Lacity in 2017

91. Personal interview with Mary Lacity in 2017

92. Personal interview with Mary Lacity and Kate Moloney in 2017

93. One blockchain study was completed in Fall 2017 and two more studies are underway. Three studies https://www.c4scs.org/dscsa-blockchain-2-teams/

94. Iansiti, M., Lakhani, K., (2017), The Truth About Blockchains, *Harvard Business Review*, 95(1), 118-127

95. Kelly, J. (September 15th 2015), *Nine of world's biggest banks join to form blockchain partnership*, https://www.reuters.com/article/us-banks-blockchain-idUSKCN0RF24M20150915

96. Hackett, R. (November 21st 2016), *Why Goldman Sachs and Santander Are Bailing on R3's Blockchain Group, Fortune Magazine,* http://fortune.com/2016/11/21/goldman-sachs-r3-blockchain-consortium/

97. Personal interview with Mary Lacity and Kate Moloney in 2017

98. Personal interview with Mary Lacity and Kate Moloney in 2017

99. Personal interview with Mary Lacity and Kate Moloney in 2017

100. https://hyperledger.org/about/charter

101. Castillo, M. (May 23rd 2017), *The startup trying to bring blockchain to Wall Street has raised $107 million*, http://www.businessinsider.com/r3-consortium-has-raised-107-million-2017-5

102. Personal interview with Mary Lacity in 2017

103. Personal interview with Mary Lacity and Kate Moloney in 2017

104. Personal interview with Mary Lacity in 2017

105. Orsini, L. *Industry Impact: Peer-to-Peer Energy Transactions*, presentation Principal and Founder, LO3 Energy at the Business of Blockchain conference, April 18th 2017, http://events.technologyreview.com/video/watch/lawrence-orsini-lo3-industry-impact/

106. Personal Interview with Lawrence Orsini, December 21st 2017

107. Personal Interview with Lawrence Orsini, December 21st 2017

108. Regenor, J. (April 18th 2017), *Industry Impact: Aerospace Supply Chain*, presentation at the Blockchain for Business Conference at MIT, Cambridge Massachusetts

109. National Defense Authorization Act for Fiscal Year 2018, https://www.congress.gov/bill/115th-congress/house-bill/2810/text - toc-HBA0AA81CFC4F410E95EF87129909DC2A

110. Personal interview with Mary Lacity in 2017

111. Mizruchi, M., and Fein, L. (1999) The Social Construction of Organizational Knowledge: A Study of the Uses of Coercive, Mimetic, and Normative Isomorphism, *Administrative Science Quarterly*, Vol. 44, 4, 653-683

112. DiMaggio, P. and Powell, W. (1991) The Iron Cage Revisited: Industrial Isomorphism and Collective Rationality in Organizational Fields, *The New Institutionalism in Organizational Analysis*, (Powell, W. and DiMaggio, editors), University of Chicago Press, Chicago, 63-82

113. DiMaggio, P. and Powell, W. (1991) The Iron Cage Revisited: Industrial Isomorphism and Collective Rationality in Organizational Fields, *The New Institutionalism in Organizational Analysis*, (Powell, W. and DiMaggio, editors), University of Chicago Press, Chicago, 63-82

114. Greenspan, G. (March 17th 2016), *Blockchains vs centralized databases*, https://www.multichain.com/blog/2016/03/blockchains-vs-centralized-databases/

115. Personal interview with Mary Lacity in 2017

116. DiMaggio, P. and Powell, W. (1991) The Iron Cage Revisited: Industrial Isomorphism and Collective Rationality in Organizational Fields, *The New Institutionalism in Organizational Analysis*, (Powell, W. and DiMaggio, editors), University of Chicago Press, Chicago, 63-82

117. Ibid, p. 71
Mizruchi, M., and Fein, L. (1999) The Social Construction of Organizational Knowledge: A Study of the Uses of Coercive, Mimetic, and Normative Isomorphism, *Administrative Science Quarterly*, Vol. 44, 4, 653-683

118. Marie Wieck, *GM of IBM Blockchain, speaking at Consensus 2017*: https://ibmgo.com/interconnect2017/search/?q=blockchain&tags=all&categoryType=video

119. Personal interview with Mary Lacity in 2017

120. Personal interview with Mary Lacity and Kate Moloney in 2017

121. Lacity, M., Moloney, K., and Ross, J. (2018), *Blockchain at BNP Paribas: The Power of Co-Creation*, CISR Case Study

122. Email interview with Mary Lacity in 2018

123. Personal interview with Mary Lacity in 2017

124. Quote from Amber Baldet's presentation, *Building Tomorrow's Financial Markets Today*, MIT Blockchain for Business, April 18th 2017, https://events.technologyreview.com/video/watch/amber-baldet-jpmorgan-building-tomorrows-financial-markets/

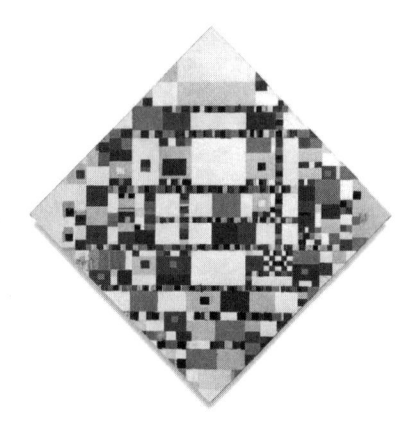

Glossary

This glossary covers terms, major events, and supplemental information.

Action principle: A management practice that facilitates the success of a business project. Action principles are similar to 'best practices' in that both seek to share knowledge from prior experiences. However, whereas 'best practices' imply that mimicry is always recommended and will always produce similar results, action principles recognize that context matters.

Application Programming Interface (API): An API is a piece of software that connects two software applications so that one application can send a message to and receive a response from another application. In the context of a blockchain application, enterprises use an API to connect their own systems of record to a blockchain application.

Asymmetric key algorithm: A type of cryptography that uses a pair of mathematically related numbers called 'keys' – one public key and one private key. Users can digitally sign messages by encrypting them with their private keys. 'This is effective since any message recipient can verify that the user's public key can decrypt the message, and thus prove that the user's secret key was used to encrypt it. If the user's secret key is, in fact, secret, then it follows that the user, and not some impostor, really sent the message.'[1] RSA, DSA, and ECC are three specific examples of asymmetric key algorithms (see entries below for each).

Bitcoin: This term bitcoin refers to both the Bitcoin application as a whole and to its native digital asset, the bitcoin cryptocurrency.

Bitcoin (application): The Bitcoin application is a peer-to-peer payment application. Conceived of by Satoshi Nakamoto in 2008,[2] it was launched live in 2009. Among its advances were a digital ledger structured as a chain of blocks, the creation of a native digital asset called bitcoins, public-private key encryption to authenticate asset ownership, a proof-of-work consensus protocol and the use of hashes to validate and continually secure transactions within a completely distributed, peer-to-peer, public network.

Bitcoin (cryptocurrency): Bitcoins are the native digital asset within the Bitcoin blockchain. Bitcoin was designed to be a scarce resource with a maximum money supply of 21 million bitcoins. The first 50 bitcoins were released in 2009, and the last will be released in the year 2140. Bitcoins are added to the money supply, on average, every ten minutes to reward miners for creating a new block of transactions. Every 210,000 blocks, the miner's reward cuts in half, so that more bitcoins are released in its earlier years than in later years. As of early 2018, about 80 percent of the money supply has been released.

Block header: Blocks contain headers with important information such as the block's unique ID hash, the number of transactions in the block, when the block was created, the size of the block (in terms of computer storage), and the pointer to the previous block. Figure G.1 provides and example of Bitcoin's block header.

Block #507980

BlockHash 0000000000000000002ac0fd Bitcoin Block 507980 | Bitcoin Block Explorer ↑154a398

Summary

Number Of Transactions	1838	Difficulty	2603077300218.5933
Height	507980 (Mainchain)	Bits	176c2146
Block Reward	12.5 BTC	Size (bytes)	973919
Timestamp	Feb 6, 2018 10:23:10 AM	Version	536870912
Mined by		Nonce	3997532233
Merkle Root	6334a61743821be369a74b116a50b...	Next Block	507981
Previous Block	507979		

Figure G.1: Example of a block header for Bitcoin

In this example, we are looking at the 507,980th block created in the Bitcoin blockchain. The summary data in the header indicates that there are 1,838 transactions in the block's payload; its '*height*' is equal to its sequence in the blockchain (block 507980); '*block reward*' indicates that the winning miner earned 12.5 bitcoins for using its computer's resources to validate the transactions and to create the block; the '*timestamp*' indicates the exact second the block was created on February 6th 2018; the '*Merkle Root*' shows the result of the Merkle hashing sequences (see 'Merkle Root' explanation below) used to secure the block; the *'previous block'* is the pointer to this block's predecessor. The *'bits'* and *'size'* indicate how much computer storage is required to store this block. The *'version'* indicates which set of Bitcoin's blockchains rules to follow. The *'difficulty'* and *'nonce'* are associated with Bitcoin's proof-of-work consensus algorithm. Functionally, the difficulty indicates the number of lead zeros the miner's computer(s) had to find (after trillions of random tries) in order to find a unique *'blockhash'*. In this block, notice the blockhash has 18 lead zeros. The difficulty is part of the proof that the miner's computer did some serious calculations to earn the block reward (see separate entry for 'Proof-of-Work').

Blockchain: This term is used several ways. Sometimes the term refers broadly to what we are calling a 'blockchain application'. For example, people call Bitcoin and Ethereum 'blockchains'. The term can also be used to describe the structure of the digital ledger. With a blockchain structure, newly submitted transactions are sequenced and collected into a block (see Figure G.2). The block comprises a header and payload of transactions. The block header includes a pointer to the previous block of transactions, forming a chain of sequenced blocks over time all the way back to the first block, called the 'genesis block'.

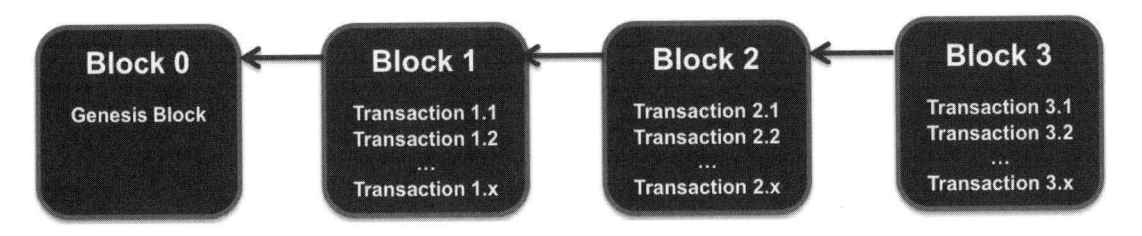

Figure G.2: Distributed ledger structured as a chain of blocks

Blockchain application: A distributed, peer-to-peer system for validating, time-stamping, and permanently storing transactions on a distributed ledger; it uses cryptography to authenticate digital asset ownership and consensus protocols to add validated transactions to the ledger, and to ensure the ongoing integrity of the ledger's complete history. Nearly all enterprise blockchains also use smart contracts that apply rules to automatically execute transactions based upon pre-agreed conditions.

Byzantine fault tolerance of a system: The ability of a distributed network to function properly given that a certain number of nodes are faulty or even malicious. A general rule is that peer-to-peer distributed systems like blockchains can function properly even when up to a third of the participating nodes are faulty.

Byzantine fault tolerance as a consensus protocol: As a class of consensus algorithms, there are many versions of Byzantine Fault Tolerance (BFT), including Redundant Byzantine Fault Tolerance (RBFT) used by Hyperledger Indy[3]; Delegated Byzantine Fault Tolerance used by Antshares;[4] Quorum used by JP Morgan;[5] and Federated Byzantine Agreement used by Stellar[6] – to name but a few. BFT versions differ by how authorized nodes are chosen and by how nodes are assigned roles. Ripple and Stellar, for example, allow participants to pick which nodes they want as validators;[7] Antshares separates bookkeeping nodes from user nodes, with the former being operated by professionals; Quorum delegates nodes to observer, voter, and maker roles;[8] R3 Corda authorizes notary and observer nodes; Hyperledger Fabric defines endorser, orderer, and committer nodes.

Byzantine generals' problem: A conceptual situation described by Leslie Lamport, Robert Shostak, and Marshall Pease (1982) to investigate how decentralized communication networks can reach agreement if some unknown number of nodes is faulty. In their metaphor, a Byzantine General represents a computer node; some generals are loyal (i.e. not faulty) and some generals are disloyal (i.e. faulty). Lamport et al. (1982) proved that decentralized networks could reach a consensus provided that two thirds of the nodes function properly[(i)] .

Centralized network: See entry for Network Structures

Chain: Chain refers to both the company and its blockchain codebase, Chain Core. The company was founded in 2014. According to its website, '*Chain Core is enterprise software that enables institutions to issue and transfer financial assets on permissioned blockchain networks. Using Chain Core, institutions can launch and operate a blockchain network, or connect to a growing list of other networks that are transforming how assets move around the world.*' [9]

Code base: The set of programming instructions based on the agreed upon rules, i.e. protocols.

(i) Lamport, L., Shostak, R., Pease, M. (1982), The Byzantine Generals Problem, *ACM Transactions on Programming Languages and Systems*, Vol. 4/3, 382-401

Coercive influences: See entry for Institutional Isomorphism

Consensus protocol: Consensus protocols are rules for making sure copies of the distributed ledger agree. Consensus protocols are used to counteract 'the tragedy of the commons' and the 'Byzantine Generals Problem' (see separate entries). Although consensus protocols vary in their validation procedures, in general, all consensus protocols seek to authenticate ownership and ensure that transactions are funded (i.e. no double spending) before adding them to the official distributed ledger. The process of validation begins when a new transaction is broadcast to the network. Computer algorithms on the other nodes verify legitimate ownership of the asset (based on the owner's digital signature with his or her private key) and check that the asset has not been given away before by scanning the ledger, thus preventing double spending. Which node gets to collect verified transactions and add them to the official ledger depends on the network's consensus protocol. Many consensus protocols have been used and proposed, including proof-of-work; proof-of-stake; proof-of-activity (which combines proof-of-stake with proof-of-work); proof-of-authority; proof-of-burn; proof-of-capacity; proof-of-elapsed;[10] time; proof-of-listening; and proof-of-luck.[11]

Consortium-led innovation: An innovation that aims to improve the performance of inter-organizational exchanges among trading partners. In the context of a blockchain, a consortium provides a legal way for competitors to cooperate to define, build, govern, and/or operate a shared blockchain application.

Corda: An open-source, distributed ledger platform developed by the R3 Consortium. Corda was designed to increase privacy, reduce data redundancy (not everyone needs to see a transaction), and increase scalability. Corda uses public-private key encryptions and hashes, and creates permanent, immutable records between trading partners. As a private protocol, participants are assigned a cryptographic identity, which will be tied to a 'real world' identity, such as a legal entity identifier.[12] Once on-boarded, a party can transform a legal contract into smart contract code to transact with another Corda party or parties. Rather than distribute the entire ledger to everyone on the network, Corda creates node-to-node transactions directly between/among the parties involved in the transaction as defined in the smart contract.[13] Each Corda participant only sees the subset of data for which they are privy. This feature is implemented using multiple composite keys (see entry below).[14]

Corda has configurable consensus, meaning parties to a contract can pick their preferred consensus protocol, which is likely to be Byzantine Fault Tolerance (BFT) or Raft.[15] The Corda ledger is built on relational database technology, and thus does not use a block structure. It chose this structure so that participants could easily query the ledger using SQL. Data is considered 'on-ledger' if at least two parties in the system agree about the transaction's validity, whereas data held by only one party is 'off-ledger'. Corda's design is scalable since there is less network traffic and data storage, more private than most DTL protocols, and settles transactions as soon as nodes agree.[16]

As time went on, Corda's architecture evolved to the point where some people no longer consider it a blockchain; Corda lacks some of the defining characteristics of public blockchains: It does not have a native digital asset, it does not broadcast transactions, and it does not distribute a shared ledger. Indeed, Corda's main architects call Corda 'blockchain-inspired'.[17] The initial version was released in November of 2016.[18]

Counterparty risk: The risk each trading party bears that the other party will not fulfill its contractual obligations.

Cryptography: The science of securing data in the presence of third party adversaries using mathematical and computer algorithms.

CryptoNotes: A protocol that aims to increase the anonymity of blockchains.

Decentralized Autonomous Innovation (DAO): A special kind of smart contract that runs an entire organization automatically based on codified rules in a smart contract. 'The idea of a DAO is to create a completely independent entity that is exclusively governed by the rules that you program into it and 'lives' on the chain. This is more than using the blockchain to manage a company: instead, the code is the entire company. And it cannot be stopped.'[19]

Decentralized network: See entry for **Network Structures**

Denial of Service (DoS) attack: A type of malicious attack that floods a network with so many transactions that it disrupts service for legitimate users.

Digital signature: A way to sign a transaction using a computer rather than a hand signature, thus proving one is authorized to do so (see Chapter 2 for more details).

Digital wallet: Software that stores private keys associated with addresses that hold digital assets. A digital wallet is an entry point, or interface, to many blockchains. Stored off a blockchain, the private keys are the only way to prove that one owns an asset on the distributed ledger. If the digital wallet is destroyed or hacked, there is no way to retrieve it. Thus digital wallets are the main source of vulnerability for blockchain applications.

Directed acyclic graphs (DAG): A type of graph that flows in just one direction with no feedback loops. In the context of blockchains, one-way graphs can be used to represent the time sequence of transactions. Iota's 'tangle' structures its ledger based on a DAG (see Figure G.3).

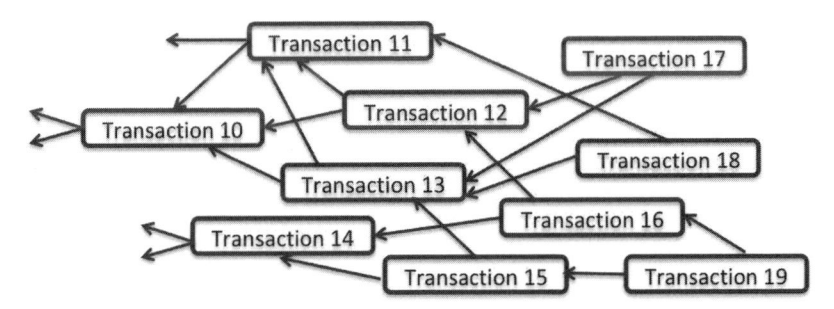

Figure G.3: Distributed ledger structured as a tangle of transactions

Distributed ledger: As a component of a blockchain, a distributed ledger is a time-stamped, permanent record of all valid transactions that have occurred within a given blockchain application. Each node of the blockchain network has an identical copy; no node is in charge.

Distributed network: See entry for Network Structures

Disruptive Innovation: An innovation based on a new business model that targets underserved customers or creates new markets that may eventually threaten the traditional competitors' market shares. The term comes from Clayton Christensen's Theory of Disruptive Innovation.[20]

DSA (Digital Signature Algorithm): An asymmetric key algorithm that generates private-public key pairs. Designed by David Kravitz, an NSA (National Security Agency) employee, the National Institute of Standards and Technology adopted it in the 1990s.[21]

Elliptic Curve Cryptography (ECC): ECC is a common method for generating private-public key pairs in blockchain applications. Basically, an ECC algorithm transforms a private key into a public key by bouncing around a large elliptic curve **n** number of times, where **n** is equal to the private key. It's theoretically impossible to figure out the private key if one only has the public key. The specific EC curve used in Bitcoin is $y^2 = x^3 + 7$ (see Figure G.4). This is called SECP256K1. If we give someone the starting point G and the ending point public key (x, y), one cannot easily determine the n (the private key) even if one has this equation for the graph.

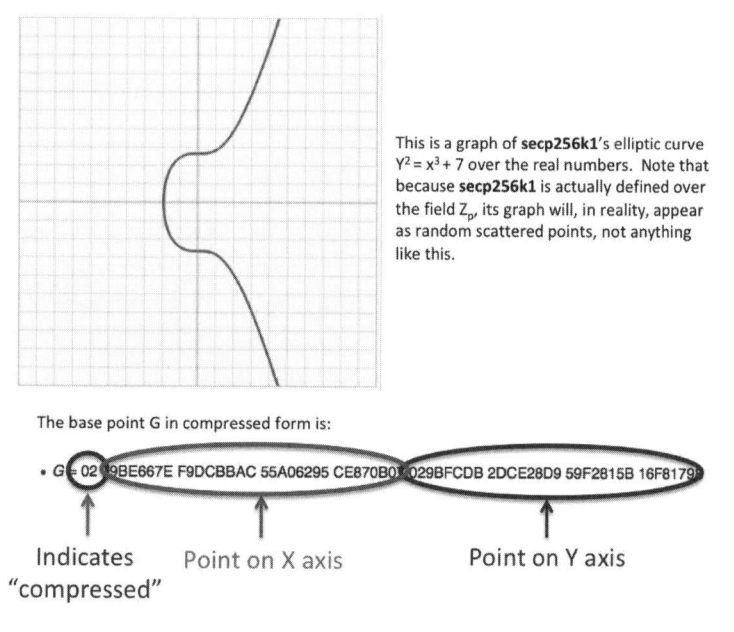

This is a graph of **secp256k1**'s elliptic curve $Y^2 = x^3 + 7$ over the real numbers. Note that because **secp256k1** is actually defined over the field Z_p, its graph will, in reality, appear as random scattered points, not anything like this.

The base point G in compressed form is:

• GE 02 9BE667E F9DCBBAC 55A06295 CE870B0 029BFCDB 2DCE28D9 59F2815B 16F8179

Indicates "compressed"   Point on X axis   Point on Y axis

Figure G.4: Bitcoin's elliptic curve cryptography

The algorithm begins at base point G and moves across the graph trillions upon trillion of times equal to the private key to land on a final (x,y) coordinate that becomes the public key

Source: https://en.bitcoin.it/wiki/Secp256k1

Ethereum: According to the Ethereum Foundation: *"Ethereum is a community-driven project aiming to decentralize the Internet and return it to its democratic roots. It is a platform for building and deploying applications which do not need to rely on trust and cannot be controlled by any central authority."*[22] Vitalik Buterin wrote the 2013 Ethereum white paper that would become the Ethereum platform when he was only 19 years old. Ethereum's smart contracts are the primary innovation that extends Bitcoin's blockchain from a transaction verification and settlement protocol, to a full-fledged 'Turing Complete'[23] platform.

Ethereum Foundation: Vitalik Buterin, Gavin Wood and Jeffrey Wilcke began work on Ethereum by launching The Ethereum Foundation, a non-profit organization based in Switzerland. The foundation was first funded in August 2014 using an Initial Coin Offering for its native digital asset called "ether". They raised $18 million.[24] Ethereum went live in July of 2015, with a presale release of 60 million ether, and 20 million ether retained by The Ethereum Foundation.[25]

Ether: Ethereum's native digital asset. Ether is not intended so much as a cryptocurrency, as much as it is a 'crypto-fuel', meaning it's a token whose main function is to pay for the Ethereum platform.[26] Like Bitcoin, ether is released through the process of mining blocks, and miners also receive the ether that senders append to their transactions to pay for them to be validated and added to the ledger. Ethereum's block reward is 5 ether – but new blocks are created more frequently than in Bitcoin. The total ether money supply amount is unclear;[27] a maximum of 18 million ether can be mined per year.[28]

Fabric: See Hyperledger Fabric entry

Fork: A divergence of a blockchain into two or more separate paths. Soft forks are temporary, whereas hard forks are permanent (see Figure G.5).

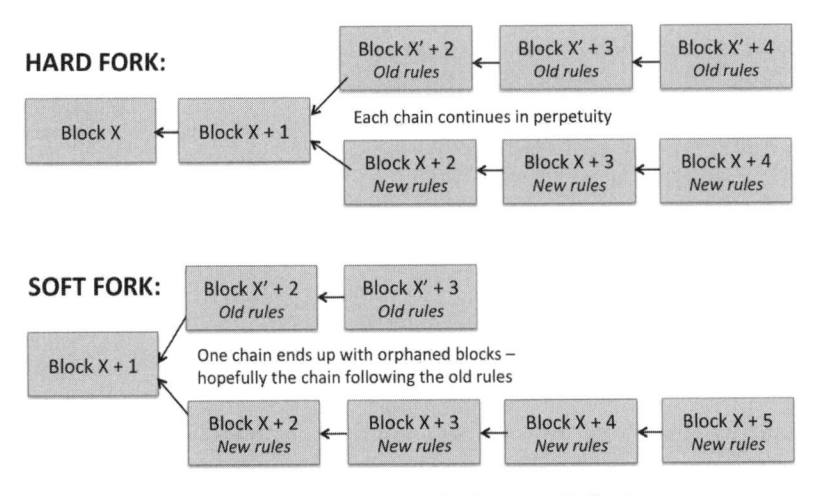

Figure G.5: Hard fork vs. soft fork

A hard fork is a permanent divergence in a blockchain. A soft fork is a temporary divergence in a blockchain while nodes upgrade to the new rules; mining under old rules will not win blocks, so nodes will eventually join the new chain if everything goes as planned.

Fork (Hard): Hard forks are permanent, divergent paths of a blockchain. Hard forks typically occur under two circumstances. First, someone may create their own blockchain or digital asset by copying and modifying source code. Second, hard forks can occur when the open source community disagrees on the rules of the next version of the protocol. For example, Bitcoin forked into 'Bitcoin' and 'Bitcoin Cash' when miners disagreed over a proposed upgrade in 2017. In another example, Ethereum split into 'Ethereum' and 'Ethereum Classic' when the community disagreed about remediating The DAO hack (see story in Chapter 4).

Fork (Soft): Soft forks also occur during planned upgrades to the open source software. A temporary divergence in the blockchain happens when non-upgraded nodes do not follow the new consensus rules.[29] The non-upgraded nodes can still mine for a set time period, so it is up to the upgraded nodes to mine faster and become the longest, and thus, most valid chain.[30] In practice, the open source community tries to get most people to agree to the soft fork in advance.

Hash: An algorithm for transforming one input into a different output. Given a specific input, the identical output will always be reproduced. A good hash algorithm makes it practically impossible to determine the input value based on the output value, which is why hashes are called 'one way' functions. SHA-256 is commonly used in blockchains (see entry below). Blockchains use hashes in many places to add layers of security. Public keys are hashed into addresses; addresses and amounts within a transaction are hashed to create a unique and secure transaction ID; transaction IDs with a block are hashed together multiple times to produce a Merkle Root (see entry below) that resides in a block header; and all the data in the block header is hashed to create a unique and secure block ID.

Heisenbug: A computer programming logic error that changes its behavior unpredictably;[31] the bug is named after the Heisenberg Uncertainty Principle which asserts that the more precisely one thing is known about a particle – like its position – the less precisely another thing is known about the particle – like its momentum.

Hyperledger Fabric: Hyperledger Fabric is one of the projects sponsored by the Hyperledger Project, a non-profit organization launched by the Linux Foundation in December of 2015 to advance the application of enterprise-grade blockchains across industries.[32] Although the Hyperledger Project has four other major blockchain frameworks (Sawtooth, Iroha, Burrow, and Indy), Fabric has received considerable media attention, thanks to its adoption by enterprises such as IBM, Wal-Mart, and Maersk.[33] Digital Asset Holdings and IBM initially contributed to Hyperledger Fabric's code base. Twenty-six other companies – including Fujitsu, GE, Hitachi, State Street, and SAP – contributed to the open source code that was released in 2017.[34] Fabric's ledger is structured as a chain of blocks and has two subsystems: 'the world state' and the 'transaction log' of all the transactions that led up to the current world state. Fabric also has a smart contracting feature, called Chaincode, that allows participants to create their own channels, which is a separate transaction ledger. Within a channel, every node gets copies of the same ledger. [35]

Immutability: As it relates to blockchains, immutability means that a transaction or smart contract that has been added to the blockchain can never be changed. The benefit of immutability is that trading partners can rely on one historical record for data provenance and auditability. The downsides are: errors cannot be fixed unless 51 percent of the nodes agree to the fix; immutability may conflict with regulations or corporate policies that require data destruction after an elapsed period of time.

Interface (blockchain): An access point to a blockchain application, such as through digital wallets or application programming interfaces.

Internet-of-Things (IoT): A term that refers to connecting devices with unique identifiers to the Internet so that data can be collected from and sent to those devices.

Initial Coin Offering (ICO): With an ICO, startups announce that they want to raise cash using an ICO by launching a new coin, i.e. a new cryptocurrency. Investors buy the coins instead of shares in a company, which bypasses many onerous regulations. While there are many legitimate ICOs, investors are warned to fully vet ICO projects to avoid being scammed.

Interoperability: The ability for one system to use another system.[36] In relation to blockchains, interoperability means one blockchain could be connected to different blockchains or different systems of record, such as an enterprise resource planning application.

Institutional Isomorphism: A theory that describes the process by which competitors within an industry become more alike in structure and adopt similar practices over time. The theory identifies three pressures that lead institutions to conform: mimetic, coercive, and normative. *Mimetic influences* arise from the perception that peer organizations are more successful; by mimicking peer behavior, the organization aims to achieve similar results. ***Coercive influences*** come from both formal and informal political pressures exerted on an organization by other organizations upon which they are dependent. Government regulations, legal requirements, and ceremonial practices to boost legitimacy, are examples of coercive influences. ***Normative influences*** arise from duties, obligations, and norms of professionalism, including formal education and professional and trade associations that seek to legitimize their existence. DiMaggio and Powell wrote, "*Many professional career tracks are so closely guarded, both at the entry level and throughout career progression, that individuals who make it to the top are virtually indistinguishable*".[37] Paul DiMaggio and Walter Powell first articulated the theory.[38]

Lighting Network: A protocol that tracks intermediate transfers of funds off a blockchain and only posts the value of the initial credit and the final account balance transfers to the blockchain. The solution helps unclutter the blockchain with intermediate transactions.

Mandelbug: A computer programming logic error that is obscure and complex and therefore hard to detect;[39] it is named after the mathematician Benoit Mandelbrot, who showed that complex phenomena can arise from simple rules.

Merkle root: Named after the US computer scientist, Ralph Merkle, the Merkle root is the result of a sequence of hashes between pairs of numbers. In blockchain applications, the numbers are pairs of transactions, which make up a 'Merkle tree' (see Figure G.6). The process to calculate the Merkle root produces a very secure block because if a single digit is altered in any individual transaction, a subsequent calculation check of the Merkle root would reveal an alteration. For a given block, the Merkle root is added to the block's header.

Mimetic influences: See entry for Institutional Isomorphism

Multiple composite keys: In contrast to a single private-key pair, multiple private keys are needed to authorize a transaction. It's a way for multiple parties to share an asset.

Network Structures: A network structure describes the relationships among nodes in a network (see Figure G.7). With a centralized structure, one node is in control; the centralized node (server) receives all incoming data from other nodes and, in turn, routes data to other nodes. In a distributed network, all nodes are peers; no one node is in charge. Data travels to its closest neighbors until all targeted recipient nodes receive the data. In computer science, a

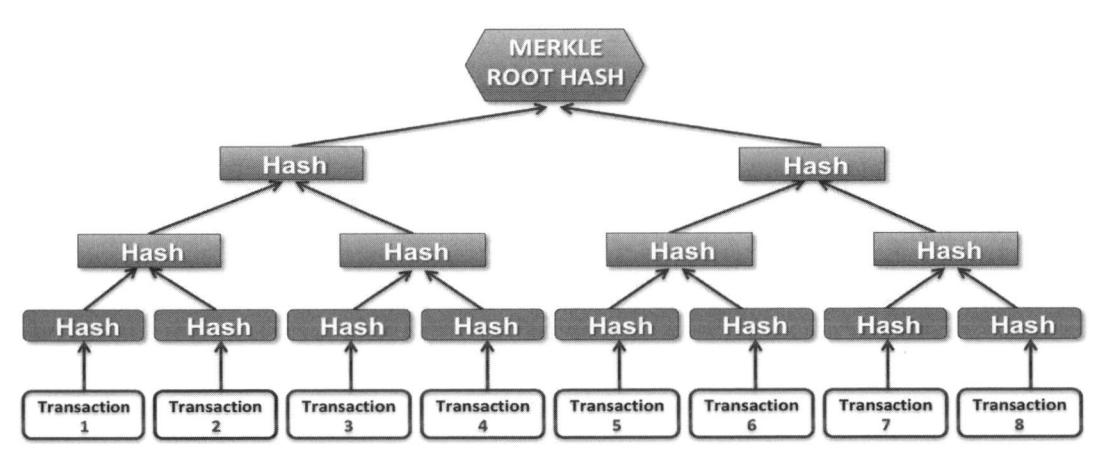

Figure G.6: Merkle tree

In the above example, a block comprises 8 transactions. Each transaction is secured with a hash. Then, the transaction hashes are secured again by hashing four pairs of transactions. Next, two pairs of the hashes are hashed. Then the last hash pair is hashed again, resulting in the root hash called the Merkle root.

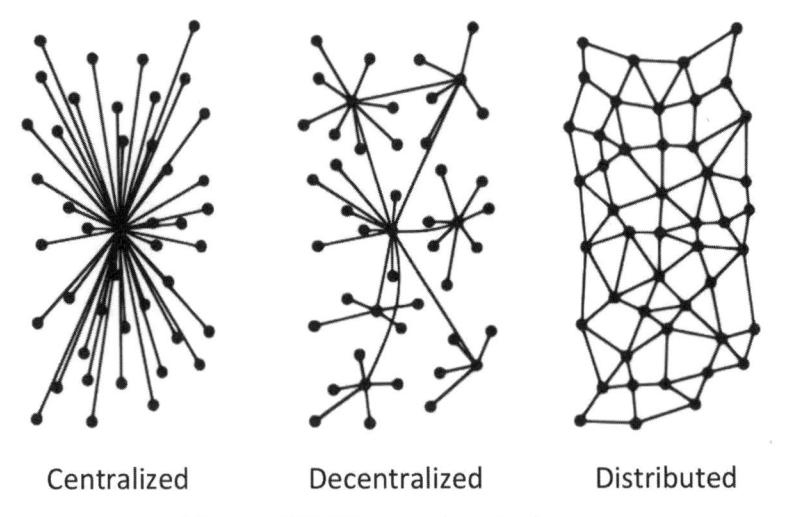

Centralized   Decentralized   Distributed

Figure G.7: Three network structures
Source: http://www.truthcoin.info/images/cent-dec-dist.jpg

decentralized network is a hybrid, resulting in a distributed network of centralized networks.[40] However, many people use the terms 'decentralized' and 'distributed' as synonyms in common vernacular.

Normative influences: See entry for **Institutional Isomorphism**

Mining: See entry for **Proof-of-work**

Money laundering with cryptocurrencies: Criminals around the world have used cryptocurrencies for money laundering, which converts profits from crimes into what appears to be a legitimate source of cash. For example, ten men were arrested in the Netherlands in January 2016 for laundering large sums of money using bitcoins.[41] More recently, a Russian man was arrested in Greece for laundering $4 billion into virtual currency.[42] The US Drug Enforcement Agency (DEA)[43] is concerned about the increased use of cryptocurrencies as a way to launder the revenue generated from crime, which is worth approximately $300 billion annually in the US. In a 2017 report, the DEA stated, *"Emerging as a money laundering vulnerability, Bitcoin and other virtual currencies enable TCOs (Transnational Criminal Organizations) to easily transfer illicit proceeds internationally."*[44]

Within the UK, the UK Treasury Department wants to require cryptocurrency exchanges to reveal the identities of their customers as well as to report suspicious activities.[45] Ripple has been in trouble for not complying with anti-money laundering regulations. In 2015, Ripple was fined $700,000 by the US Department of the Treasury for violating the Bank Secrecy Act of 1970, specifically charging that Ripple willfully failed to implement an anti-money laundering program and failed to report suspicious activity.[46] Ripple agreed to enhance its protocol to meet current banking regulations.[47] For businesses that use blockchain services, managers will certainly need to make sure their blockchain provider adheres to all laws and regulations.

MultiChain: MultiChain is the code base developed by Coin Sciences Ltd. According to its whitepaper, *"MultiChain is an off-the-shelf platform for the creation and deployment of private blockchains, either within or between organizations. It aims to overcome a key obstacle to the deployment of blockchain technology in the institutional financial sector, by providing the privacy and control required in an easytouse package. Rather than supporting a single blockchain like Bitcoin Core, MultiChain is easy to configure and can work with different blockchains at the same time."*[48] Its consensus protocol relies on 'mining diversity'; a round robin schedule of pre-authorized nodes assigned the tasks of validating new transactions and adding them to the ledger.

Node: Any device connected to a network that has a unique identifier.

Oracle: In a blockchain application, an oracle is an agent that finds and verifies real-world occurrences and submits this information to a blockchain to be used by smart contracts.[49]

Performance: See entry for **Systems Performance**.

Permissioned Protocol: Within a blockchain application, a permissioned protocol restricts access and confines which nodes are allowed to observe, transact, validate and add transactions to the permanent record (i.e. the distributed ledger).

Permissionless Protocol: Within a blockchain application, a permissionless protocol does not restrict access. Anyone with access to the Internet can observe a blockchain. Anyone can submit transactions to the blockchain provided they obtained some of the native digital assets (e.g. cryptocurrency). Anyone can operate a full node and compete (or be semi-randomly assigned) to validate and add transactions to the permanent record (i.e. the distributed ledger).

Private-public key pair: Two numbers that are mathematically related such that it is nearly impossible to figure out the private key if one only has access to the public key. Both keys are needed to prove ownership of a digital asset. Together, the pair serves as a digital signature. In practice, the owner of the digital asset holds the private key off the blockchain, either in a wallet the owner stores on his/her own device or in a wallet stored on an exchange or third-party provider. The public key is stored on the blockchain. (In Bitcoin, the public key is transformed into an address using a hash function.) Both keys need to 'turn' to send value.

Proof-of-stake: Sunny King and Scott Nadal created the 'proof-of-stake' consensus protocol for blockchains in a 2012 white paper.[50] Instead of 'mining' for coins, the protocol selects a member to 'forge' new currency as a reward for validating the transactions and creating the next block. Essentially, the selected member node is awarded a transaction fee. The member node is selected in a semi-random way; it's called a 'proof-of-stake' because the members with the highest 'stake' (i.e. have the largest account balances) are giving priority in the selection algorithm. Participants in the blockchain can estimate with some certainty which member will likely be the next 'forger'. A 'proof-of-stake' process uses much less energy than a 'proof-of-work' process. However, critics claim it is less secure than proof-of-work because people with small stakes have little to lose by voting for multiple blockchain histories, which leads to consensus never resolving.[51] Another downside is that the 'richest' participants are given the easiest mining puzzle. Peercoin and Nxt use proof-of-stake.

Proof-of-work: Cynthia Dwork and Moni Naor created the 'proof-of-work' protocol in 1993 to prevent junk email.[52] Satoshi Nakamoto adopted the 'proof-of-work' consensus protocol for Bitcoin in the 2008 white paper.[53] Ethereum also uses proof-of-work (for now). Nakamoto needed a way to find independent verifiers to validate transactions and add blocks to the blockchain without relying on trusted third parties. Nakamoto proposed to reward other nodes in the network with newly issued bitcoins when they validate all recently submitted transactions and create the next block. So that validator nodes take the task seriously, Nakamoto proposed a competition among computer nodes in the blockchain network to be the first to collect recently verified transactions into a block and then to find an acceptable block identification number (known as the blockhash) for the next block in the blockchain. It's not easy to find an acceptable number... it takes a lot of computing power to perform the brute force guesses to find a hash number that is less than the current mining 'difficulty'. The difficulty is part of the proof that the miner's computer did a significant amount of work to earn the block reward. Figure G.8 shows how it works.

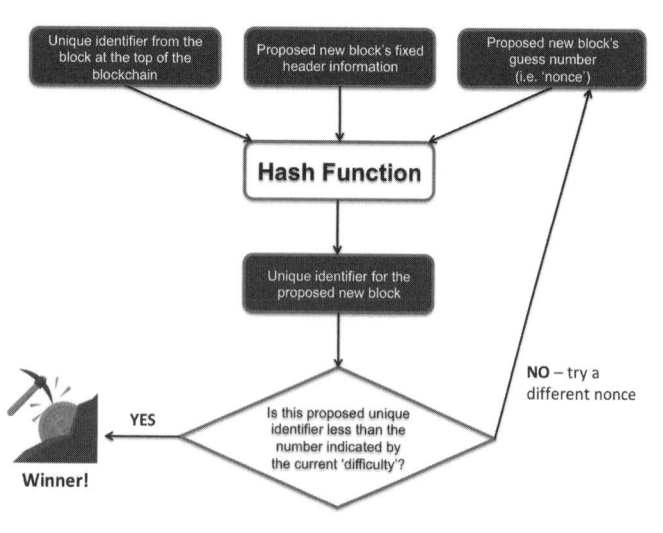

Figure G.8: The 'proof-of-work' mining competition algorithm

A miner's computer takes the unique identifier (i.e. the blockhash) from the block at the top of the chain and hashes that number with the proposed next block's header of fixed information – the protocol version number, the root hash of the Merkle tree, the current time, and the difficulty – and a randomly selected number called a 'nonce'. The hash is then checked to see if it is less than the current mining difficulty. If the hash is greater than the target difficulty, the algorithm tries another guess. If it is less than the target difficulty, the miner wins the competition and is awarded newly created coins.

For the Bitcoin blockchain, a block's winning miner – or more likely, the winning mining pool – receives a set amount of bitcoins, which was 12.5 bitcoins as of December 2017, plus all the small fees that people offered miners to include their transactions in the block. On July 30 2017, for example, a bitcoin was worth $2,796, so winning miners were paid $34,950 per block. A new block is mined every ten minutes on average. The miner's block reward halves every 210,000 blocks, so miners earn fewer coins with time, but the value of those coins might be substantially higher over time.

For the Ethereum blockchain, winning miners are awarded five ether per block, which are created about every 15 seconds. On July 30 2017, an ether was worth $197.46, so winning miners were paid $987 per block. Sometimes two to three ether is sent to a miner who found a solution but whose block was not included, called an uncle (or aunt) reward.[54]

The proof-of-work protocol creates a highly secure ledger, as an attacker would need to gain control of more than 50 percent of the nodes, rewrite history and find all new hashes that adhere to the protocol before other nodes notice. The cons of the protocol include slower transaction settlement times and higher electricity consumption compared to other protocols.

Protocol: A common set of rules that allow different nodes in a computer network to communicate. For example, the Internet uses the Transmission Control Protocol/Internet Protocol (TCP/IP), which is a set of protocols that specify how data should be structured, addressed, transmitted, routed, and received by nodes on the Internet. Blockchain protocols specify rules for how transactions are structured; addressed; transmitted; routed; validated; sequenced; secured; and added to the permanent record (i.e. the distributed ledger) by nodes in a blockchain network.

Quorum: Quorum is an enterprise-ready distributed ledger and smart contract platform based on Etherum.[55] The Enterprise Ethereum Alliance officially supports Quorum,[56] but Quorum is being led by J.P. Morgan, the world's third largest financial services firm, by assets of over $2.5 trillion, as an open-source, enterprise grade version of Ethereum.[57] Quorum is a private/permissioned blockchain that requires institutions to apply for permission to operate a node.[58] A key benefit is that it is designed to process and settle hundreds of transactions per second. J.P. Morgan licensed Quorum with a General Purpose License (GPL) so that the platform will be free to use. It plans to co-evolve in cooperation with Ethereum.[59] Quorum's architecture sits on top of the public Ethereum blockchain. QuorumChain is the original consensus protocol, with other Raft and Istanbul BFT protocols[60] added later.[61] As an open source project, any person or enterprise can download Quorum for experimentation. Notable adopters include Reuters;[13] Markit;[62] Microsoft;[63] Synechron;[64] BlockApps;[65] AMIS Technologies;[66] and Chronicled. Microsoft added Quorum to the Azure cloud marketplace and can be used with Microsoft's Coco framework for a trusted execution environment that is an additional layer of security.[67]

QuorumChain: The main consensus protocol used in Quorum. QuorumChain is a time-based, majority-voting algorithm that uses a smart contract to identify which nodes participate in consensus. QuorumChain has three types of nodes: voter nodes, maker nodes, and observer nodes. Voter nodes vote on which block should be added to the blockchain. Maker nodes are authorized to add the blocks after enough votes have been cast. Observer nodes receive and validate blocks, but do not vote or make blocks.[68] The ledger is segmented into a private state database and a public state database. Participants can execute private and public smart contracts. While all nodes validate public transactions, nodes can only validate private transactions if they are party to the private smart contract.[69]

R3: A blockchain consortium founded in 2014 by David Rutter, with the aim to develop a blockchain platform that could be used by global financial institutions. See Chapter 1 for more information.

Raft: A consensus protocol used in several blockchains, including Quorum. According to the Quorum white paper, "*Raft separates the key elements of consensus, such as leader election, log replication, and safety, and it enforces a stronger degree of coherency to reduce the number of states that must be considered.*"[70] The elected leader node accepts requests from client nodes, replicates them to the network, and responds to the client when a quorum (>50 percent) has been reached. Raft can ensure settlement finality and has throughput of over a thousand transactions per second.

Raiden Network: A protocol that builds another layer on top of a blockchain. It was initially launched to allow for micropayments on Ethereum.[71] Described as similar to the Lightning Network, the basic idea is to switch from a model where all transactions hit the shared ledger on the blockchain (which is the bottleneck) to a model where users can privately exchange messages which sign the transfer of value. Raiden nodes connect to Ethereum nodes using an API, and claims a million transactions per second of confidential transactions are possible (because they are not added to the blockchain).[72]

RSA: RSA is an asymmetric key algorithm designed by three MIT professors –Rivest, Shamir, and Adleman –in 1977 based on multiplying two really large prime numbers.

Sandbox: A test environment that isolates software code from the live production environment, allowing people to test and experiment with the software.

Schrödinbug: An error in computer programming logic which manifests only when somebody debugging it finds out that it shouldn't work at all.[73] The name comes from Schrödinger's cat thought experiment, which essentially described situations where we cannot know whether something is true or false until we observe it. (The actual thought experiment went something like this: *If a cat and something that could kill the cat was left in a sealed box, one cannot ascertain whether the cat is dead or alive until one opens the box. Until the box is opened, it's equally valid to surmise that the cat is both dead and alive.*)

Scalability: See entry for System Scalability

Segregated Witness (SegWit): A protocol that aims to increase the number of transactions that can be included in a block. Instead of appending a digital signature to each address within a transaction, the protocol calls for a single digital signature at the transaction level, thus reducing the size of transactions, enabling more transactions per block.[74]

SHA-256: A secure, one-way hash function commonly used in blockchains. It was designed by the US National Security Agency. It takes any-sized input value and produces a 32-byte output value using hexadecimal notation. The output looks nonsensical, but the same input will always produce the exact same output. Figure G.9 shows three examples. The first example transformed the name 'MaryLacity' into a 32-byte output. The second example, 'Marylacity', merely changed a capital 'L' to a small 'l', yet the output is completely different from the first example. The third example shows how a block of text greater than 32 bytes can still be transformed to a unique 32-byte output. It's quite remarkable!

Example	Input (m)	SHA-256 Output H(m) in hex (base 16)
1	MaryLacity	681794341783bb9b8e0c310ec316643bb3d1000 766bdb5b32c63d3ffb7bad161
2	Marylacity	de850a9d2f7d47163333ba3455cb94ea0209324 470944df4c3d97dde99b5ad02
3	Dr. Mary Lacity is Curators' Professor of Information Systems and an International Business Fellow at the University of Missouri-St. Louis. She is also a Senior Editor of MIS Quarterly Executive and on the Editorial Boards for Journal of Information Technology, MIS Quarterly Executive, IEEE Transactions on Engineering Management, Journal of Strategic Information Systems, and Strategic Outsourcing: An International Journal.	9c819a612575844b8ea04017efc56ef5d4aea8aa 83934dc72d679eb6b65e92b9

Figure G.9: Three examples of the SHA-256 hash function

As a cryptographically secure one-way hash function,
SHA-256 takes any size input and produces a unique 32-byte output

Source: http://www.xorbin.com/tools/sha256-hash-calculator

Sharding: A protocol that segments the validation process for new transactions in a blockchain so that not every node validates every transaction. Its purpose is to improve system performance.

Silk Road: Silk Road was an anonymous marketplace, and Bitcoin's most visible example of a nefarious use case. Ross William Ulbricht founded Silk Road in 2011, when he was just 27 years old.[75] The marketplace combined the anonymity of Bitcoin with the obscurity of Tor, the network protocol that masks the identity of servers. (One can spot a Tor website by the website address's suffix '.onion'). One can hardly believe the audacity of Silk Road's openness (see Figure G.10 for a screen shot showing illegal drugs available for sale). After an intense search that comprised cyber and behavioral investigative methods – such as posing as drug buyers – the US Federal Bureau of Investigation (FBI) arrested Ulbricht in 2013. He was sentenced to life in prison without the possibility of parole.[76] This story is nuanced in a way that will not be covered here, but the documentary firm, Deep Web, by Director Alex Winter, provides thorough coverage of the rise and fall of Silk Road.

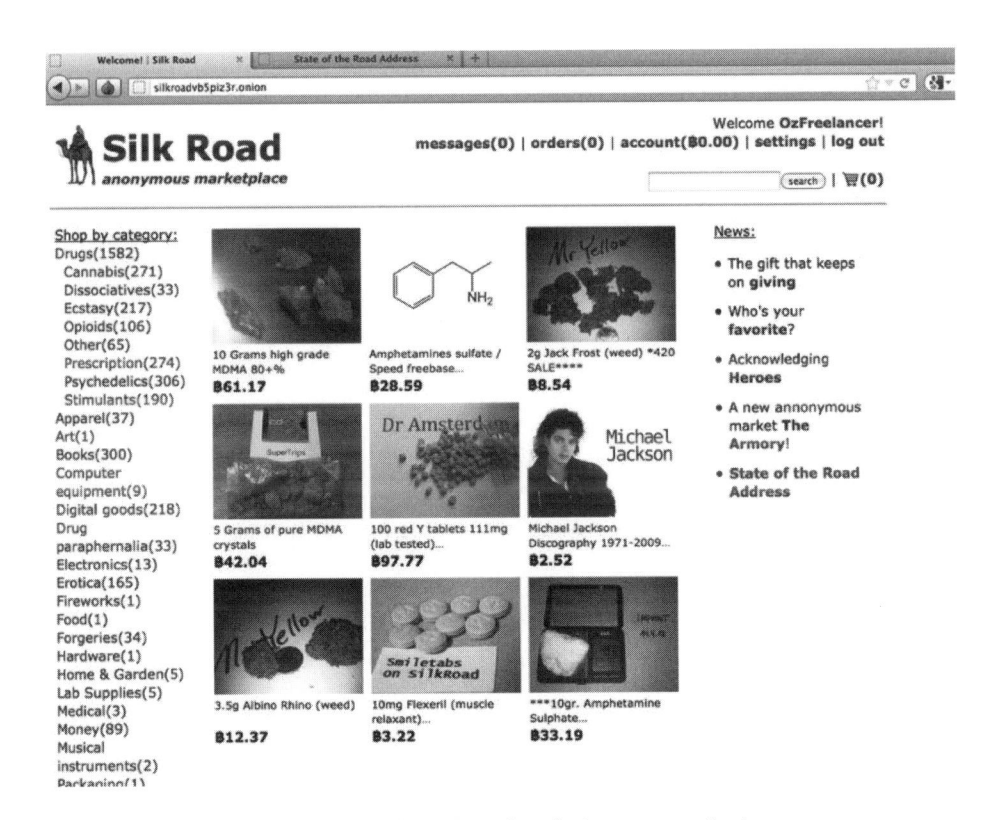

Figure G.10: Silk Road website screenshot

Source: Techrepublic[77]

Smart Contract – Deterministic: Once deployed on the blockchain, a deterministic smart contract can execute autonomously without the need for any outside information. See Chapter 2 for more information.

Smart Contract – Non-Deterministic: Once deployed on the blockchain, a deterministic smart contract requires outside information to execute the terms of the agreement. The outside information is called an 'oracle'. See Chapter 2 for more information.

Smart contract: A smart contract – a concept developed by Nick Szabo in 1994 – is a piece of software that stores rules for negotiating the terms of a contract, automatically verifies the contract and then executes the terms.[78] See Chapter 2 for more information.

Sustaining innovation: An innovation that improves the performance of an enterprise's current product or services to meet the needs of its most demanding customers. The term comes from Clayton Christensen's Theory of Disruptive Innovation.[79]

Sybil attack: A single malicious node in a network that replicates itself so many times, it takes over the network. Blockchains like Bitcoin, Ethereum and Stellar use cryptocurrencies to prevent Sybil attacks, as a Sybil attacker would run out of money.

System performance: A term used to measure how long it takes a network to process a transaction. Blockchain applications generally vary in their performance from minutes to seconds.

System scalability: A system's ability to handle an increase in workload, such as when new users are added to a system.[80]

Tragedy of the Commons: This concept is defined as a situation within a shared-resource system where individual users acting independently according to their own self-interest behave contrary to the common good of all users by depleting or spoiling that resource through their collective action.[81]

Transaction costs: The effort, time, and costs incurred in searching, creating, negotiating, monitoring, and administrating a contract between trading partners.

Trust: In general, trust is the confidence in another party's benevolence. In reference to blockchains, trust often refers to the confidence that records on the distributed ledger agree.

Trust protocol: In the context of a blockchain application, the term 'trust protocol' is defined to mean the reliance on computer algorithms rather than trusted third party institutions to verify transactions and to ensure all copies of the digital ledgers agree across nodes.

Trusted third parties: Trusted third parties – like banks, certificate authorities, and credit card companies – exist to mitigate counterparty risks, i.e. the risk each party bears that the other party will not fulfill its contractual obligations. Trusted third parties perform many vital functions, such as authenticating asset ownership and making sure accounts are funded to prevent double spending.

Turing complete: A term that refers to a computer programming language that has a full set of commands to execute every algorithm that another Turing complete programming language can execute. For example, a simple calculator with basic arithmetic functions is not Turing complete because it cannot execute if-then-else or loop logic. As it relates to blockchain codebases, a Turing complete, smart contracting feature provides the ability to code many types of agreements; but with more coding capabilities comes more risks of software vulnerabilities. Ethereum and Hyperledger Fabric, for example, do have Turing complete programming languages to code smart contracts; Ethereum's smart contracting language is called Solidity; Hyperledger Fabric's is called Chaincode. Bitcoin and Stellar do not have Turing complete smart contracts.

Zero knowledge proof: A method by which one party can verify possession of a piece of information to other parties without revealing the information. See Chapter 4 for more information.

zk-SNARK (Zero-Knowledge Succinct Non-Interactive Argument of Knowledge): A zero-knowledge proof used in some blockchain protocols. Here is an explanation of zk-SNARKs:

*'Suppose Bob is given a hash **H** of some value, and he wishes to have a proof that Alice knows the value s that hashes to **H**. Normally Alice would prove this by giving s to Bob, after which Bob would compute the hash and check that it equals **H**. However, suppose Alice doesn't want to reveal the value s to Bob but instead she just wants to prove that she knows the value. She can use a zk-SNARK for this. We can describe Alice's scenario using the following program, here written as a Javascript function:*

```
function C(x, w) {
return ( sha256(w) == x );
}
```

*In other words: the program takes in a public hash **x** and a secret value **w** and returns true if the **SHA–256 hash** of w equals **x**. Translating Alice's problem using the function C(x,w) we see that Alice needs to create a proof that she possesses s such that **C(H, s) = true**, without having to reveal s. This is the general problem that zk-SNARKs solve.'* [82]

Citations

1. *Definition of Asymmetric Encryption*, http://hitachi-id.com/resource/itsec-concepts/asymmetric_encryption.html
   Mapt course, *Asymmetric Cryptography*, https://www.packtpub.com/mapt/book/big_data_and_business_intelligence/9781787125445/3/ch03lvl1sec28/asymmetric-cryptography

2. Nakamoto, S. (2008), *Bitcoin: A Peer-to-Peer Electronic Cash System*, https://bitcoin.org/bitcoin.pdf

3. Hyperledger Foundation, *Hyperledger Architecture, Volume 1*, https://www.hyperledger.org/wp-content/uploads/2017/08/HyperLedger_Arch_WG_Paper_1_Consensus.pdf

4. Connell, J. (June 2017), *On Byzantine Fault Tolerance in Blockchain Systems*, https://cryptoinsider.com/byzantine-fault-tolerance-blockchain-systems/

5. Quorum White Paper, https://github.com/jpmorganchase/quorum-docs/blob/master/Quorum Whitepaper v0.1.pdf

6. Maziières, D. (2016), *The Stellar Consensus Protocol: A Federated Model for Internet-level Consensus*, White Paper, https://www.stellar.org/papers/stellar-consensus-protocol.pdf

7. Maziières, D. (2016), *The Stellar Consensus Protocol: A Federated Model for Internet-level Consensus*, White Paper, https://www.stellar.org/papers/stellar-consensus-protocol.pdf

8. Maziières, D. (2016), *The Stellar Consensus Protocol: A Federated Model for Internet-level Consensus*, White Paper, https://www.stellar.org/papers/stellar-consensus-protocol.pdf

9. https://chain.com/faq/

10. Proof-of-Elapsed-Time (PoET) was created by the Hyperledger Sawtooth project. https://www.hyperledger.org/projects

11. Chan, R. (May 2nd 2016), *Consensus mechanisms used in blockchains*, https://www.linkedin.com/pulse/consensus-mechanisms-used-blockchain-ronald-chan

12. *How is Consensus achieved in Corda?* https://discourse.corda.net/t/how-is-consensus-achieved-on-corda/1148

13. *Welcome to Corda*, https://docs.corda.net/

14. Corda survey responses as reported in Seibold, S., and Samman, G. (2016), *Consensus: Immutable Agreement for the Internet of Value*, KPMG White Paper

15. Brown, R., Carlyle, J., Grigg, I., and Hearn, M. (2016), *Corda: An Introduction*, Corda White Paper, https://docs.corda.net/_static/corda-introductory-whitepaper.pdf

16. Corda survey responses as reported in Seibold, S., and Samman, G. (2016), *Consensus: Immutable Agreement for the Internet of Value*, KPMG White Paper

17. *Welcome to Corda*, https://docs.corda.net/

18. Lee, P. (November 30th 2017), *R3 releases Corda as Blockchain strains start to show*, https://www.euromoney.com/article/b12kqb9hqwgp2d/r3-releases-corda-as-blockchain-strains-start-to-show

19. Diedrich, H. (2016), *Ethereum: blockchains, digital assets, smart contracts, decentralized*

autonomous organizations, Wildfire Publishing.

20. Clayton Christensen has developed the theory of disruptive innovation over two decades, beginning with this first book, published in 1997, *The innovator's dilemma: when new technologies cause great firms to fail,* (Boston, Massachusetts, Harvard Business School Press). For a thoughtful and current synopsis of the theory, see Christensen, C., Raynor, M., and McDonald, R. (2015), *Disruptive Innovations, Harvard Business Review*, 93(12): 45-53

21. https://en.wikipedia.org/wiki/Digital_Signature_Algorithm

22. http://wiki.p2pfoundation.net/Ethereum
A Next-Generation Smart Contract and Decentralized Application Platform, https://github.com/ethereum/wiki/wiki/White-Paper

23. In layman's terms, 'Turing complete' means a programming language has a comprehensive instruction set such that it can be programmed to perform all the other functions of Turing complete programming languages/ Bitcoin's scripting tool is not 'Turing complete' because it has no way to program logic loops, among other missing features. (See https://en.bitcoin.it/wiki/Script for Bitcoins command set.) Buterin proposed that Ethereum would include a Turing complete programming language to enable coding of smart contracts

24. Levi, A. (May 21st 2017), *Corporate Trends in Blockchain*, CB Insights webinar presentation

25. *Is the ether supply infinite?* https://www.ethereum.org/ether

26. Beigel, O. (March 3rd 2017), *What is Ethereum?*, https://99bitcoins.com/guide-buy-ether-ethereum/

27. According to discussions within the open source community, the total money supply for ether has not been established, https://ethereum.stackexchange.com/questions/443/what-is-the-total-supply-of-ether

28. *Is the ether supply infinite?* https://www.ethereum.org/ether

29. *The Differences Between Hard and Soft Forks*, We Use Coins, August 23rd 2016, https://www.weusecoins.com/hard-fork-soft-fork-differences/

30. *Hard & Soft Forking Explained*, by Loshil and @MLPFrank, https://www.youtube.com/watch?v=pdaXY1OOiWQ

31. Martin, L. (2016) *Blockchain for developers: Is it right for your application?*, Techbeacon, https://techbeacon.com/blockchain-it-right-your-app

32. The Linux Foundation (January 22nd 2016), *The Hyperledger Project Charter*, https://www.hyperledger.org/about/charter

33. Connell, J. (June 2017), *On Byzantine Fault Tolerance in Blockchain Systems*, https://cryptoinsider.com/byzantine-fault-tolerance-blockchain-systems/

34. Groenfeldt, T. (July 13th 2017), Linux Foundation's Hyperledger Fabric 1.0 Ready For Production, *Forbes Magazine,* https://www.forbes.com/sites/tomgroenfeldt/2017/07/13/linux-foundats-hyperledger-fabric-1-0-ready-for-production/ - 624d7632902e

35. Hyperledger Foundation, *Hyperledger Architecture, Volume 1*, https://www.hyperledger.org/wp-content/uploads/2017/08/HyperLedger_Arch_WG_Paper_1_Consensus.pdf

36. Ross, C. (December 5ᵗʰ 2016), *Blockchain Brings Us Into The Future, But Only After It Drags Up The Past: Interoperability Becomes An Actual Issue Again,* http://www.horsesforsources.com/blog/christine-ferrusi-ross/the-interoperability-problems-blockchain-brings_120616
Ross, C. (April 18ᵗʰ 2017), *Simplify Blockchain by Refusing to Let Interoperability Issues Bog You Down*, http://www.horsesforsources.com/Simplify-Blockchain-Refusing-Interoperability-Issues_041817

37. DiMaggio, P., and Powell, W. (1991), The Iron Cage Revisited: Institutional Isomorphism and Collective Rationality in Organizational Fields, *The New Institutionalism in Organizational Analysis,* (Powell & DiMaggio eds), The University of Chicago Press, 63-82

38. DiMaggio, P., and Powell, W. (1991), The Iron Cage Revisited: Institutional Isomorphism and Collective Rationality in Organizational Fields, *The New Institutionalism in Organizational Analysis,* (Powell & DiMaggio eds), The University of Chicago Press, 63-82

39. Martin, L. (2016) *Blockchain for developers: Is it right for your application?,* Techbeacon, https://techbeacon.com/blockchain-it-right-your-app

40. Institute of Network Cultures, *Beyond distributed and decentralized: what is a federated network?,* http://networkcultures.org/unlikeus/resources/articles/what-is-a-federated-network/

41. The Guardian (January 20ᵗʰ 2016), *Ten arrested in Netherlands over bitcoin money-laundering allegations*, https://www.theguardian.com/technology/2016/jan/20/bitcoin-netherlands-arrests-cars-cash-ecstasy

42. Lee, T. (July 26ᵗʰ 2017), *Officials arrest suspect in $4 billion Bitcoin money laundering scheme*, https://arstechnica.com/tech-policy/2017/07/officials-arrest-suspect-in-4-billion-bitcoin-money-laundering-scheme/

43. De, N. (Oct 25ᵗʰ 2017), *DEA Report: Bitcoin Used for Trade-Based Money Laundering*, https://www.coindesk.com/dea-report-bitcoin-used-trade-based-money-laundering/

44. The US Department of Justice Drug Enforcement Administration (October 2017), *2017 National Drug Threat Assessment*, https://www.dea.gov/docs/DIR-040-17_2017-NDTA.pdf

45. Musaddique, S. (December 4ᵗʰ 2017), *UK Government plans Bitcoin crackdown amid money laundering concerns*, http://www.independent.co.uk/news/business/news/uk-bitcoin-regulation-money-laundering-crytocurrency-european-union-eu-a8090791.html

46. Press release by the United States Department of the Treasury on May 5ᵗʰ 2016: https://www.fincen.gov/sites/default/files/shared/20150505.pdf

47. Todd, S. and McKendry, I. (2015), What Ripple's Fincen Fine Means for the Digital Currency Industry, *American Banker*, https://www.americanbanker.com/news/what-ripples-fincen-fine-means-for-the-digital-currency-industry

48. MultiChain White Paper (2015), https://www.multichain.com/download/MultiChain-White-Paper.pdf

49. https://blockchainhub.net/blockchain-oracles/

50. King, S., and Nadal, S. (2012), *PPCoin: Peer-to-Peer Crypto-Currency with Proof-of-Stake*, https://peercoin.net/assets/paper/peercoin-paper.pdf

51. *Distributed Consensus from Proof of Stake is Impossible, Andrew Poelstra,* https://www.smithandcrown.com/open-research/distributed-consensus-from-proof-of-stake-is-impossible/

52. Dwork, C., and Naor, M. (1993), *Pricing via processing: Combatting Junk Mail,* http://www.hashcash.org/papers/pvp.pdf

53. Nakamoto, S. (2008), *Bitcoin: A Peer-to-Peer Electronic Cash System,* https://bitcoin.org/bitcoin.pdf

54. Beigel, O. (March 3rd 2017), *What is Ethereum?,* https://99bitcoins.com/guide-buy-ether-ethereum/

55. J.P. Morgan, Quorum, https://www.jpmorgan.com/country/US/EN/Quorum

56. Enterprise Ethereum Alliance (July 7th 2017), *Enterprise Etherum Alliance Announces Support for Blockchain Consensus Algorithm Integration,* https://entethalliance.org/enterprise-ethereum-alliance-announces-support-blockchain-consensus-algorithm-integration/

57. The Quorum White Paper, https://github.com/jpmorganchase/quorum-docs/blob/master/Quorum Whitepaper v0.1.pdf

58. Hackett, R. (October 4th 2016), Why J.P. Morgan Chase Is Building a Blockchain on Ethereum, *Fortune Magazine,* http://fortune.com/2016/10/04/jp-morgan-chase-blockchain-ethereum-quorum/

59. J.P. Morgan, Quorum, https://www.jpmorgan.com/country/US/EN/Quorum

60. https://www.ethnews.com/amis-technologies-new-algorithm-handles-more-transactions-per-second
https://github.com/ethereum/EIPs/issues/650
https://ethereumfoundation.org/devcon3/sessions/bft-for-geth/

61. Quorum White Paper, https://github.com/jpmorganchase/quorum-docs/blob/master/Quorum Whitepaper v0.1.pdf

62. http://www.ibtimes.co.uk/how-ihs-markits-syndicated-loans-blockchain-arrived-cash-1622304

63. Castillo, M (February 28th 2017), *Microsoft Adds JPMorgan's 'Quorum' Blockchain to Azure Platform,* https://www.coindesk.com/microsoft-azure-jpmorgans-quorum-blockchain/

64. http://www.financemagnates.com/cryptocurrency/innovation/synechron-releases-quorum-maker-enterprise-ethereum-alliance/

65. http://blockapps.net/

66. Nation, J. (July 5th 2017), *AMIS Technologies' New Algorithm Handles More Transactions-Per-Second,* https://www.ethnews.com/amis-technologies-new-algorithm-handles-more-transactions-per-second

67. Castillo, M (February 28th 2017), *Microsoft Adds JPMorgan's 'Quorum' Blockchain to Azure Platform,* https://www.coindesk.com/microsoft-azure-jpmorgans-quorum-blockchain/

68. *QuorumChain Consensus,* https://github.com/jpmorganchase/quorum/wiki/QuorumChain-Consensus

69. Quorum White Paper, https://github.com/jpmorganchase/quorum-docs/blob/master/Quorum Whitepaper v0.1.pdf

70. Raft White Paper, Ongaro, D., and Ousterhout, J. (2014) *In Search of an Understandable Consensus Algorithm,* https://raft.github.io/raft.pdf

71. Hertig, A. (May 31st 2016), *Will Ethereum Beat Bitcoin to Mainstream Microtransactions?*, https://www.coindesk.com/ethereum-bitcoin-mainstream-microtransactions/

72. *The Raiden Network: High Speed Asset Transfers for Ethereum*, http://raiden.network/

73. https://en.wiktionary.org/wiki/schroedinbug

74. For a technical explanation of segregated witness, see http://learnmeabitcoin.com/faq/segregated-witness

75. Popper, N. (2015), *Digital Gold: Bitcoin and the Inside History of the Misfits and Millionaires Trying to Reinvent Money*, Harper, New York.

76. Weiser, B. (May 29th 2015), Ross Ulbricht, Creator of Silk Road Website, Is Sentenced to Life in Prison, *The New York Times*, posted https://www.nytimes.com/2015/05/30/nyregion/ross-ulbricht-creator-of-silk-road-website-is-sentenced-to-life-in-prison.html

77. Reese, H. (May 10th 2017), *How the founder of the Silk Road made millions on his illegal startup on the Dark Web*, https://www.techrepublic.com/article/how-online-marketplace-silk-road-became-the-craigslist-for-illegal-drugs/
https://tr2.cbsistatic.com/hub/i/r/2017/05/10/709e488c-6c51-407f-ae13-5115b14d86c4/resize/770x/ac1af617d15f84b986b574770d9a67de/screen-shot-2012-04-24-at-2-02-25-am.png

78. *The Future of Blockchains: Smart Contracts*, Technode, http://technode.com/2016/11/14/the-future-of-blockchain-technology-smart-contracts/

79. Clayton Christensen has developed the theory of disruptive innovation over two decades, beginning with this first book, published in 1997, *The innovator's dilemma: when new technologies cause great firms to fail,* (Boston, Massachusetts, Harvard Business School Press). For a thoughtful and current synopsis of the theory, see Christensen, C., Raynor, M., and McDonald, R. (2015), *Disruptive Innovations, Harvard Business Review*, 93(12): 45-53

80. Castor, A. (June 14th 2017), *Hyperledger Takes on Blockchain Scaling with New Working Group,* https://www.coindesk.com/hyperledger-takes-on-blockchain-scaling-with-new-working-group/

81. 'The tragedy of the commons' is defined as 'an economic theory of a situation within a shared-resource system where individual users acting independently according to their own self-interest behave contrary to the common good of all users by depleting or spoiling that resource through their collective action.' https://en.wikipedia.org/wiki/Tragedy_of_the_commons

82. Lundkvist, C. (2017), *Introduction to zk-SNARKs with examples*, https://media.consensys.net/introduction-to-zksnarks-with-examples-3283b554fc3b

Robotic Process Automation and Risk Mitigation: The Definitive Guide

Robotic Process Automation and Risk Mitigation:
The Definitive Guide

Mary C. Lacity & Leslie P. Willcocks

Softback, 108 pages (Pub. 2017)
(ISBN: 978-0-995682-03-0)

This pioneering guide offers the first comprehensive analysis to Robotic Process Automation (RPA)risks as actually experienced and dealt with by organizations. The authors present analysis and findings from a two-year study. As more organizations adopt RPA, they find that best practice companies are able to gain a 'triple win' from RPA: a win for shareholders, a win for customers, and a win for employees. But while such results are impressive, they are far from guaranteed.

Service automation, like all organizational initiatives, is fraught with risks that need to be mitigated. The RPA risk mitigation framework reveals the significant RPA risks, and identifies 30 key risk mitigation practices that the research found to be successful. Whether an organization is just beginning its RPA journey or has reached maturity, this definitive guide serves as a key source of knowledge.

This title can be purchased from

www.sbpublishing.org

Email: sales@sbpublishing.org
Tel: +44(0)1789 267124

Worldwide shipping is available

SB Publishing

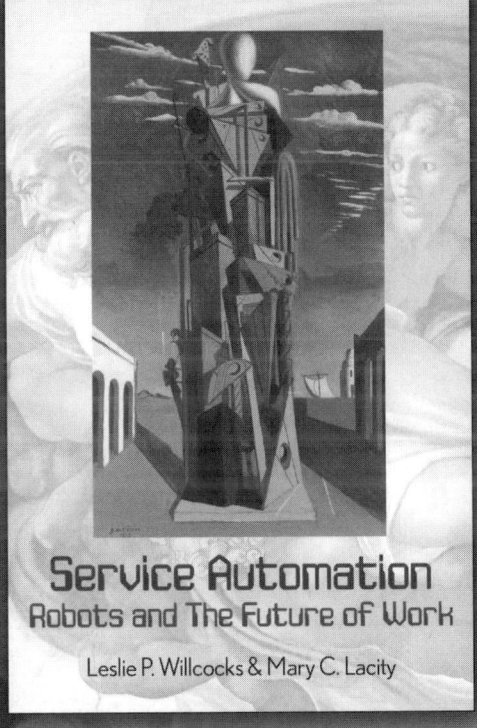

This is an invitation to join us on our new website:

www.RoboticandCognitiveAutomation.com

Despite the massive hype surrounding robotic process automation, cognitive automation, artificial intelligence (AI), and blockchain, these emerging technologies are becoming more real, relevant and impactful every day.

Our objective on this website is to dispel myths and misinformation about risks and effective practices, through insightful, researched-based commentary that is independent, objective, rigorous, ahead of the learning curve, and highly practical.

We are also focusing on the bigger picture consequences of automation. This will lead us into interactive discussions on major issues as they arise such as:

- The future of work
- Technology and ethics
- Physical & psychological health
- Quality of work

- Automation & the economy
- Automation & the environment
- Political & social challenges
- Emerging technologies

We will be connecting up service automation & blockchain technologies with the broader digital transformation ongoing over the next ten years or more.

Importantly, we will be running discerning and sceptical eyes and brains over emerging technologies in business and work contexts to find out their capabilities, limitations and likely diffusion, using our customary, searching, evidence-based assessments.

There is a plethora of information available on the website, including free, downloadable research papers; regular blogs; links to RPA & CA advisors and providers; and video interviews where we answer questions on robotic process, cognitive automation and blockchain.

"Robotic process automation takes the robot out of the human; cognitive automation complements and amplifies both the human, and RPA. Service automation technologies can deliver a triple-win of value for shareholders, customers and employees – but only if managed well."

Whether you are an existing adopter of RPA & CA; thinking of moving in that direction; or just have a keen interest in where the technology is currently at, you can join us on the adventure that is: **'Automation and the future of work.'**

Professor Leslie Willcocks
London School
of Economics

Professor Mary Lacity
University of
Missouri-St Louis

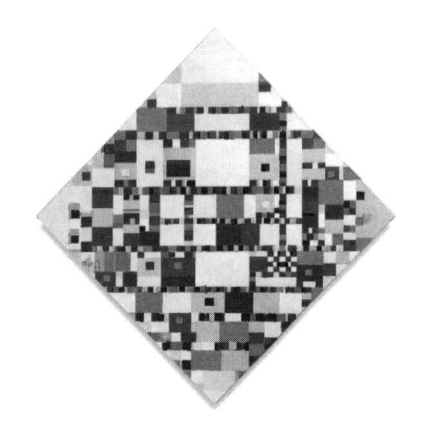